KeepersDollyD

Desig

Presents...

A Doll Clothes Pattern Collection for 16-inch

A Girl for all Time® Dolls

By Eve Coleman

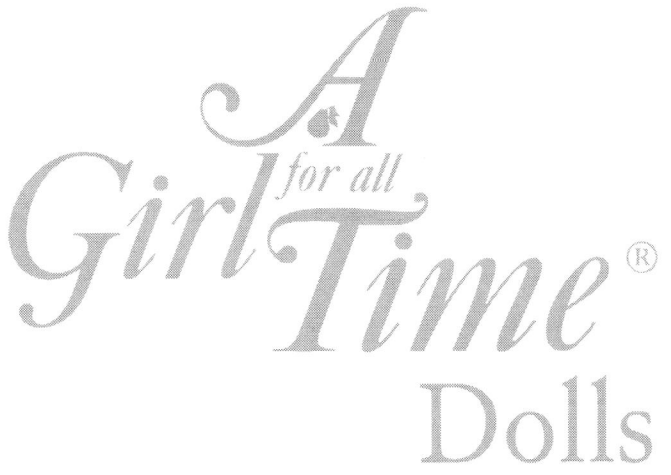

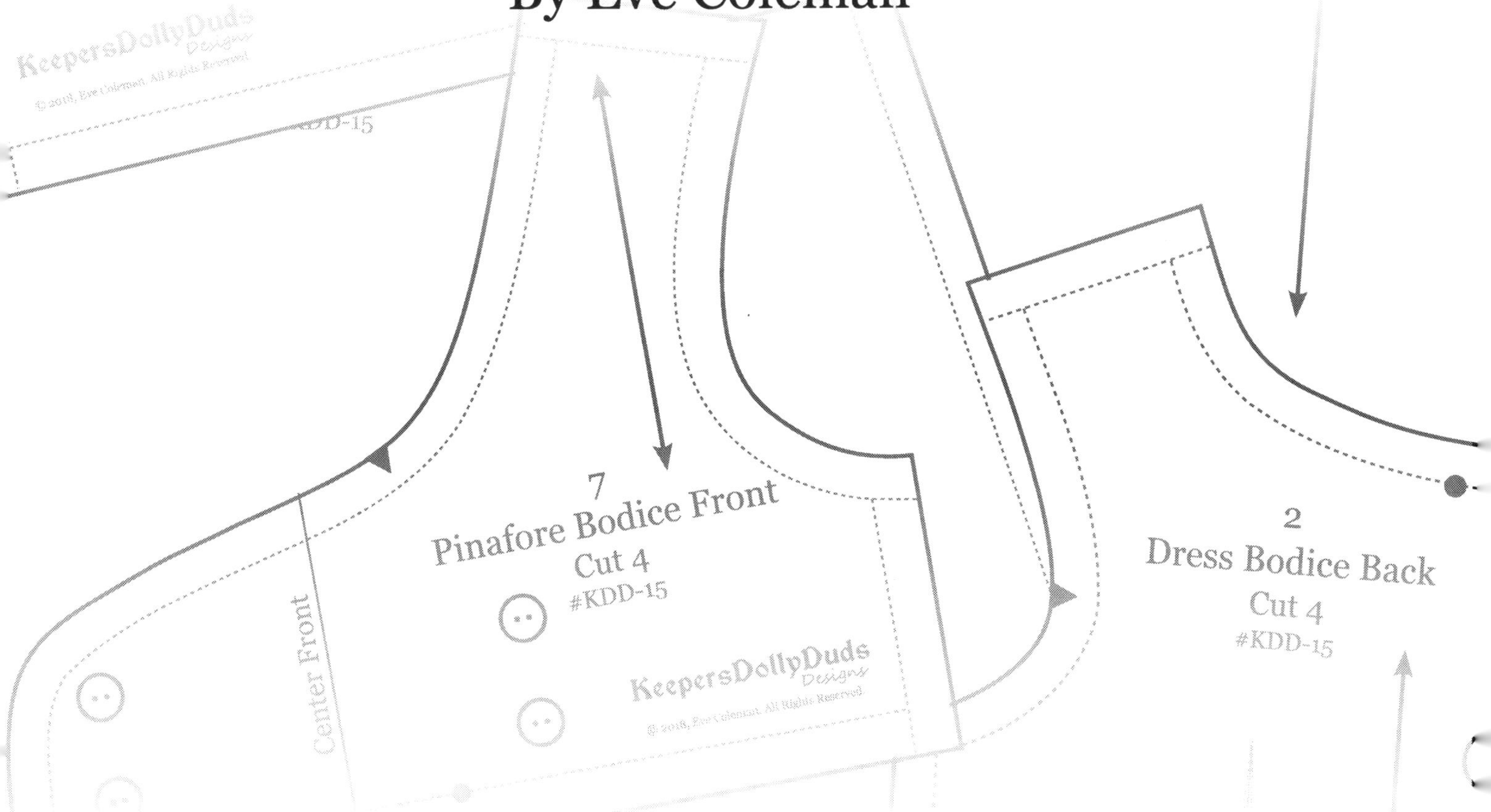

Published By Thimbles and Acorns Making History Memorable Esko, Minnesota

KeepersDollyDuds Designs
...real clothes for real dolls

www.keepersdollyduds.com
www.keepersdollyduds.etsy.com
email: keepersdollyduds@yahoo.ca

Design and Pattern © 2018 by Eve Coleman. All Rights Reserved.
Illustrations and Text © 2018 by Shari Fuller. All Rights Reserved.

These patterns may be used solely by the original purchaser. These patterns may not be duplicated in any way, in whole or in part, for redistribution, posting, advertising, or resale without prior authorization from Eve Coleman, KeepersDollyDuds, or Shari Fuller, Thimbles and Acorns. Clothing made from this pattern may be sold solely by the original purchaser.

These patterns are intended for personal use, not for large-scale commercial purposes or manufacturing.

Thimbles and Acorns Publishing
www.thimblesandacorns.com
email: sharifuller@thimblesandacorns.com

Eve Coleman, Keepers Dolly Duds, and Shari Fuller, Thimbles and Acorns, are not affiliated with any doll manufacturing company. No endorsement is implied.

ISBN: 9781693674266 (Black and White Interior)
ISBN: 9781693675416 (Full Color Interior)

Pattern photography by Eve Coleman. Images copyright 2018.

Special Thanks to Project Consultants
Linda Blaker, VintiqueDesigns
Karen Dosier, Threads of Troy
Heidi Mittiga, Flossie Potter Patterns

Table of Contents

General Information...4

Town and Country..5 - 20
    Materials List...5
    Instructions...6 - 10
    Pattern Pieces...11 - 20

Train Station...21 - 42
    Materials List..21
    Instructions...22 - 29
    Pattern Pieces...30 - 42

Bodice Details...43 - 66
    Materials List..43
    Instructions...44 - 51
    Pattern Pieces...52 - 66

Downtown 1920's..67 - 90
    Materials List..67
    Instructions...68 - 76
    Pattern Pieces...77 - 90

Victorian Caroler...91 - 118
    Materials List..91
    Instructions...92 - 98
    Pattern Pieces...99 - 118

Regency Dress and Pinafore........................119 - 144
    Materials List...119
    Instructions..120 - 127
    Pattern Pieces......................................128 - 144

Double Cape and Bonnet.............................145 - 166
    Materials List...145
    Instructions..146 - 151
    Pattern Pieces......................................152 - 166

Glossary...167 - 169

General Information

General Sewing Instructions

~ Read through the instructions before beginning.
~ Pre-wash washable fabrics to help reduce shrinkage.
~ Before sewing, transfer all pattern markings to the fabric where indicated on the pattern pieces.
~ All seams are 1/4-inch (6mm) unless otherwise indicated.
~ In the illustrations, the right side of the fabric is colored or shaded and the wrong side of the fabric is left white.

Pattern Information

These patterns are designed to fit 16-inch A Girl for All Time® dolls; however, they are suitable to use with other dolls with similar body shapes. Small variations in size can usually be accommodated with minor modifications such as adjusting the closure placements or hemlines.

	Fits 16" (40 cm) A Girl for All Time®
Bust	8.25" (21 cm)
Waist	7.5" (19 cm)
Hip	9" (23 cm)
Back-neck to Waist	3.5" (9 cm)
Shoulder to Wrist	6" (15.25 cm)
Arm	3.75" (9.5 cm)
Wrist	2.5" (6.3 cm)
Widest Hand	2.75" (7 cm)
Shoulder to Floor	12.5" (31.75 cm)
Neck	4.5" (11.5 cm)
Inseam	6.75" (17 cm)
Waist to Floor	9" (23 cm)
Head	10.75" (27 cm)

Sewing Skill Level

Skill levels vary with each project and are indicated with the title.

● **Beginner**
basic skills such as straight stitching, some hand sewing, and applying snaps

●● **Confident Beginner**
gathering, hook & loop tape

●●● **Intermediate**
fold over elastic, stretch lace, bias tape, pleats, darts, zippers, and pockets

●●●● **Experienced**
beading, buttonholes, and welt pockets

●●●●● **Advanced**
couture techniques, French seams

Town and Country

Materials List
#KDD-23-16

Suggested Fabrics: ***Dress and contrast*** in lightweight cotton, cotton blends, or any light weight woven fabric. Not suitable for knits.

Fabric Yardage:

View A Dress ~ 1/3 yard (0.33 m)
View A Contrast ~ 1/4 yard (0.25 m)
View B Dress ~ 1/2 yard (0.5 m)

Notions:

__Thread
Dress A
__four 3/8-inch (9 mm) buttons
__three 1/4-inch (6 mm) decorative buttons
Dress B
__four 3/8-inch (9 mm) buttons

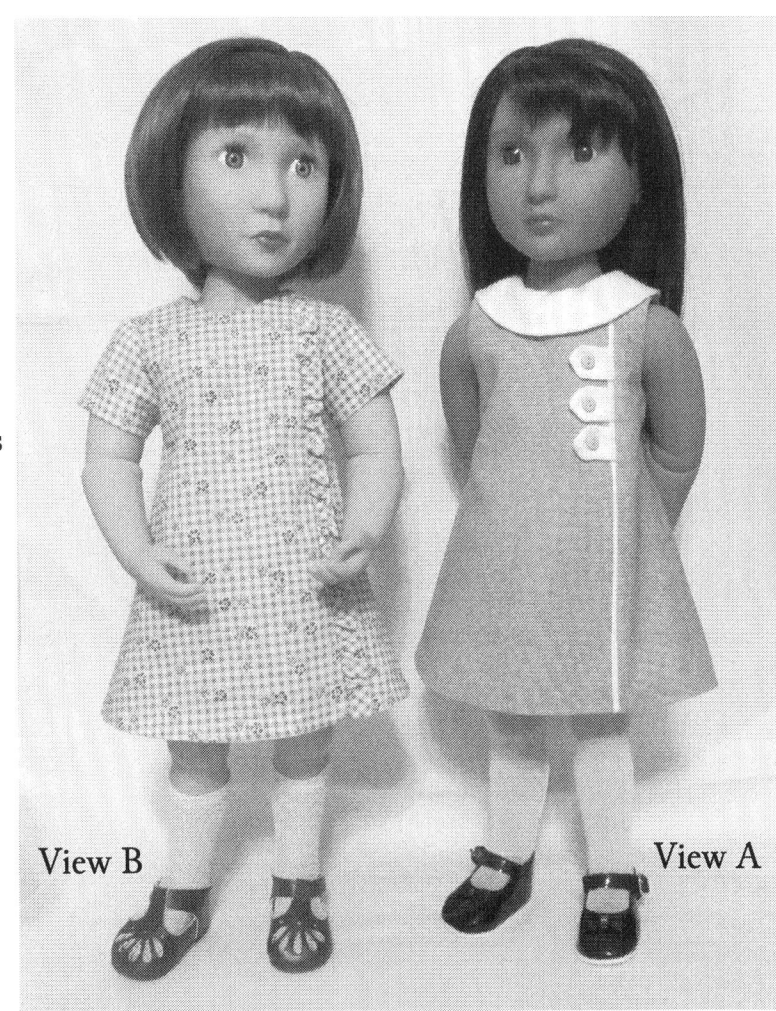

View B   View A

View A Front Trim

For View B, Skip to Step 4.

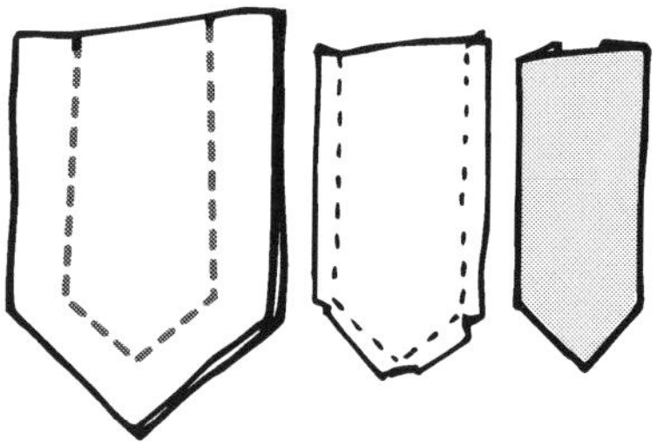

Step 1: Pin three tab sets right sides together. Stitch, leaving the flat end open. Clip the corners and trim the seam allowances to 1/8-inch (3 mm). Turn right side out, squaring the corners with a blunt needle. Press, following the seam lines.

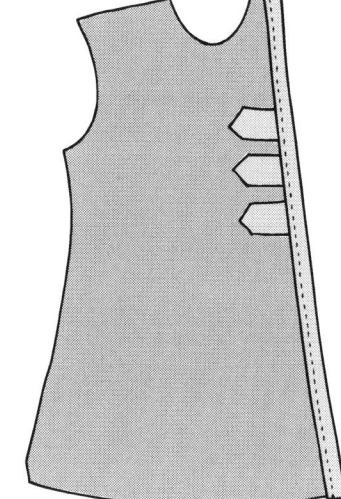

Step 2: With the right side out, fold the piping along the fold line. Press to crease.

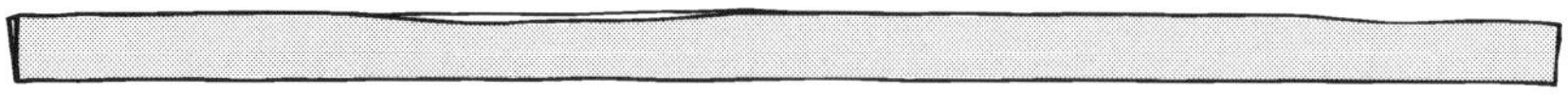

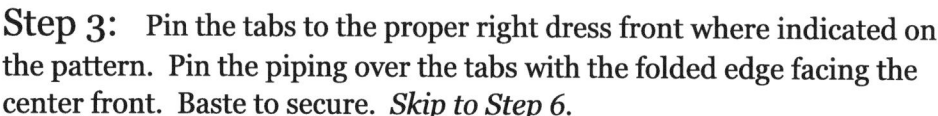

Step 3: Pin the tabs to the proper right dress front where indicated on the pattern. Pin the piping over the tabs with the folded edge facing the center front. Baste to secure. *Skip to Step 6.*

View B Front Trim

For View A, Skip to Step 6

Step 4: With the right side out, fold the ruffle along the fold line. Press to crease. Sew two rows of gathering stitches along the edge opposite the fold. Draw up the gathering stitches to fit along the proper left dress front.

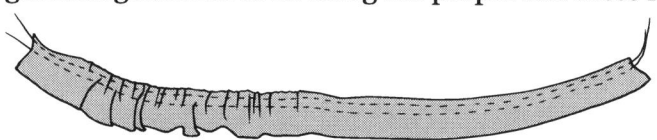

Step 5: With the right sides facing up, pin the ruffle to the proper left dress front where indicated on the pattern. Arrange the gathers evenly along the edge. Baste to secure.

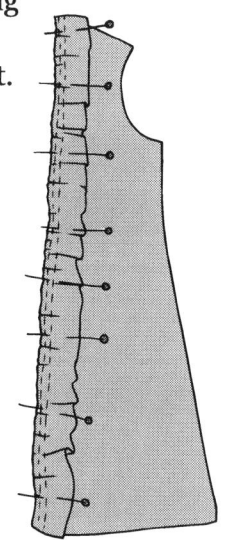

View A & B Dress Front

Step 6: Pin the proper right and proper left dress front pieces right sides together, matching the notches. Stitch. Finish the front seam allowance, if desired. Press the View A seam allowance toward the side secure the tabs to the bodice by sewing decorative buttons on the tabs where indicated on the pattern. Press the View B seam allowance toward the center.

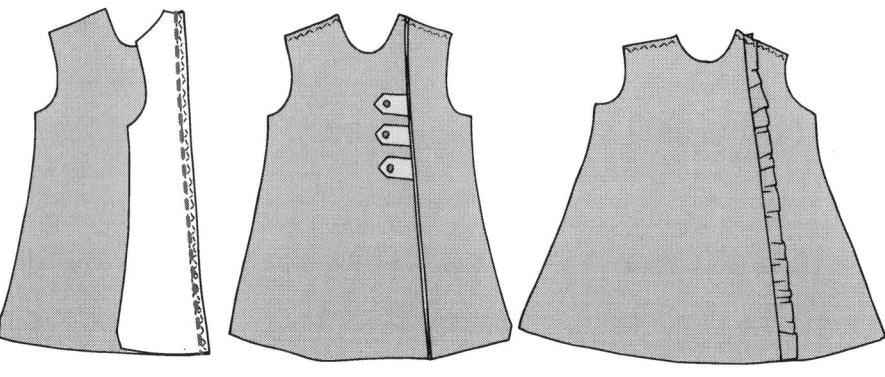

View A & B Dress

Step 7: Finish the shoulder seam allowances on the dress front, dress backs, and facings, if desired.

Step 8: Sew darts on dress backs. With the right sides together and matching the notches, pin the front facing to the back facings. Stitch. Press the seam allowances open. Finish the outside edge of the facing, if desired.

Step 9: With the rights sides together, pin the dress pieces along the shoulders. Stitch. Press the seam allowances open. Staystitch the neck opening and clip the curves up to the stitching line. *For View B, skip to Step 12*

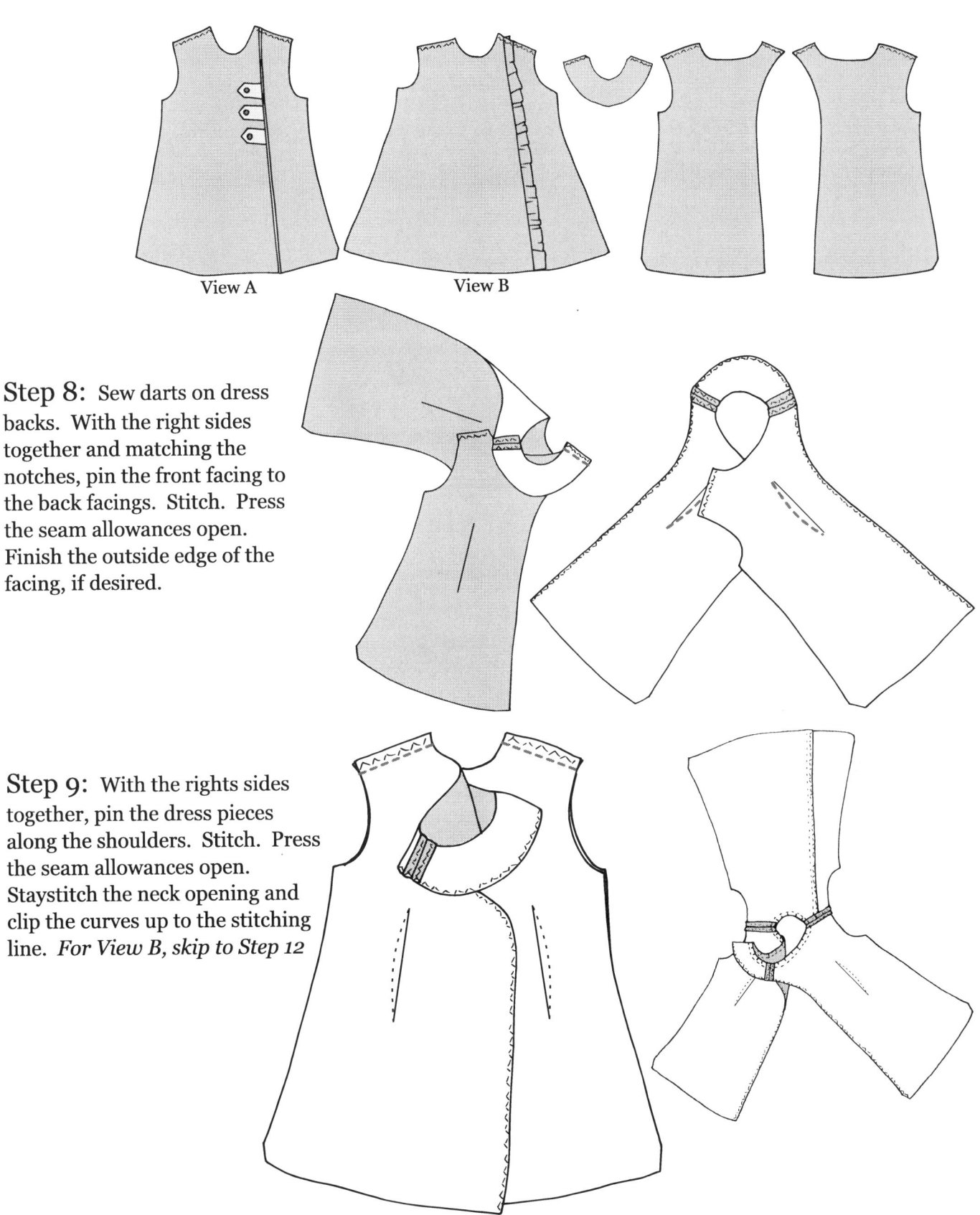

View A

View B

Page 7

View A Collar

For View B, Skip to Step 12

Step 10: With the right sides together, pin the collar pieces along the outside edges. Stitch. Notch the corners and curves and trim the seam allowance to 1/8-inch (3 mm). Turn right side out, squaring the corners with a blunt needle. Press, following the seamline.

Step 11: With the right sides facing up and matching the dots to the center front and shoulder seams, pin the collar to the bodice neckline.

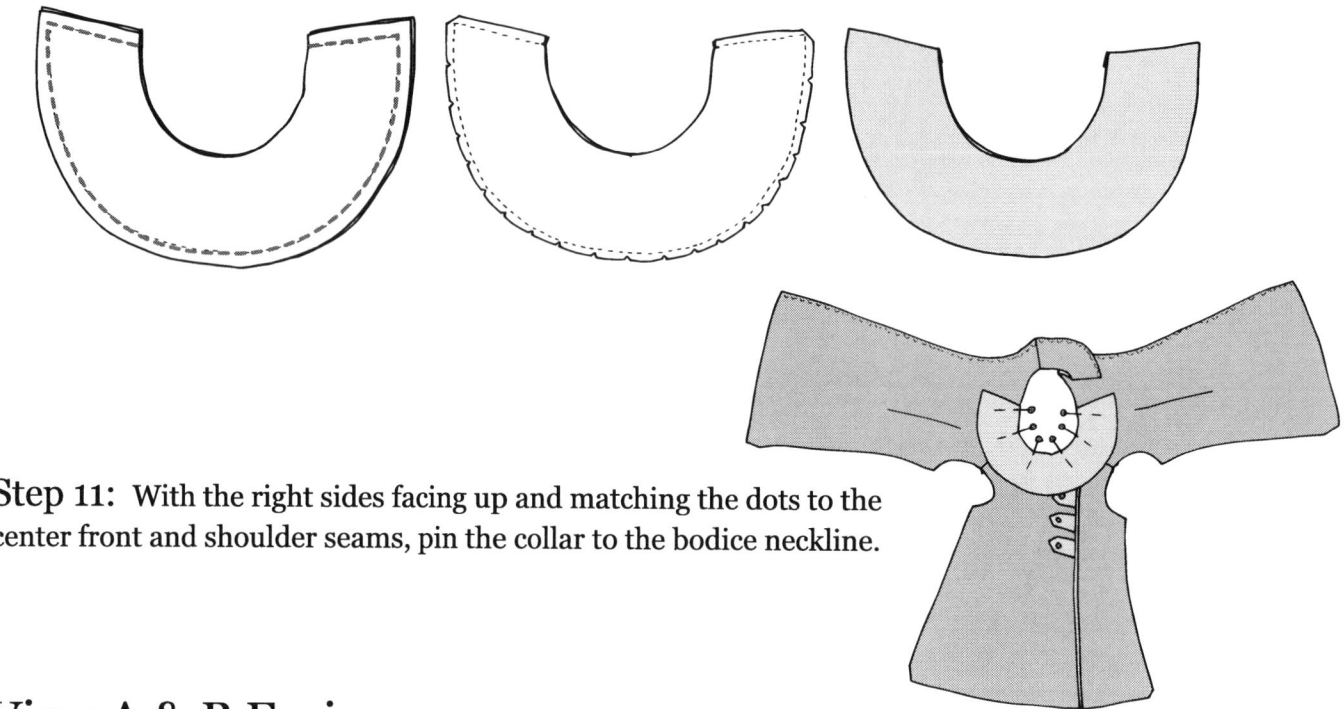

View A & B Facing

Step 12: With the right sides together, pin the facing to the neckline, taking care to line up the seamlines at the shoulders. Stitch. Clip the corners and curves and turn right side out, squaring the corners with a blunt needle. Understitch the neckline. Press, following the seamline. *For View B, skip to Step 16.*

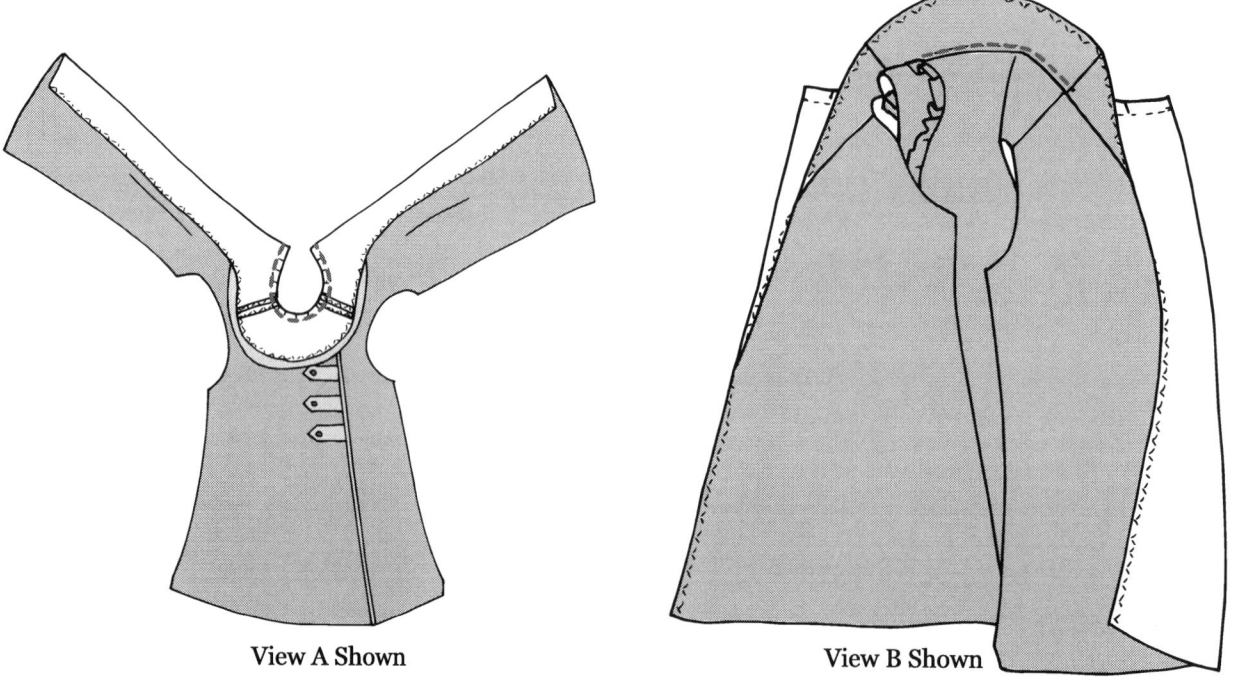

View A Shown   View B Shown

View A Armscye Facings

For View B, Skip to Step 16

Step 13: Finish the outside curves of the armscye facings.

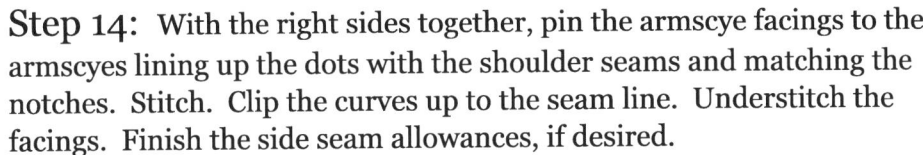

Step 14: With the right sides together, pin the armscye facings to the armscyes lining up the dots with the shoulder seams and matching the notches. Stitch. Clip the curves up to the seam line. Understitch the facings. Finish the side seam allowances, if desired.

Step 15: Pin the sides right sides together. Stitch. Press the seam allowances open. Turn the facings under along the seam lines and press, following the seam lines. Tack the armscyes to the dress at the side and shoulder seam lines. *For View A, skip to Step 20.*

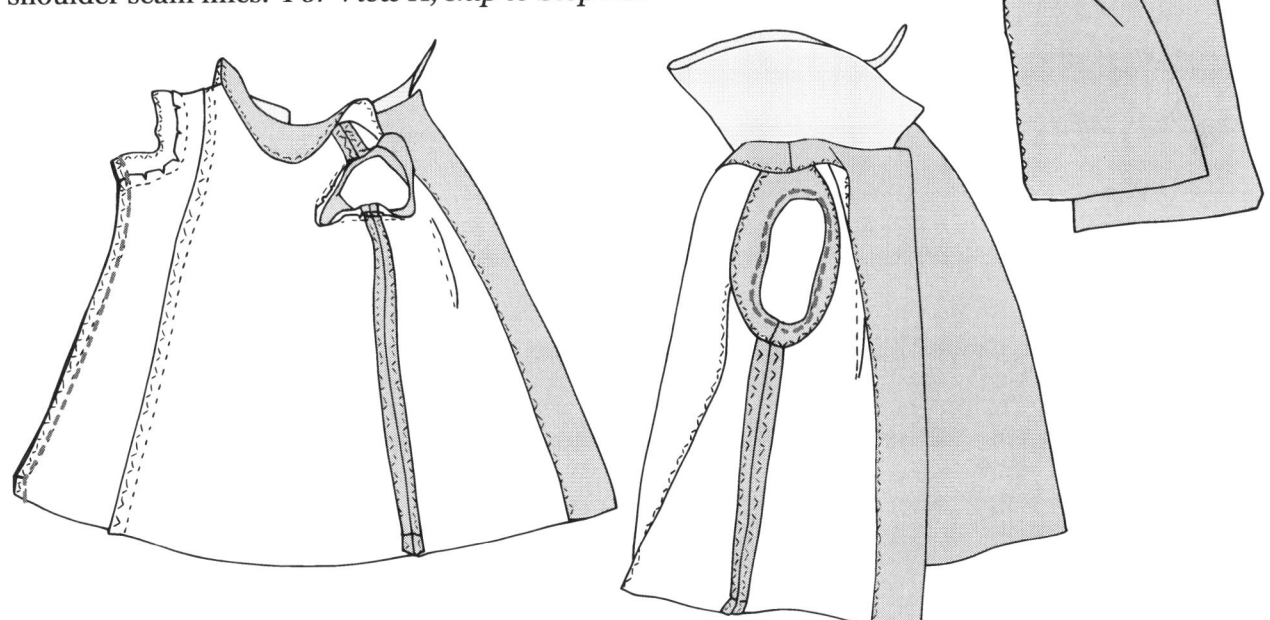

View B Sleeves

For View A, Skip to Step 20

Step 16: Fold sleeves right side out along the fold lines. Press. Sew two rows of gathering stitches along the top edge where indicated on the pattern.

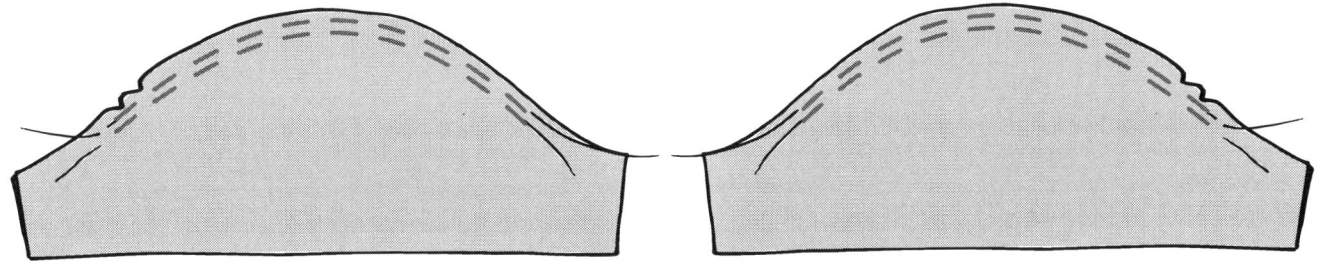

Page 10

Step 17: With the right sides together, pin the sleeves to the armscyes of the dress, lining up the dots with the shoulder seams and matching the notches. Draw up the gathering stitches to ease the fit. Stitch. Clip the curves. Finish the seam allowances, if desired. Press the seam allowances toward the dress.

Step 18: Finish the side seam allowances, if desired.

Step 19: Pin the sides right sides together, matching the seamlines of the armscyes and the bottom edges of the sleeves and dress. Stitch. Press the seam allowances open.

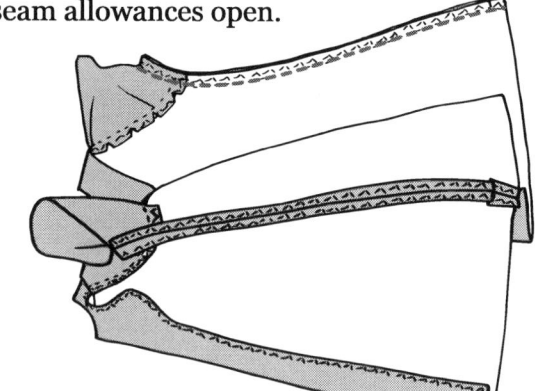

Finishing View A & B Dress

Step 20: With the right sides together, fold the back facings of the dress over along the fold line at the bottom edge. Pin in place. Stitch across the facings at the hemline using a 3/8- inch (9 mm) seam allowance. Finish the bottom edge of the dress from facing to facing. Turn the facings right side out, squaring the corners with a blunt needle. Press the back facing from the neckline to the hem along the fold line. Turn up a 3/8-inch (9 mm) hem and press to crease. Stitch the hem between the facings by hand or machine.

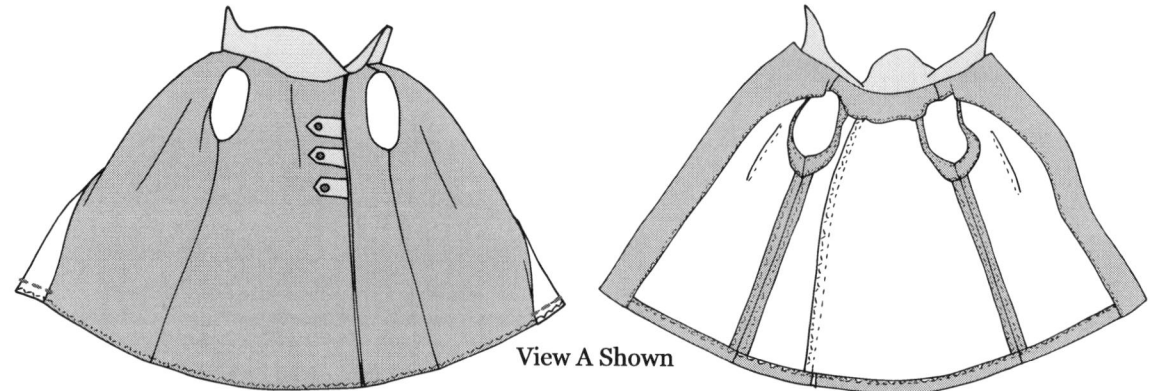

View A Shown

Step 21: Make buttonholes on the proper left and apply buttons on the proper right where indicated on the pattern.

Page 11

Town and Country
Pattern Pieces

Cutting Layout for 45-inch (1.14 m) wide Fabric
10 Pieces

1 ~ View A & B Proper Right Front
2 ~ View A & B Back
3 ~ View A & B Proper Left Front
4 ~ View A & B Front Neck Facing
5 ~ View A Collar
6 ~ View A Armscye Facing
7 ~ View B Sleeve
8 ~ View A Tab
9 ~ View B Ruffle
10 ~ View A Piping

View A Dress
Use Pieces: 1, 2, 3, 4, and 6

View A Dress Contrast
Use Pieces: 5, 8, and 10

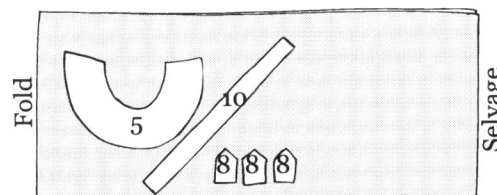

View B Dress
Use Pieces: 1, 2, 3, 4, 7, and 9

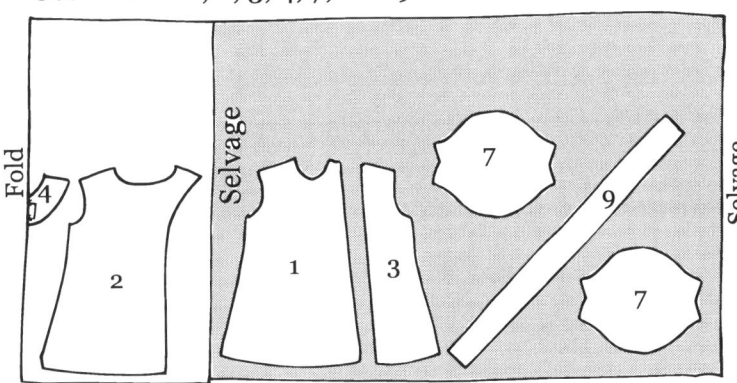

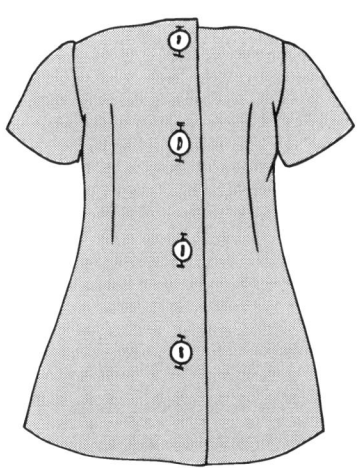

View B Back

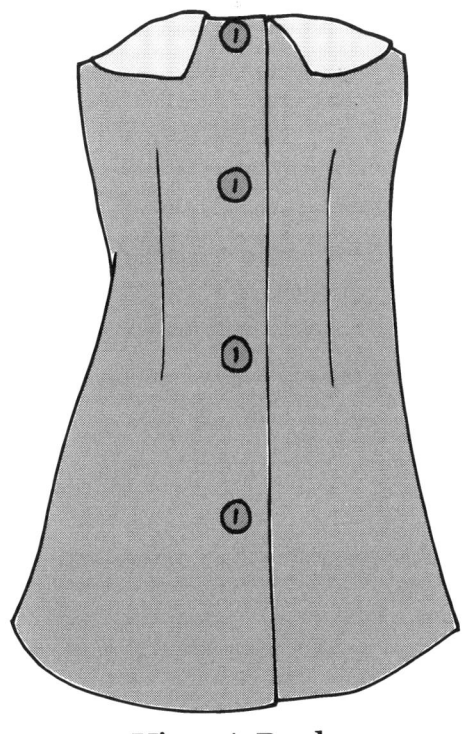

View A Back

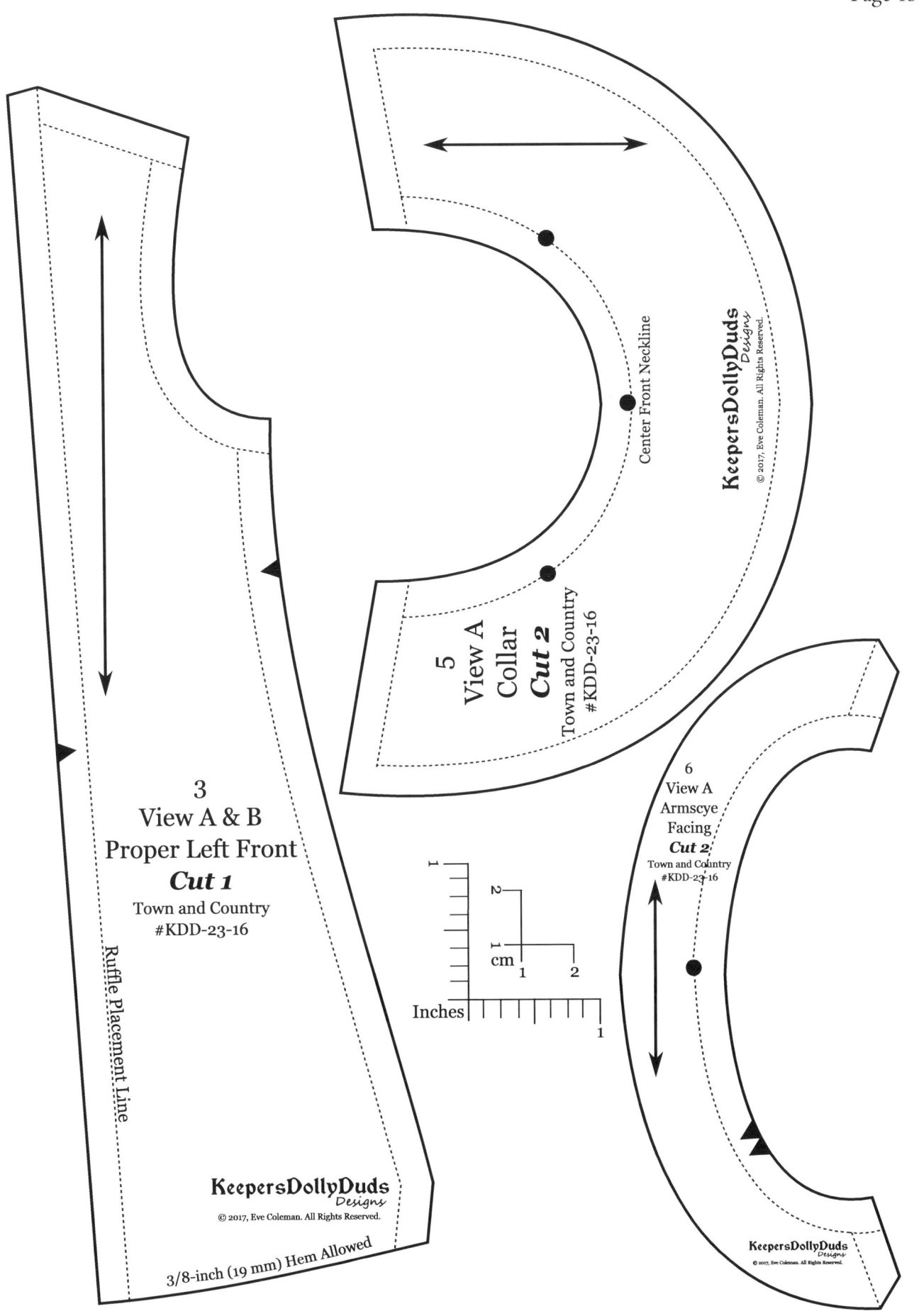

Page 15

4
View A & B
Front Neck Facing
Cut 1 on Fold
Town and Country
#KDD-23-16

Place on Fold

2
View A & B
Back
Cut 2
Town and Country
#KDD-23-16

Facing

Fold Line

KeepersDollyDuds Designs
© 2017, Eve Coleman. All Rights Reserved.

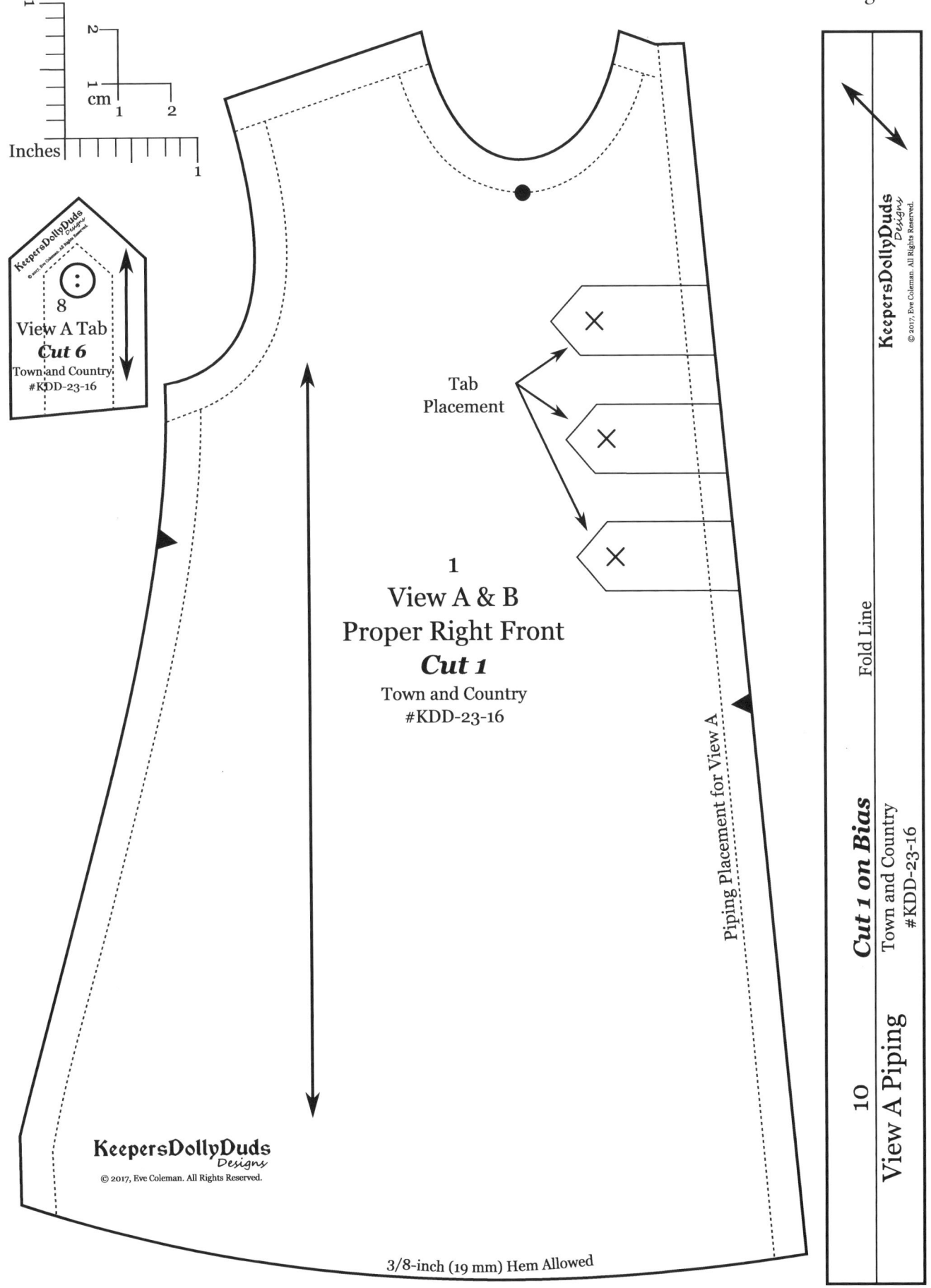

Inches
1
cm
1
2
1
2
1

7
View B Sleeve
Cut 2
Town and Country
#KDD-23-16
KeepersDollyDuds Designs
© 2017, Eve Coleman. All Rights Reserved.
Fold Line
Gather
Gather

Attach Section 1 Here
Fold Line
9
View B Ruffle
(Section 2 of 2)
Town and Country
#KDD-23-16
KeepersDollyDuds Designs
© 2017, Eve Coleman. All Rights Reserved.

9
View B Ruffle
(Section 1 of 2)
Cut 1 on Bias
Town and Country
#KDD-23-16
Attach Section 2 Here

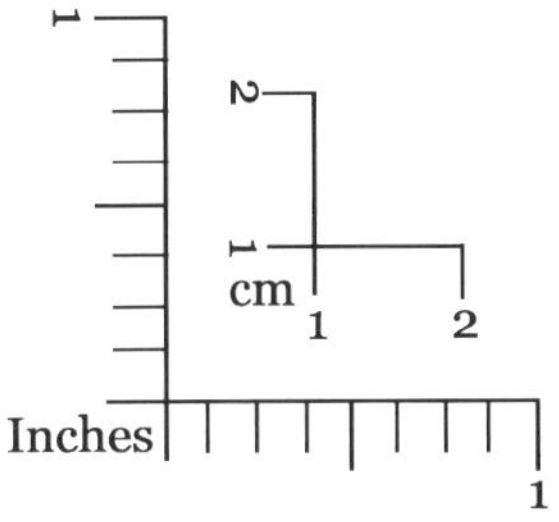

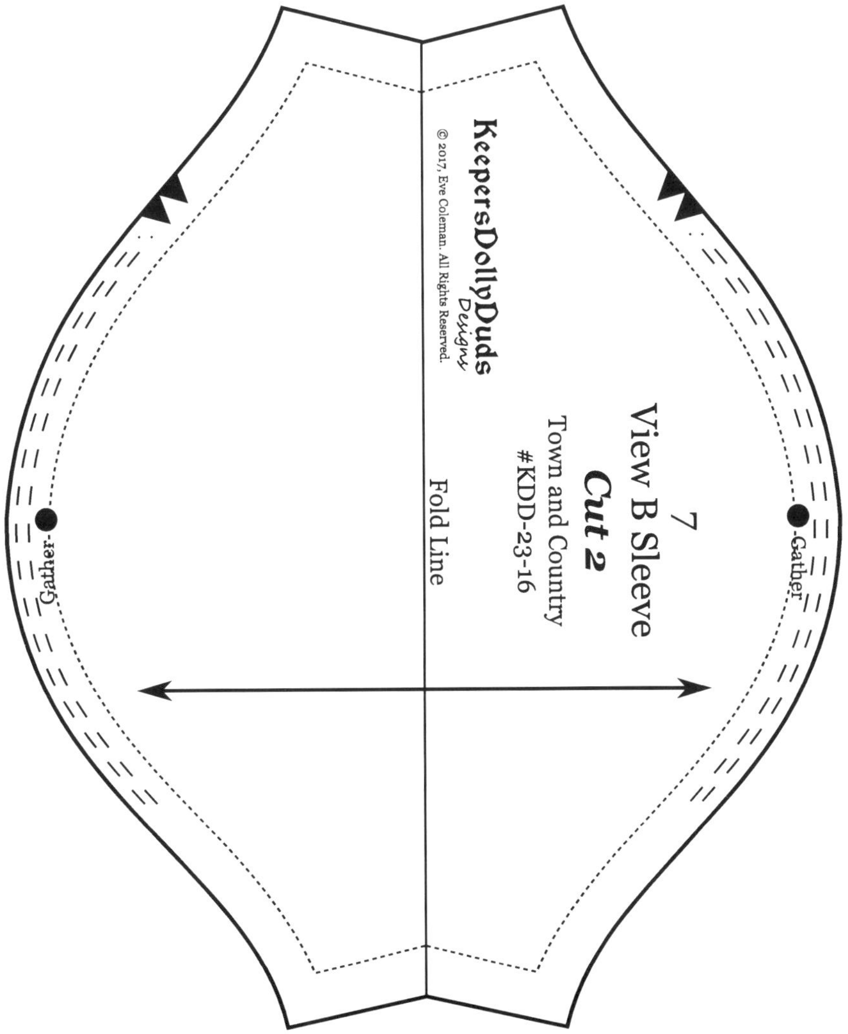

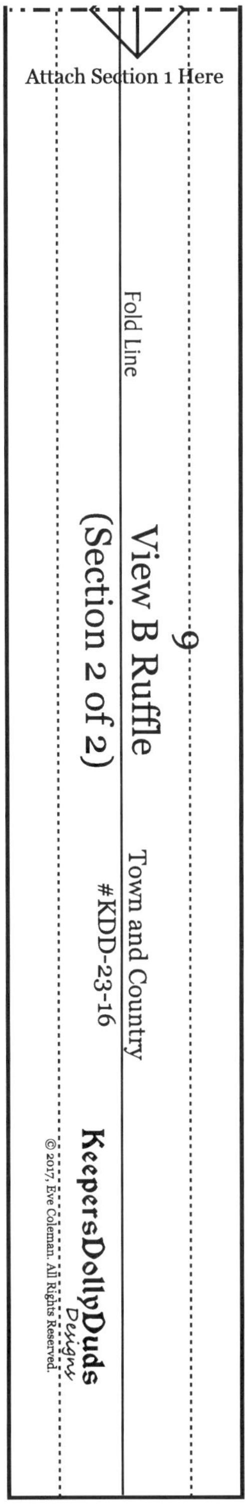

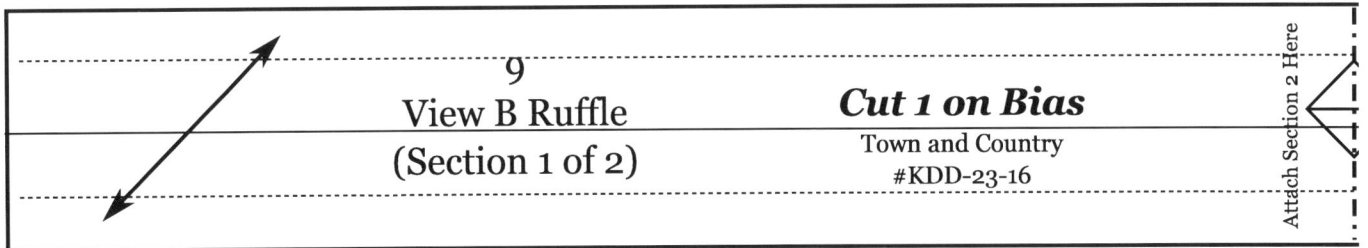

Train Station

Materials List
#KDD-22-16

Suggested Fabrics: ***Blouse*** in calico, cotton voile, batiste, cotton blends, or any light weight woven fabric. Not suitable for knits. ***Jacket and hat*** in light weight wool or wool blends, linen, twill, flannel, corduroy, gabardine, or most any medium weight woven fabric. Not suitable for knits, ***Skirt*** in homespun plaids, cotton, very light weight wool or wool blends, gingham, chambray, and linen types. Not suitable for knits.

Fabric Yardage:
Blouse ~ 1/3 yard (0.33 m)
Skirt ~ 1/3 yard (0.33 m)
Jacket and Hat ~ 1/3 yard (0.33 m)
Jacket and Hat Lining ~ 1/3 yard (0.33 m)

Notions:
___Thread
Blouse
___three 3/8-inch (9 mm) buttons
___1/3-yard (0.33 m) 1/2-inch (12 mm) wide lace
___8-inch (20 cm) square of lightweight fusible interfacing
Skirt
___four 1/4-inch (12 mm) decorative buttons
___six small snaps
Jacket and Hat
___seven 1/4-inch (6 mm) decorative buttons.

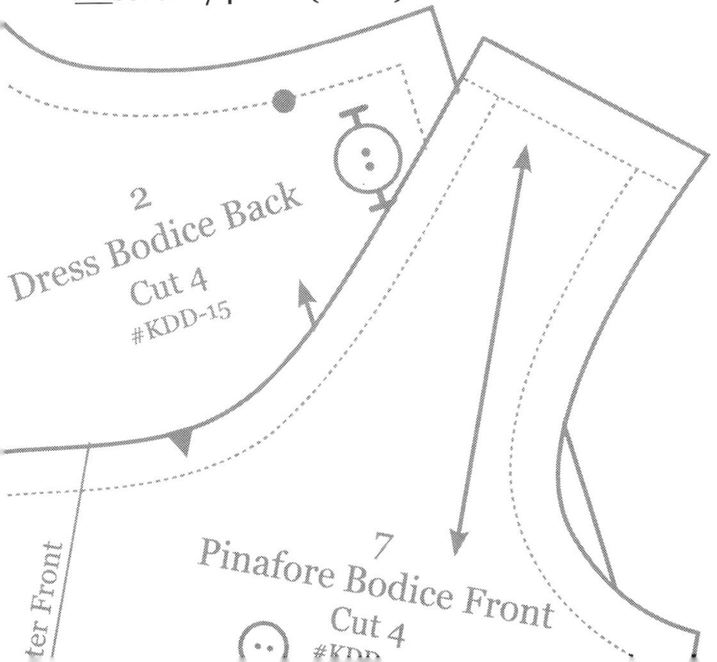

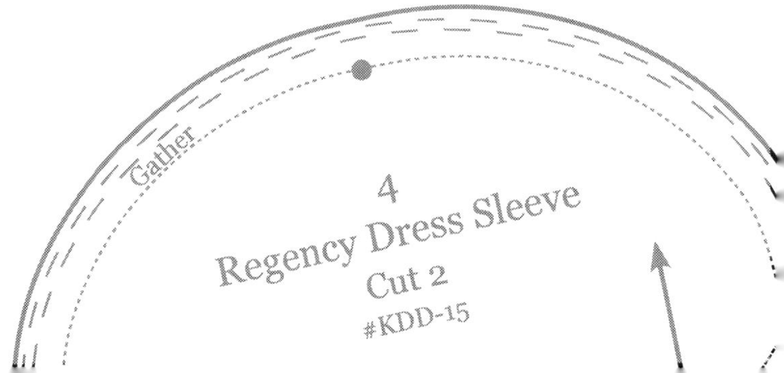

Blouse Bodice

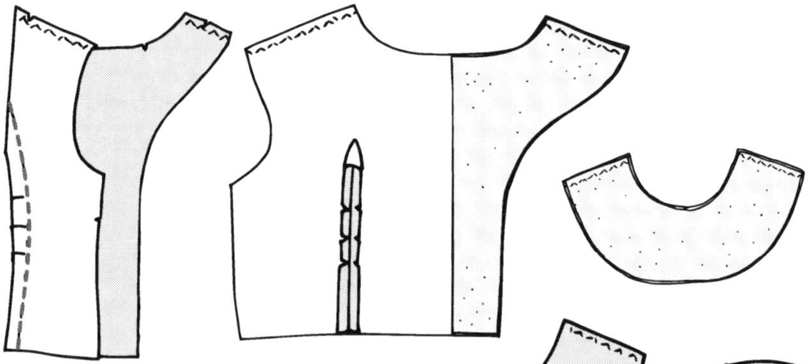

Step 1: Apply interfacing to the bodice back and front facing pieces where indicated on the pattern, following the manufacturer's instructions. Fold the bodice back pieces right sides together along the dart. Stitch. Press the seam allowances open. Finish the shoulder seam allowances on the facings, bodice back, and bodice front pieces.

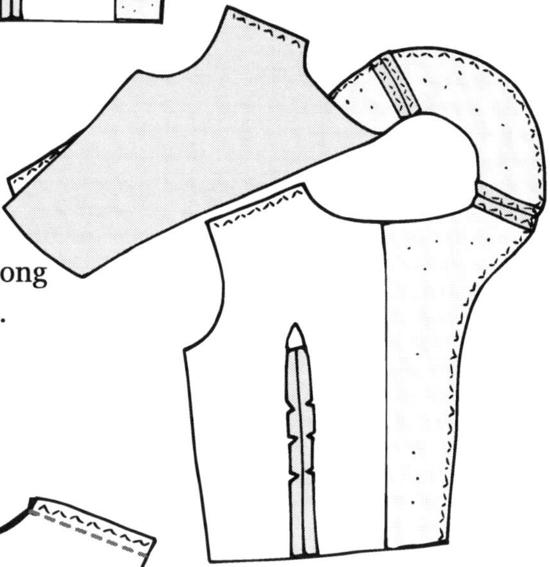

Step 2: Pin the front facing to the bodice back facings along the shoulder lines. Stitch. Press the seam allowances open.

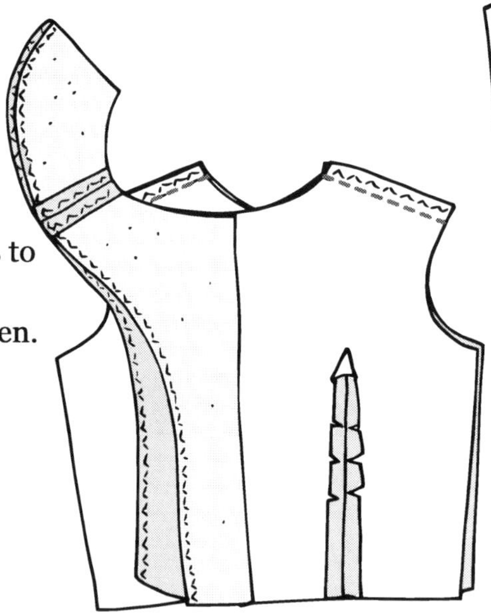

Step 3: Pin the bodice back pieces to the bodice front along the shoulders. Stitch. Press the seam allowances open.

Blouse Collar

Step 4: On the right side of two collar pieces, pin the top edge of lace just inside the seam allowance of the outside edges. With the right sides together, pin the collar pieces along the outside edges. Stitch. Notch the curves and trim the seam allowances to 1/8-inch (3 mm). Turn right side out and press, following the seamline.

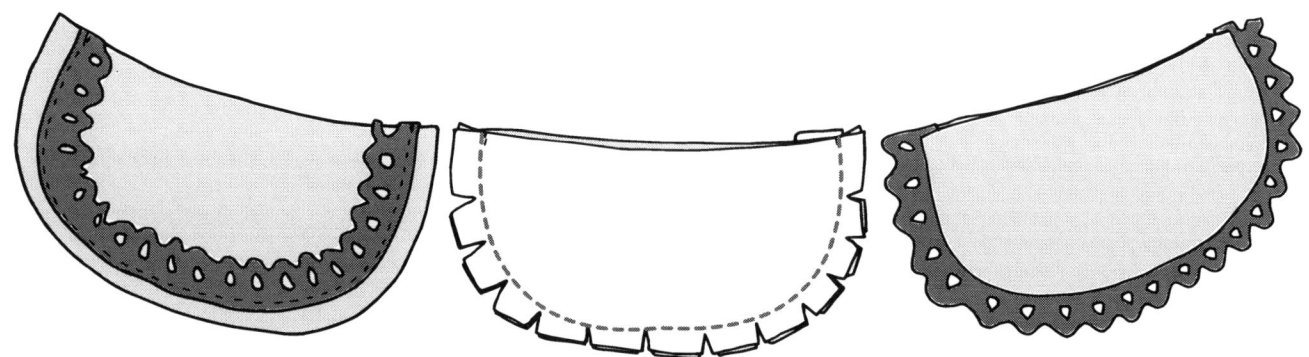

Step 5: Matching the ends of the collar to the dots, pin the collar to the right side of the bodice neckline. Pin the bodice facing along the neckline over the collar, taking care to line up the seamlines at the shoulders. Stitch. Clip the corners and curves and turn right side out, squaring the corners with a blunt needle. Understitch the neckline. Press, following the seamline.

Blouse Sleeves

Step 6: Sew two rows of gathering stitches along to the top and bottom edges of the sleeves where indicated on the pattern. With the right sides together, pin the lower edge of each sleeve to a sleeve band, drawing the gathering stitches to fit. Arrange the fullness evenly along the band. Stitch. Press the seam allowances toward the sleeve band being careful not to crush the fullness on the sleeve.

Step 7: With the right sides together, pin the sleeves to the armscyes of the bodice matching the notches. Draw up the gathering stitches to fit, arranging the fullness evenly along the armscyes. Stitch. Clip the curves and finish the seam allowances, if desired. Press the seam allowances toward the bodice.

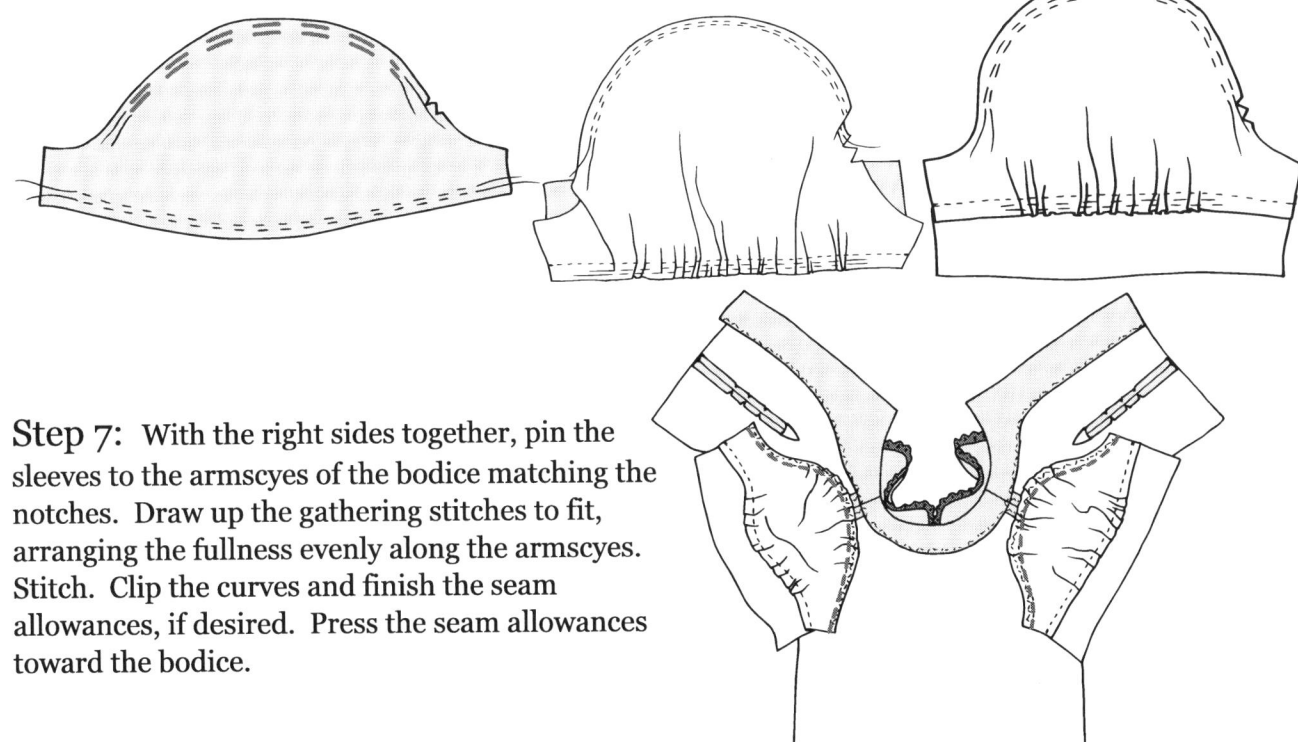

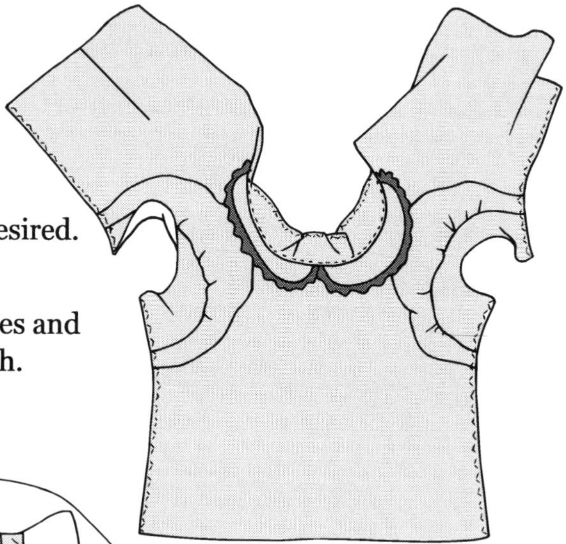

Step 8: Finish the side seam allowances, if desired.

Step 9: Pin the sides of the bodice right sides together, matching the seamlines of the armscyes and the bottom edges of the sleeve and bodice. Stitch. Press the seam allowances open.

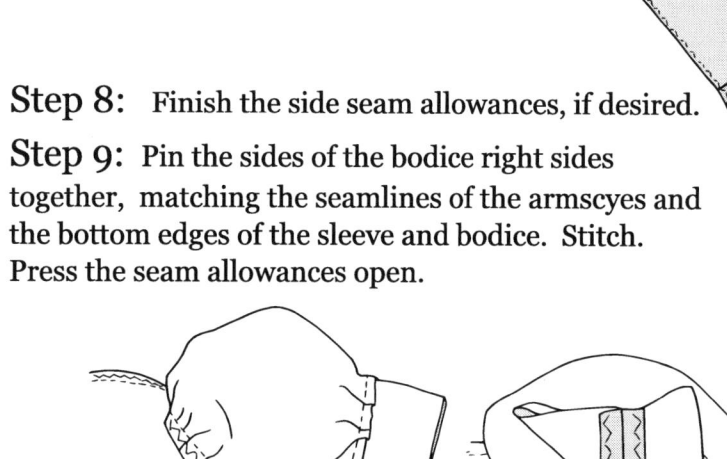

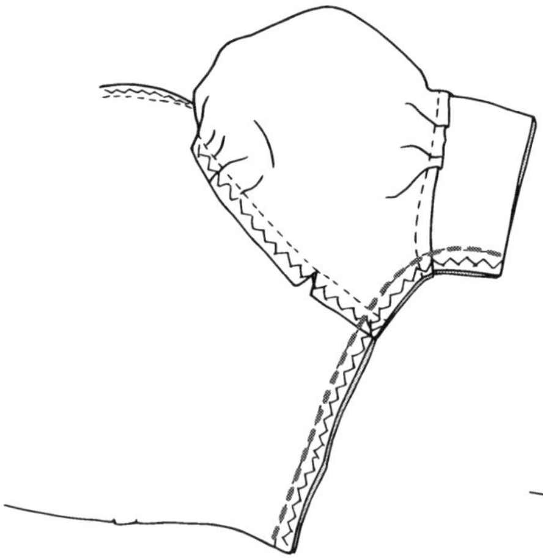

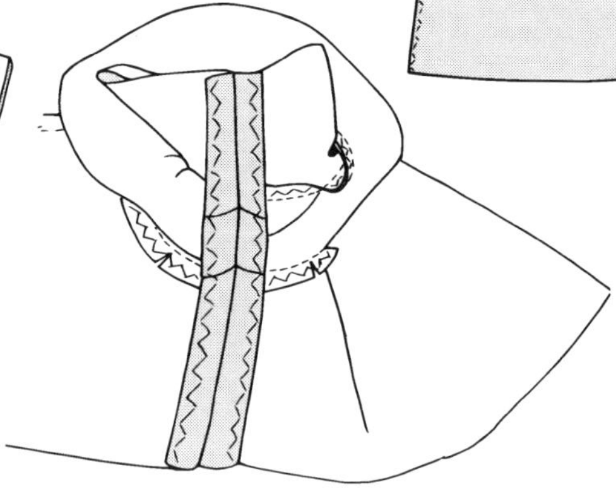

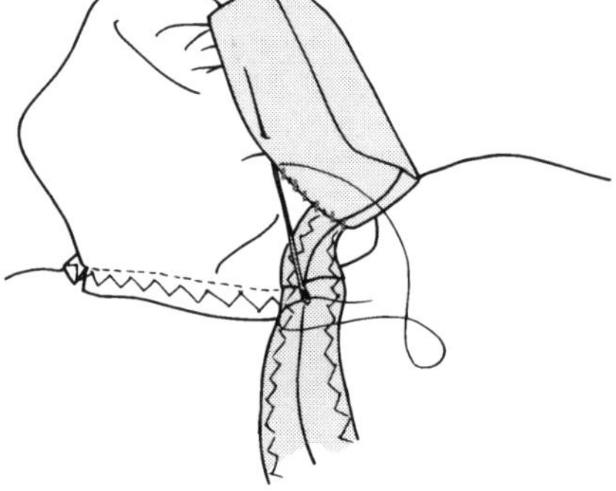

Step 10: Fold each sleeve band under along the fold line and seam allowance to form a double-fold hem. Hand stitch along the seamline to secure.

Finishing the Blouse

Step 11: With the right sides together, fold the back facings over along the fold line at the bottom edge and pin in place. Stitch across the facings at the hemline using a 3/8- inch (9 mm) seam allowance. Finish the bottom edge of the blouse from facing to facing. Turn the facings right side out, squaring the corners with a blunt needle. Press the back facing from the neckline to the hem along the fold line. Turn up a 3/8-inch (9 mm) hem and press to crease. Hand or machine stitch the hem between the facings.

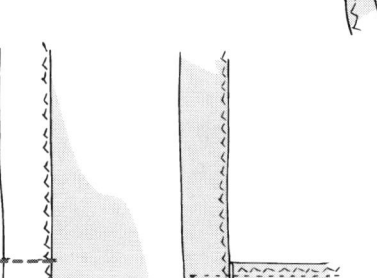

Step 12: Make buttonholes on the proper left and apply buttons on the proper right where indicated on the pattern. Attach a decorative bow under the center front collar.

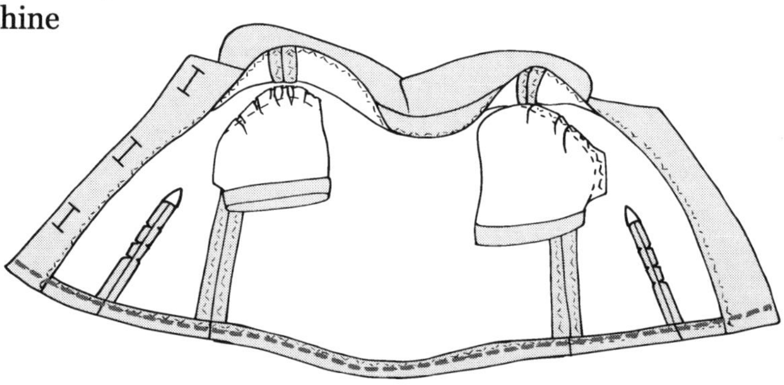

Skirt

Step 13: Mark the pleat placement lines on the right side of the skirt. Cut the back edge of the skirt along the proper left cutting line (the right edge of the fabric when viewed from the right side). Finish the back edges of the skirt.

Step 14: With the right sides together, fold the back skirt facings over along the foldlines at the bottom edge. Pin in place. Stitch across the facing at the hemline with a 1/2-inch (12 mm) seam allowance. Finish the bottom edge of the skirt. Turn right side out, squaring the corner with a blunt needle. Press the facing along the fold line. Press the hem under 1/2-inch (12 mm). Stitch the hem by hand or by machine.

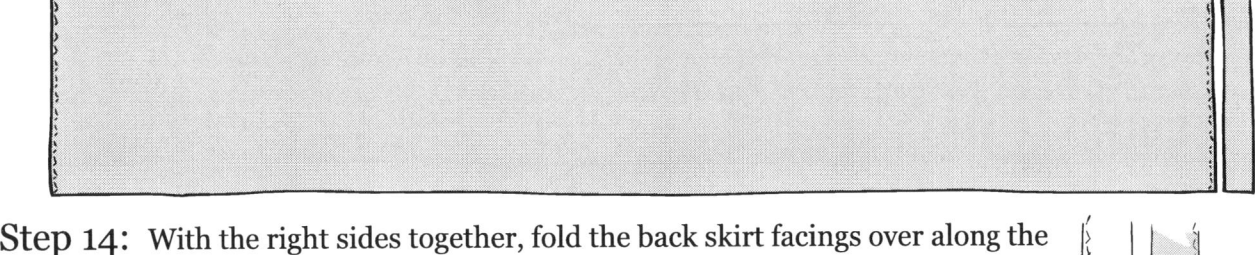

Step 15: Pin the back facings at the top edge to secure. Working from left to right, fold pleats where indicated on the pattern and press each pleat from top to bottom along the pleat lines to crease. Sew two rows of gathering stitches along the top edge of the pleats to secure.

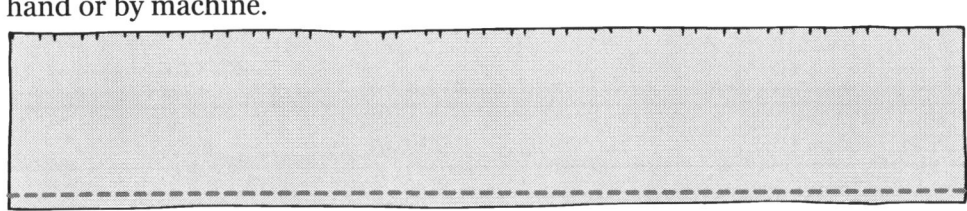

Skirt Waistband and Suspenders

Step 16: Fold the waistband in half along the fold line, wrong side out. Turn up a 1/4-inch (6 mm) seam allowance on one side and press. Stitch each end of the waisband. Turn right side out, squaring the corners with a blunt needle. Press.

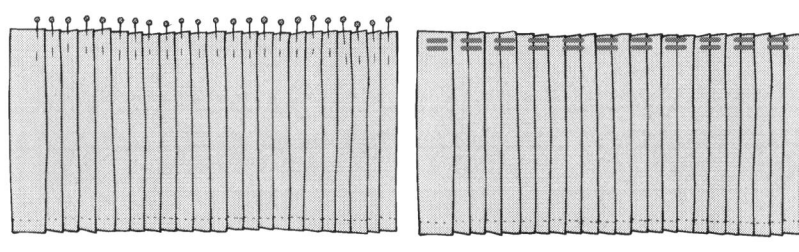

Step 17: Pin two sets of strap pieces right sides together. Stitch, leaving the angled edges open for turning. Grade the seam allowances, clip and notch the corners, and turn right side out. Square the corners with a blunt needle and press, following the seamline. Finish the raw edges of the straps by turning them inside and whipstitching the ends closed or simply serge or zigzag over the ends.

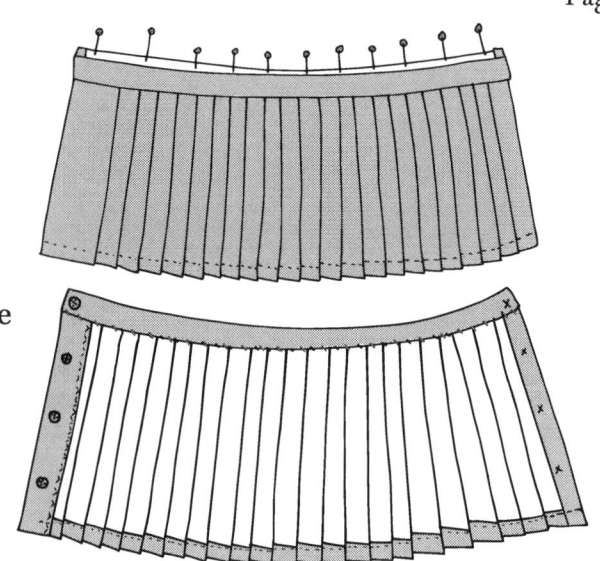

Step 18: With the right sides together, pin the waistband to the top edge of the skirt. Stitch, being careful not to catch the folded edge of the waistband in the seamline. Turn the waisband over the seam allowance and pin along the seamline. Whipstitch the folded edge along the seamline to secure. Attach snaps along the back edge where indicated on the pattern.

Step 19: Attach the straps with buttons to the front of the waistband where indicated on the pattern.

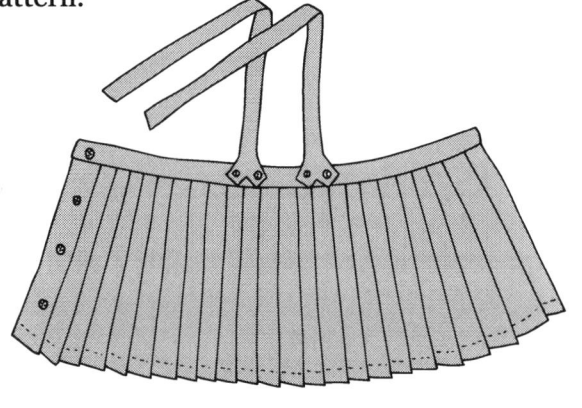

Step 20: Test fit the skirt and straps on the doll to determine where to attach the snaps at the back. Use the dots on the back of the waistband as a guide. Apply the snaps to the ends of the straps and back inside waistband.

Jacket

Step 21: With the right sides together, pin the jacket back pieces along the back edge. Stitch. Clip the curve and press the seam allowances open. Pin the jacket front and jacket back pieces right sides together along the shoulders. Stitch and press the seam allowances open. Stay-stitch the armscyes and clip the curves. Repeat for the jacket lining.

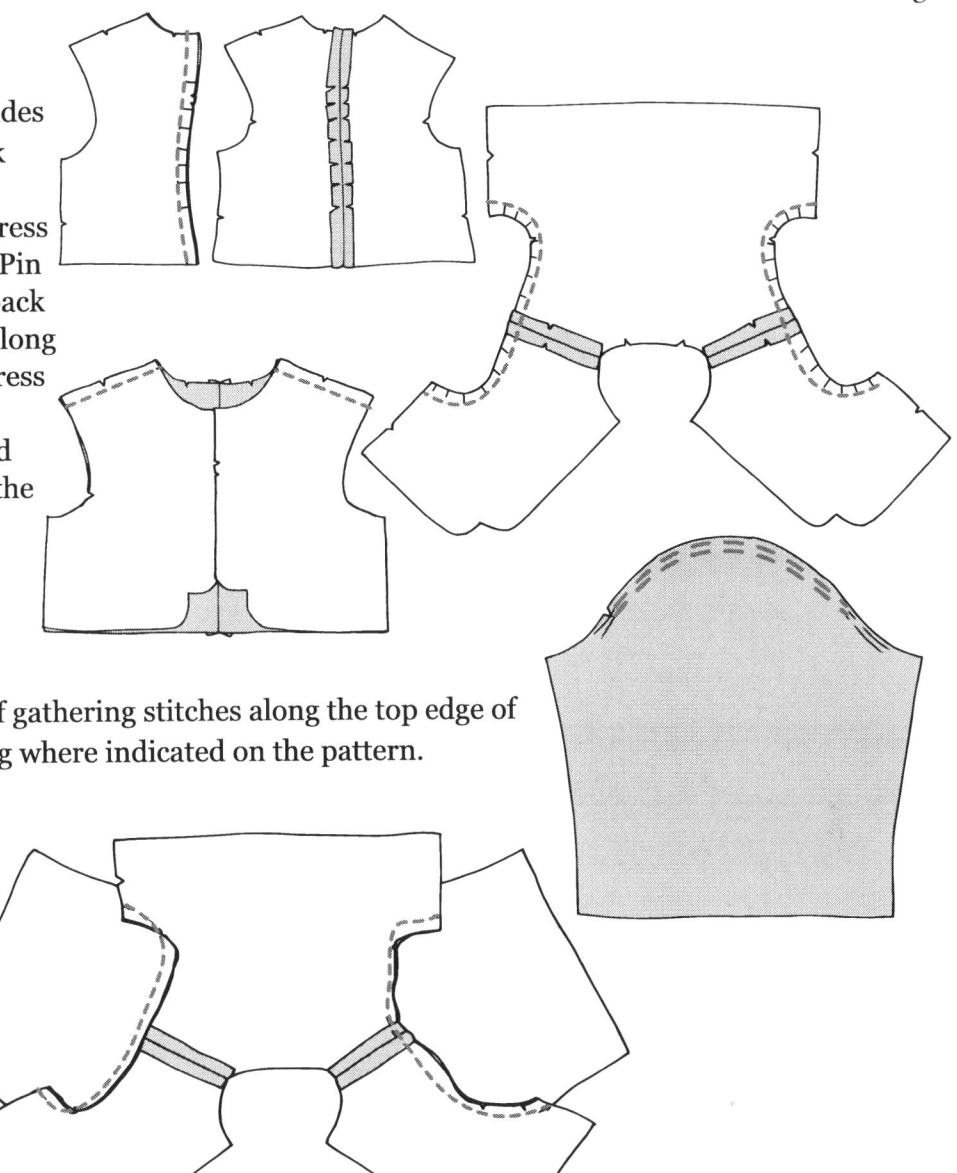

Step 22: Sew two rows of gathering stitches along the top edge of each sleeve and sleeve lining where indicated on the pattern.

Step 23: With the right sides together, pin the sleeves to the armscyes, matching the notches. Ease the top edge of the sleeves to fit. Stitch. Clip the curves and press the seam allowances toward the sleeves. Repeat for lining.

Step 24: With the right sides together, pin the jacket lining to the jacket along the front edges and neckline, the lower edges of the sleeves, and the lower edge of the back. Stitch. Clip the corners and curves. Turn the jacket right side out, squaring the corners with a blunt needle. Press following the seamlines. Finish the side seam allowances if desired.

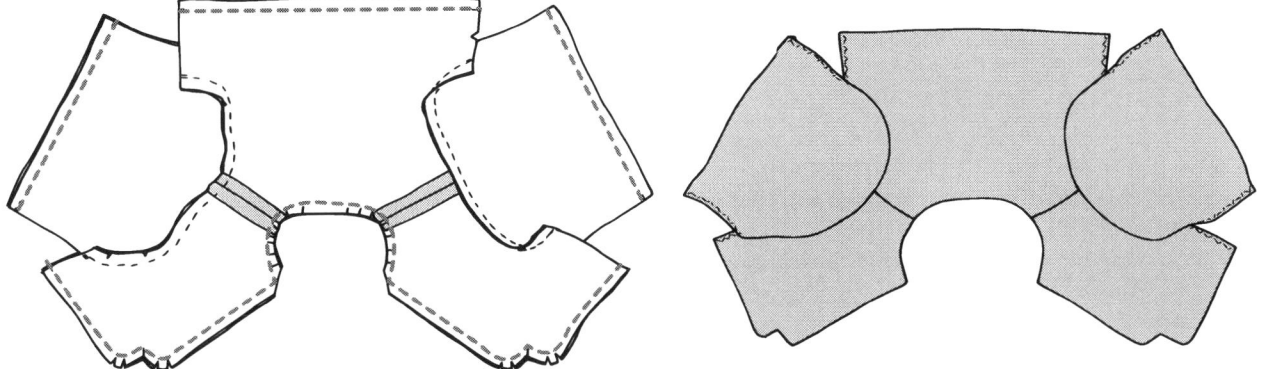

Step 25: With the right sides together, pin the sides of the bodice together, aligning the seamlines of the armscyes and the bottom edges of the bodice and sleeves. Stitch. Press the seam allowances open. Tack the ends of the seam allowances to the bottom edges of the sleeve and bodice to secure. Turn the jacket right side out.

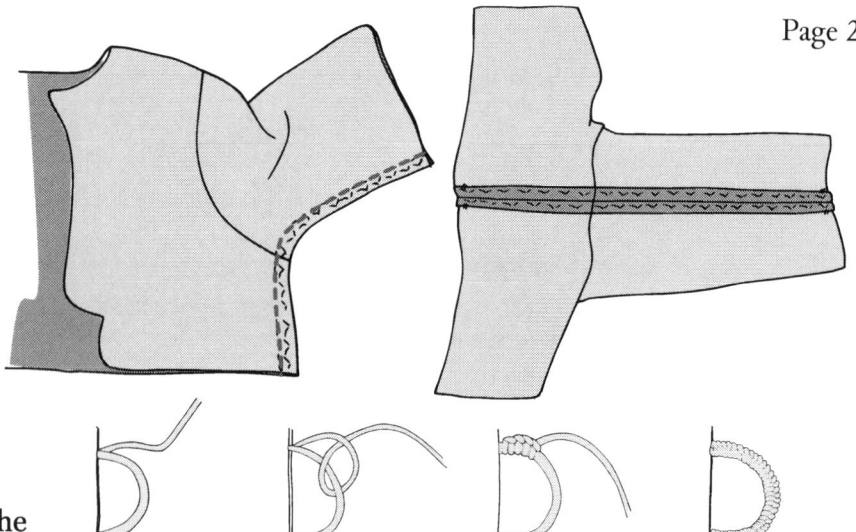

Step 26: Make a button loop on the proper right side of the jacket front and attach button where indicated on the pattern.

To make the button loop, use a single strand of button thread to make a loop that loosely fits the diameter of the button. Tack the loop in place at each end to secure. Do not cut the thread.

Starting at the end that the thread is attached, make a blanket stitch on the thread loop. Tighten the stitch snugly around the loop.

Continue adding stitches until the loop is completely covered.

Tack the end of the thread at the end of the loop and draw it through the fabric to hide. Trim off the extra thread.

Hat

Step 27: With the right sides together and matching the notches, pin two sets of hat crowns together along a side edge. Stitch. Clip the curves and press the seam allowances open. Repeat for the crown lining.

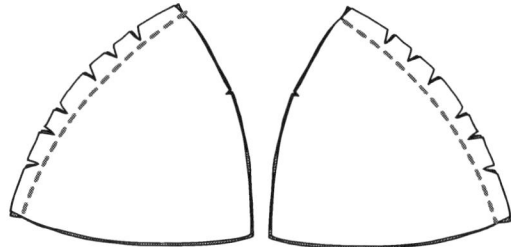

Step 28: With the right sides together and matching the notches, pin the two crown sections together along the side edges. Stitch. Clip the curves and press the seam allowances open. Repeat for the crown lining.

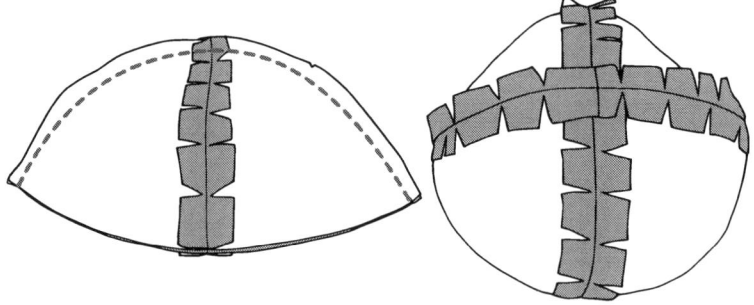

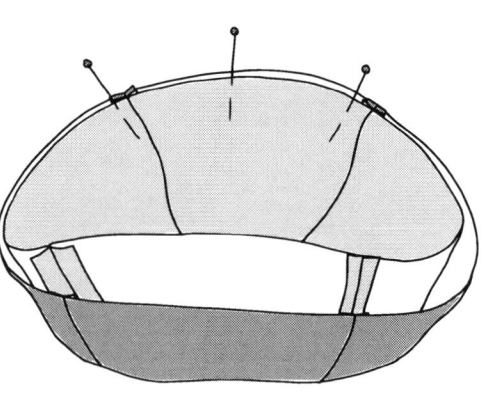

Step 29: Turn the crown right side out. Pin the crown and crown lining wrong sides together, matching the seam lines.

Step 30: With the right sides together, fold each brim piece in half, matching the notches. Stitch. Press the seam allowances open.

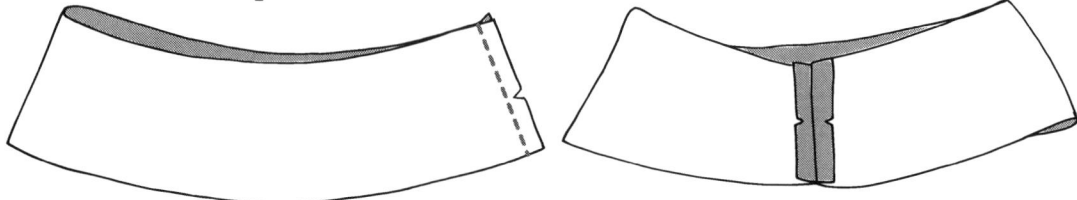

Step 31: With the right sides together, pin the inside curve of one of the hat brims along the bottom edge of the crown. To reduce bulk, the brim seam allowance should be centered on the back crown panel, not on a seam. Stitch. Clip the curve.

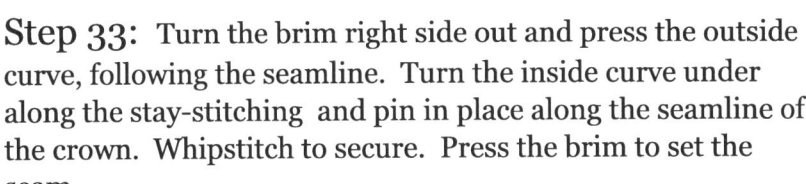

Step 32: Stay-stitch the other brim along the inside curve and clip the curve up to the stay-stitching. Turn the brim on the hat down. Pin the brim pieces right sides together along the outside curve. Stitch. Notch the curve along the seamline.

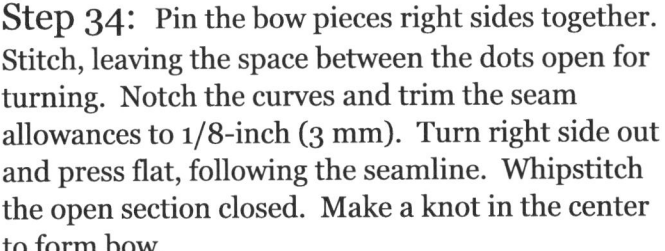

Step 33: Turn the brim right side out and press the outside curve, following the seamline. Turn the inside curve under along the stay-stitching and pin in place along the seamline of the crown. Whipstitch to secure. Press the brim to set the seam.

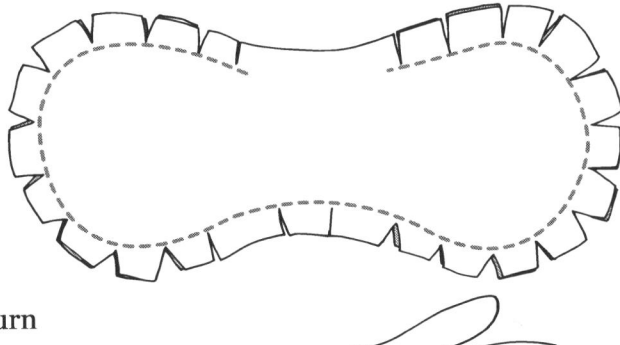

Step 34: Pin the bow pieces right sides together. Stitch, leaving the space between the dots open for turning. Notch the curves and trim the seam allowances to 1/8-inch (3 mm). Turn right side out and press flat, following the seamline. Whipstitch the open section closed. Make a knot in the center to form bow.

Step 35: Tack the bow to the top of the hat and turn the brim up to finish.

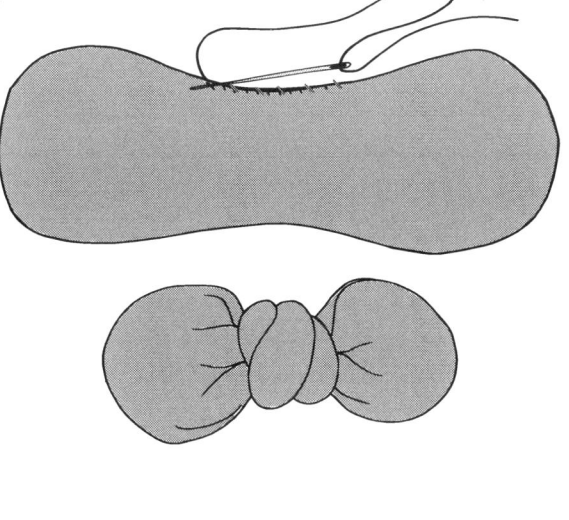

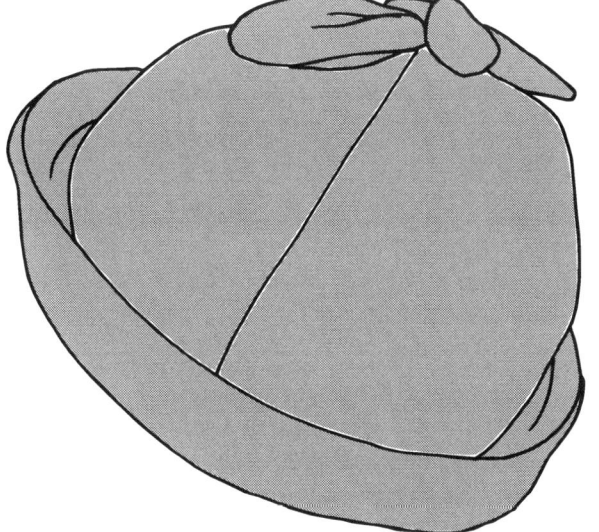

Page 30

Train Station
Pattern Pieces

Cutting Layout for 45-inch (1.14 m) wide Fabric
16 Pieces

11~ Jacket Front
12 ~ Jacket Back
13 ~ Jacket Sleeve
14 ~ Blouse Front
15 ~ Blouse Back
16 ~ Blouse Back Interfacing
17 ~ Blouse Front Facing
18 ~ Blouse Sleeve Band
19 ~ Blouse Collar
20 ~ Blouse Sleeve
21 ~ Straps
22 ~ Skirt Waistband
23 ~ Skirting
24 ~ Hat Crown
25 ~ Hat Brim
26 ~ Bow

Blouse
Pieces: 14, 15, 17, 18, 19, and 20

Skirt
Pieces: 21, 22, and 23

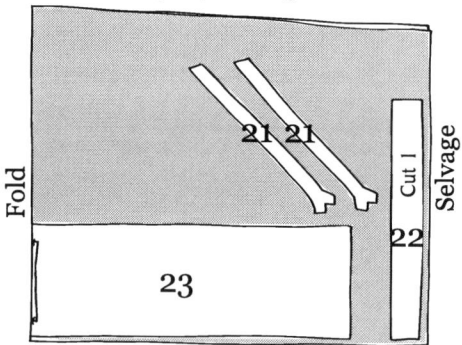

Interfacing
Pieces: 16 and 17

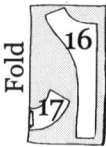

Jacket and Hat
Pieces: 11, 12, 13, 24, 25, and 26

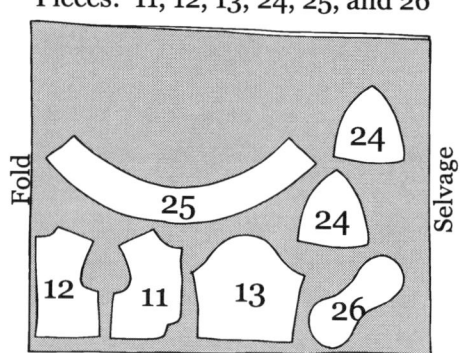

Jacket and Hat Lining
Pieces: 11, 12, 13, and 24

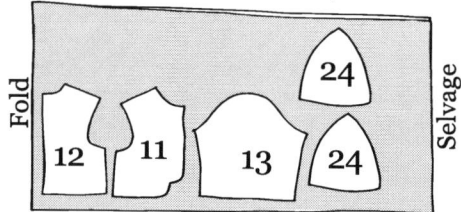

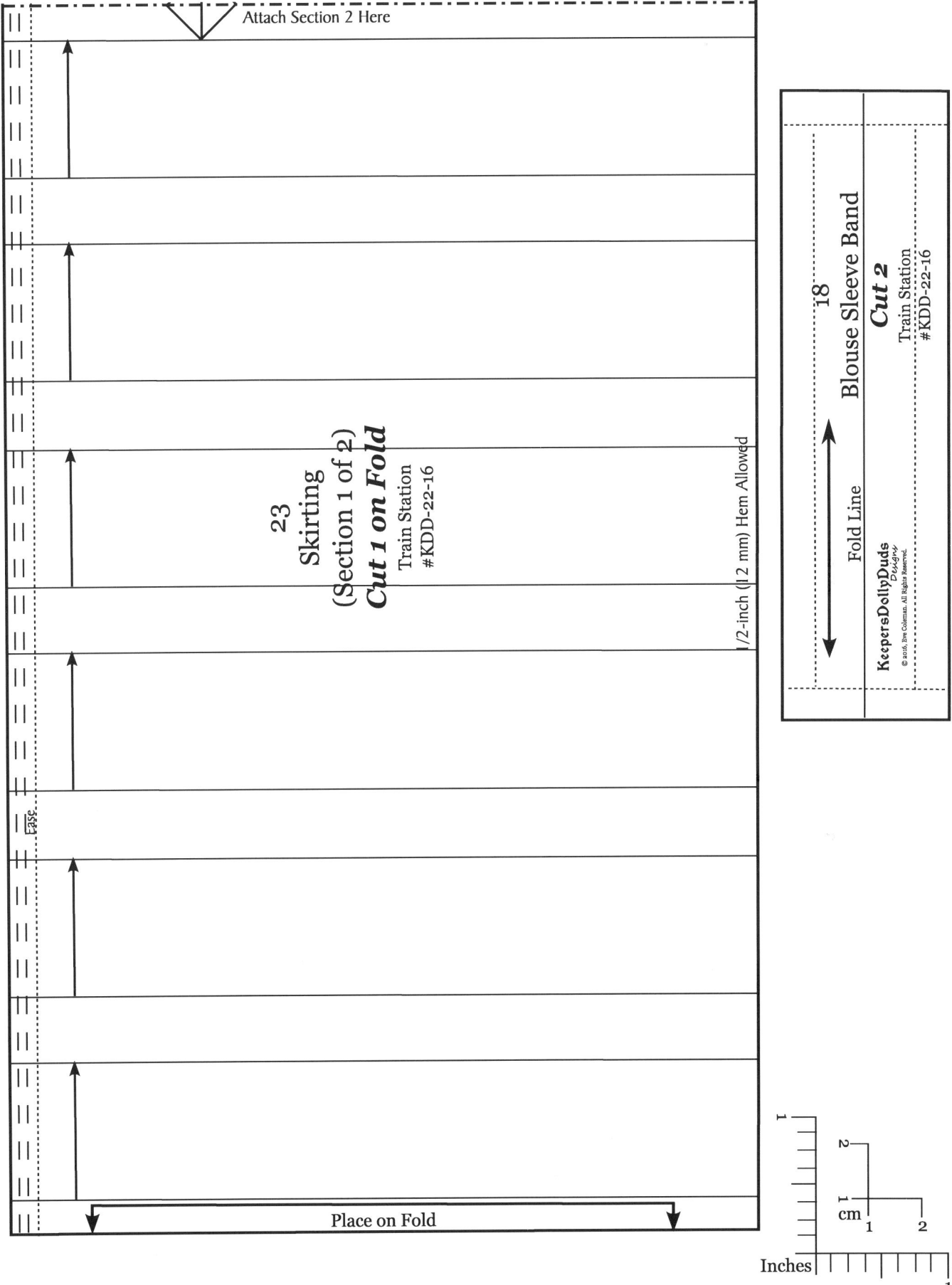

Page 33

26
Bow
Cut 2
Train Station
KDD-22-16

Leave Open Between Dots to Turn

KeepersDollyDuds
Designs
© 2016, Eve Coleman. All Rights Reserved.

cm
Inches

21
Straps
Cut 4
on the Bias
Train Station
#KDD-22-16

Proper Right Facing
Proper Left Facing
Fold Line for Proper Right
Cut Here for Proper Left
Fold Line for Proper Left

23
Skirting
(Section 2 of 2)
Train Station
#KDD-22-16

Attach Section 1 Here

KeepersDollyDuds
Designs
© 2016, Eve Coleman. All Rights Reserved.

Page 35

**13
Jacket Sleeve
Cut 2 of Fabric
Cut 2
Train Station
#KDD-22-16**

KeepersDollyDuds Designs
© 2016, Eve Coleman. All Rights Reserved.

**20
Blouse Sleeve
Cut 2
Train Station
#KDD-22-16**

KeepersDollyDuds Designs
© 2016, Eve Coleman. All Rights Reserved.

Page 37

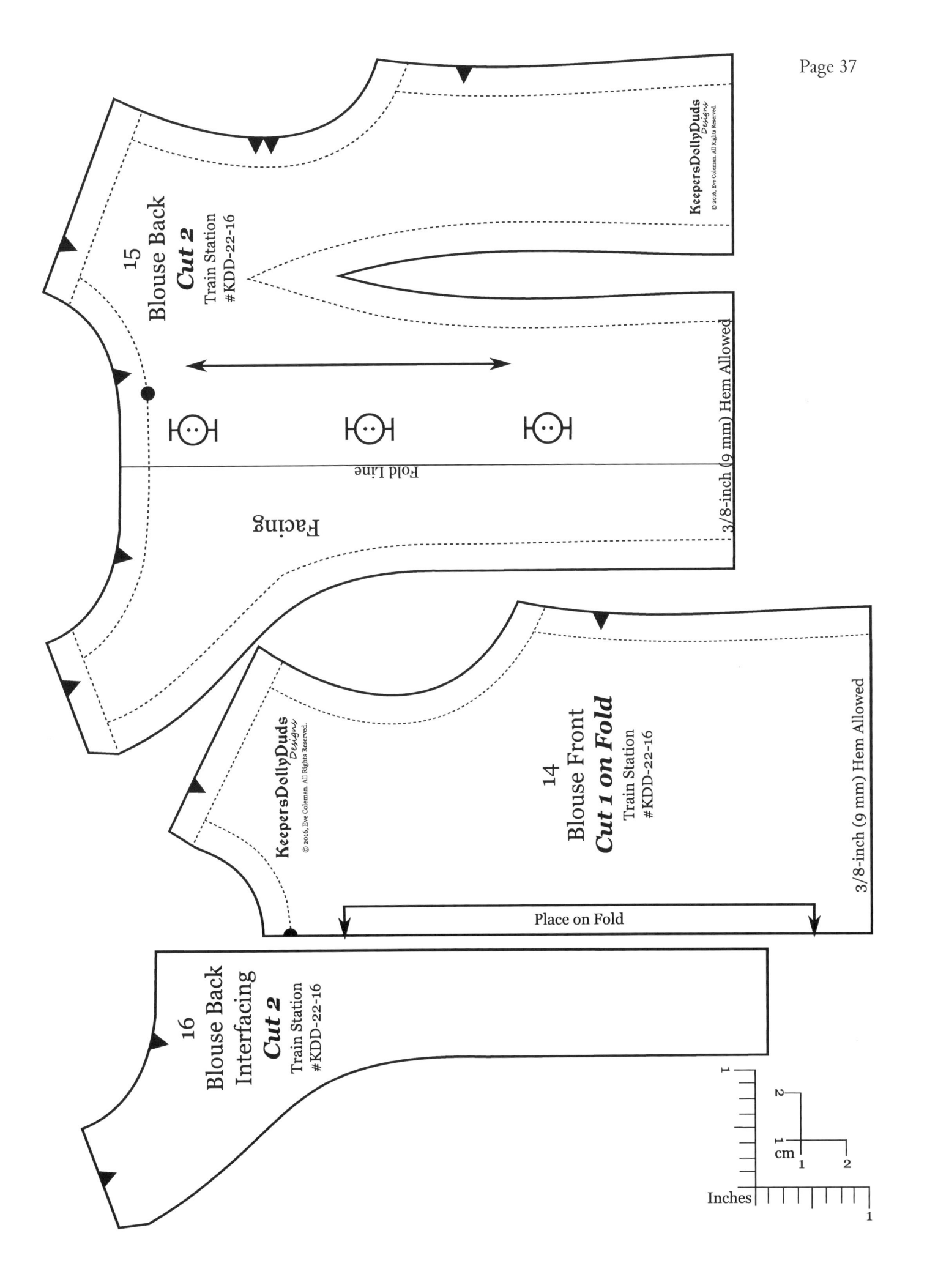

Page 39

12
Jacket Back
Cut 2 Fabric
Cut 2 Lining
Train Station
#KDD-22-16

KeepersDollyDuds
Designs
© 2016, Eve Coleman. All Rights Reserved.

19
Blouse Collar
Cut 4 on the Bias
Train Station
#KDD-22-16

KeepersDollyDuds
Designs
© 2016, Eve Coleman. All Rights Reserved.

17
Blouse Neck Facing
Cut 1 of Fabric on Fold
Cut 1 of Interfacing on Fold
Train Station

KeepersDollyDuds
Designs

Place on Fold

22
Skirt Waistband
Cut 1 of Fabric
Train Station
#KDD-22-16

Fold Line

KeepersDollyDuds
Designs
© 2016, Eve Coleman. All Rights Reserved.

11
Jacket Front
Cut 2 Fabric
Cut 2 Lining
Train Station
#KDD-22-16

KeepersDollyDuds
Designs
© 2016, Eve Coleman. All Rights Reserved.

Inches

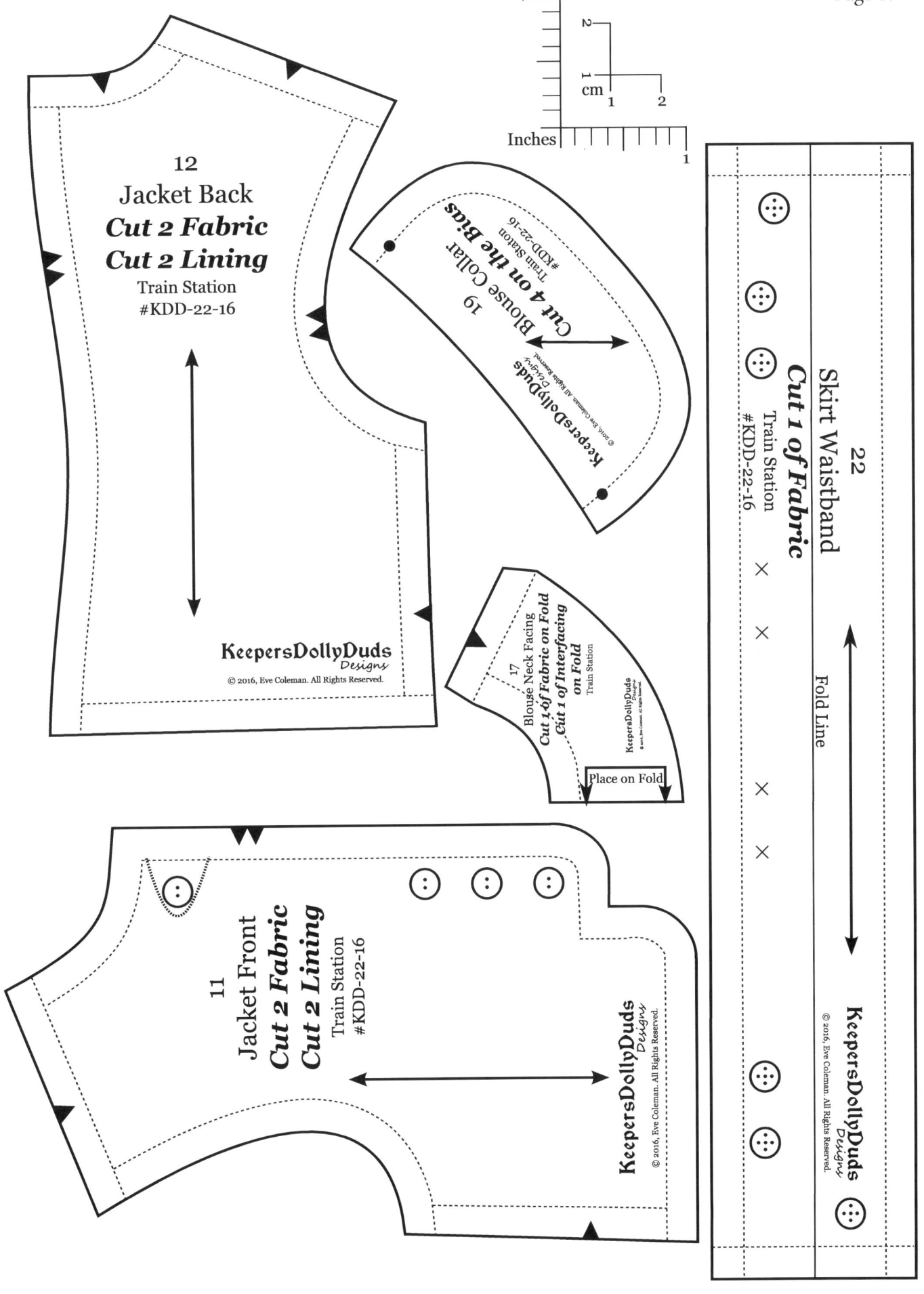

cm

Page 41

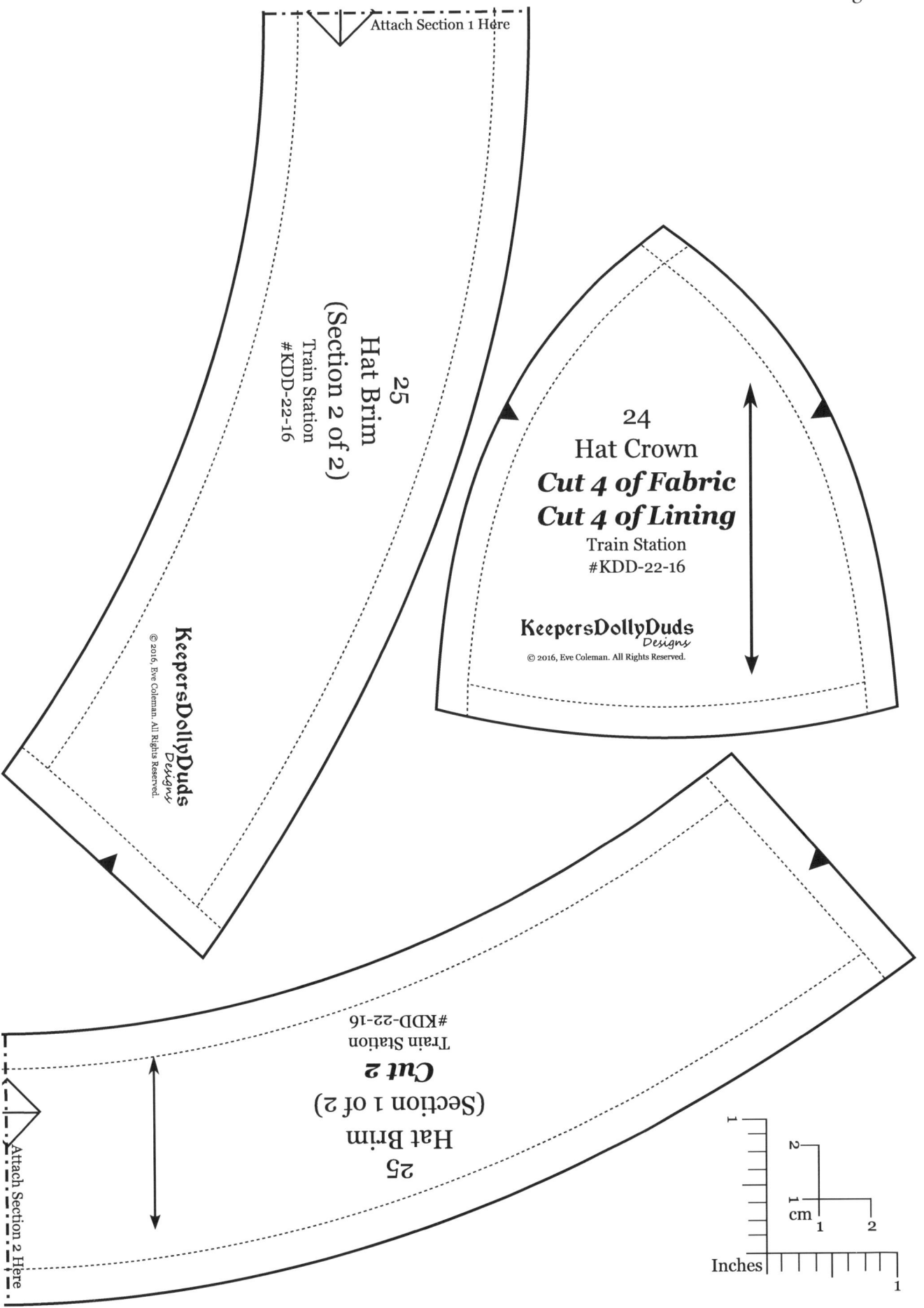

25 Hat Brim (Section 2 of 2)
Train Station
#KDD-22-16

24 Hat Crown
Cut 4 of Fabric
Cut 4 of Lining
Train Station
#KDD-22-16

KeepersDollyDuds Designs
© 2016, Eve Coleman. All Rights Reserved.

25 Hat Brim (Section 1 of 2)
Cut 2
Train Station
#KDD-22-16

Attach Section 1 Here
Attach Section 2 Here

Page 43

Bodice Details

Materials List
#KDD-14-16

Suggested Fabrics: **View A & View B Dress** in lightweight cotton, cotton blends, or linen. Not suitable for knits.

Fabric Yardage:

View A Dress ~ 1/2 yard (0.5 m)
View A Contrast ~ 1/6 yard (0.15 m)
View B Dress ~ 1/2 yard (0.5 m)
View B Contrast ~ 1/6 yard (0.15 m)

Notions:
___Thread
View A Dress
___1/4 yard (0.25 m) 1/2-inch (12 mm) wide lace or bias tape
___five 3/8-inch (9 mm) buttons
___one decorative bow
View B Dress
___6-1/2-inches of bias trim
___one slider buckle with a 1/2-inch (12 mm) opening
___five 3/8-inch (9 mm) buttons
___three 1/4-inch (6 mm) decorative buttons

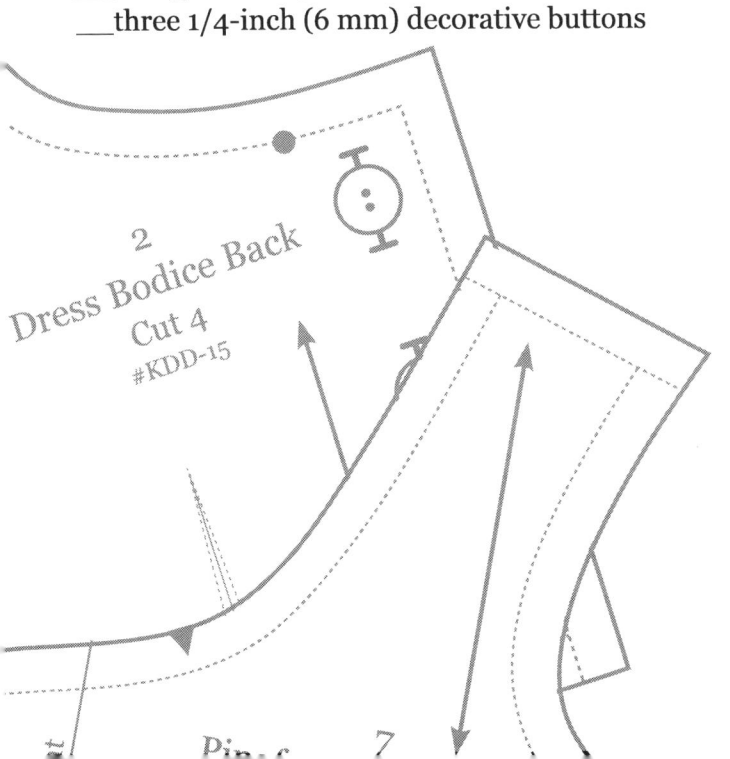

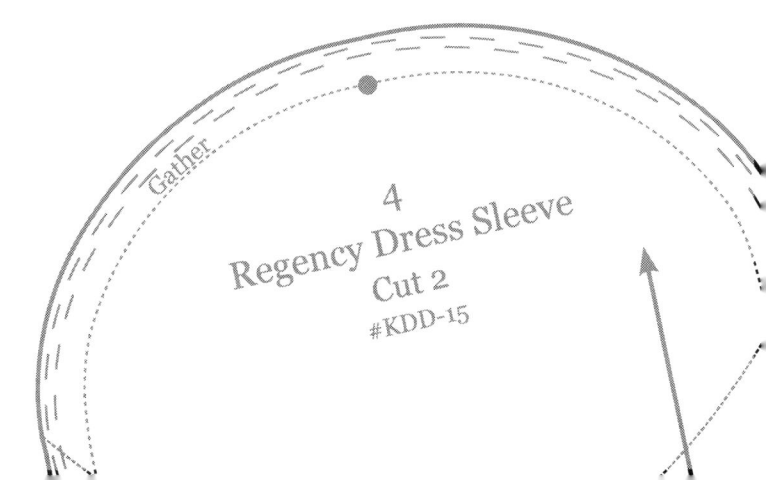

View B

Page 44

View A & View B Bodice Trim

Step 1: Apply trim along the trim line where indicated on the pattern. *For View B, skip to Step 5.*

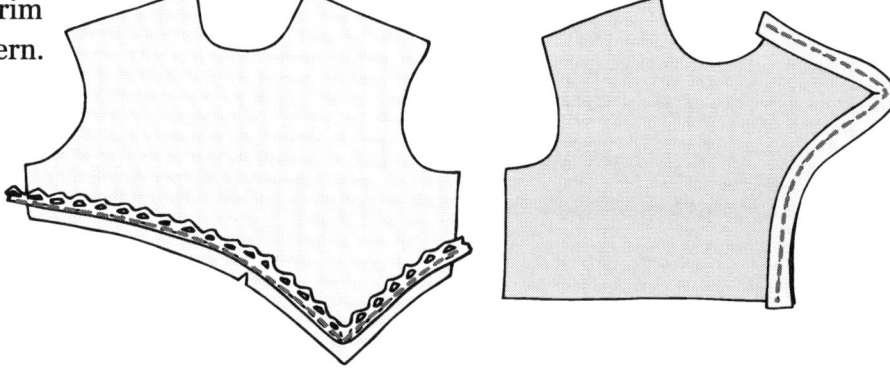

View A Bodice Front Overlay

Step 2: With the right sides together, pin the waist under-band along the bottom and front edges. Stitch. Clip the corner and curve.

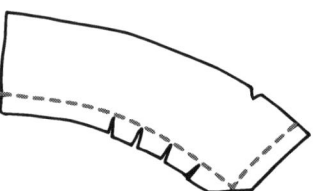

Step 3: Turn the waist under-band right side out, squaring the corner with a blunt needle. Press flat, following the seamline. Clip the notched curve on the bodice front overlay. Matching the notches, pin the waist under-band to the bodice front overlay easing the clipped edge along the curve. Baste in place.

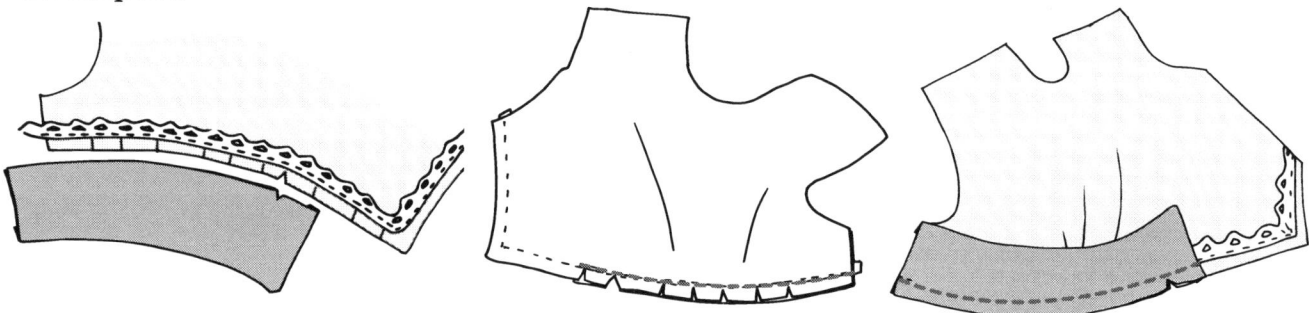

Step 4: Apply interfacing to bodice overlay facing following manufacturer's instructions. Finish the top edge of the bodice overlay facing. With right sides together, pin the facing to the bodice front overlay, matching the notches. Stitch. Clip the corners and curves. Turn right side out, squaring the corner with a blunt needle. Press flat following the seamline. *Skip to Step 6.*

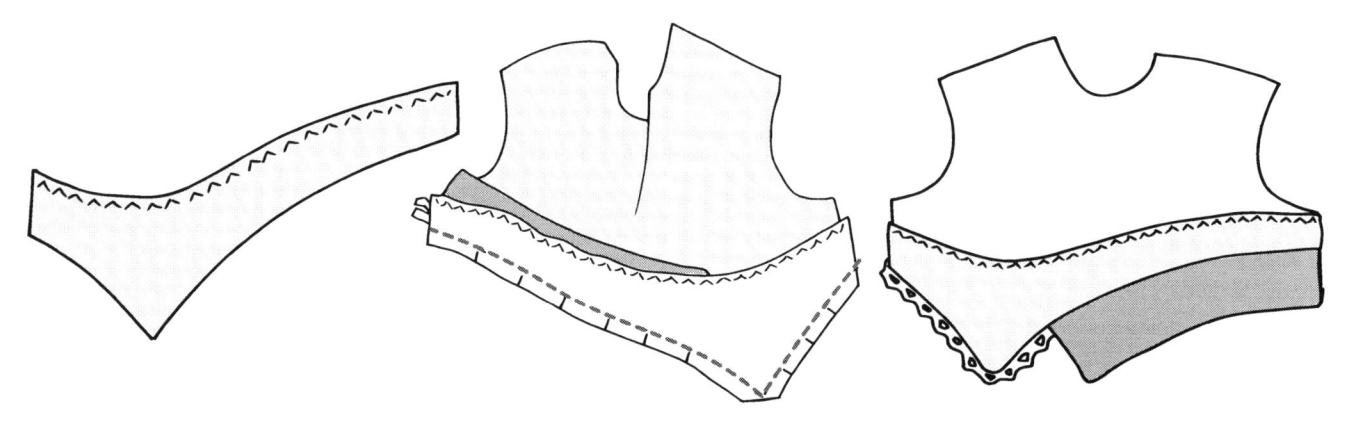

View B Bodice Front Overlay

Step 5: Finish the inside edge of the overlay facing. With the right sides together and matching the notches, pin the facing to the bodice front overlay. Stitch. Clip the corners and curves. Turn right side out, squaring the corner with a blunt needle. Press flat, following the seamline.

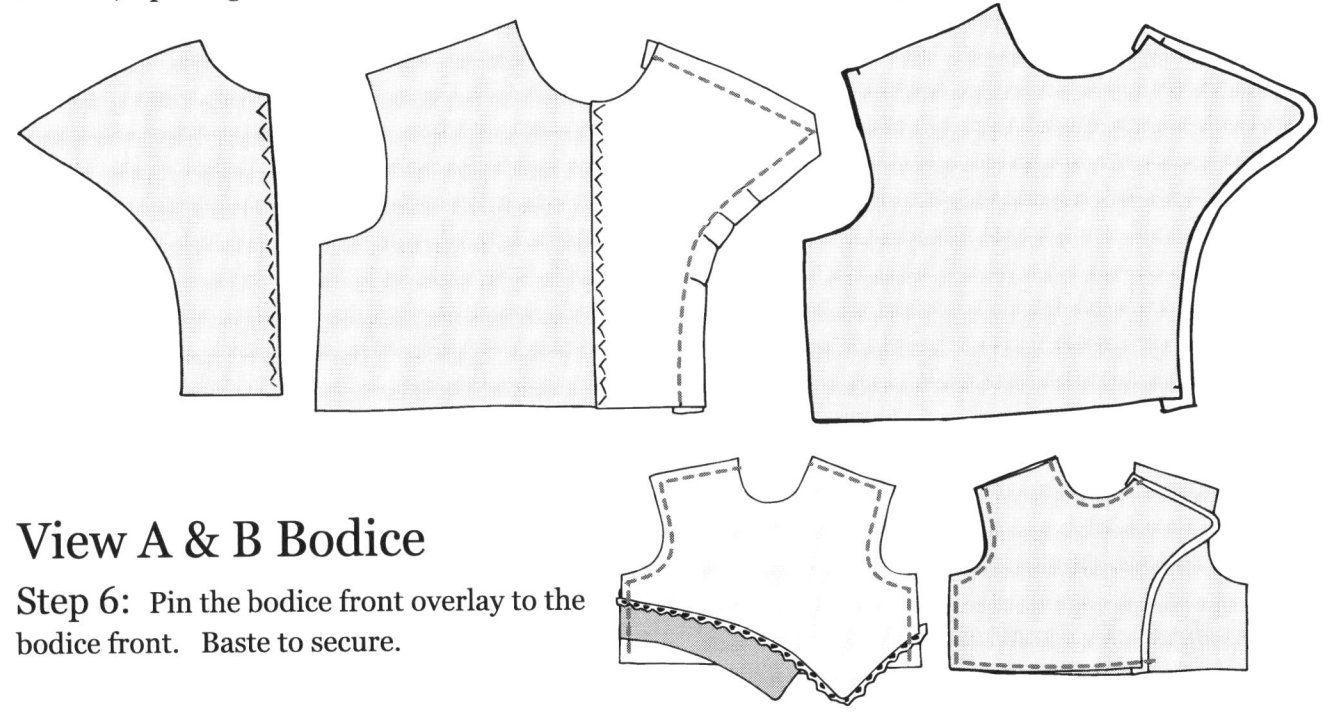

View A & B Bodice

Step 6: Pin the bodice front overlay to the bodice front. Baste to secure.

Step 7: Apply interfacing to the bodice back and front facings, following the manufacturer's instructions. Sew the darts on the bodice back pieces and press toward the back.

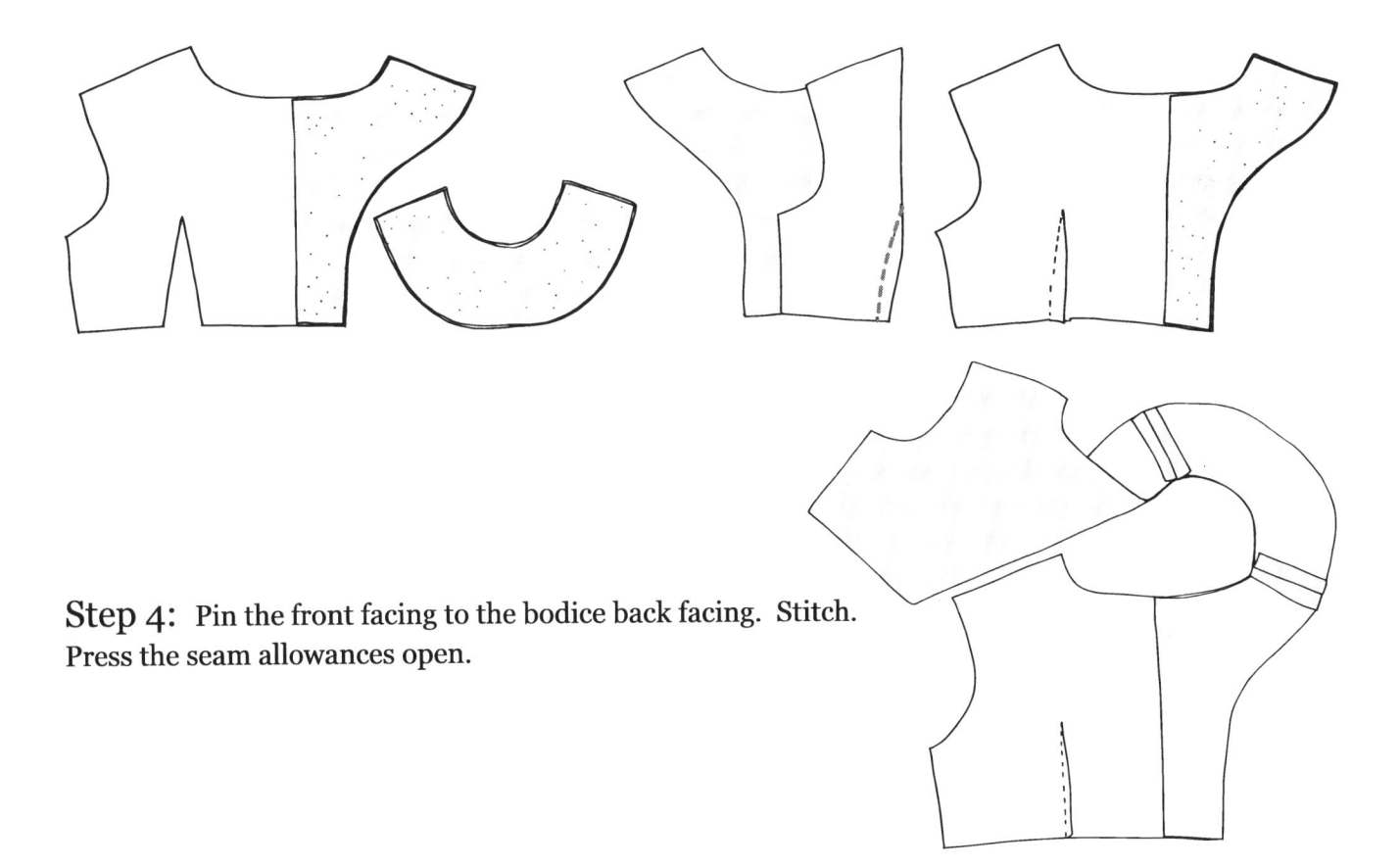

Step 4: Pin the front facing to the bodice back facing. Stitch. Press the seam allowances open.

Page 45

Step 9: Pin the bodice back pieces to the bodice front along the shoulders. Stitch. Press the seam allowances open.

View A & B Collar

Step 10: With the right sides together, pin the collar pieces along the outside edges. Stitch. Notch the curves and trim the seam allowances to 1/8-inch (3 mm). Turn right side out and press, following the seamline.

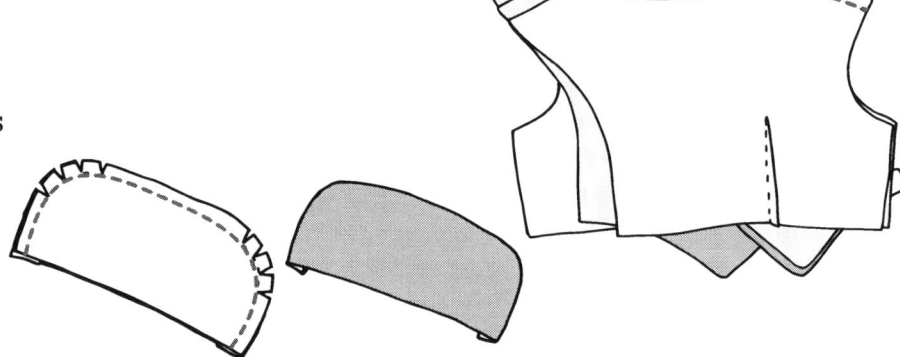

Step 11: Matching the ends of the collar to the dots, pin the collar to the right side of the bodice neckline. Bring the bodice facing over the collar and pin in place, taking care to line up the seamlines at the shoulders. Stitch. Clip the corners and curves and turn right side out, squaring the corners with a blunt needle. Understitch the neckline. Press, following the seamline. *For View B, skip to Step 16. For Alternate Long Sleeves skip to Step 25.*

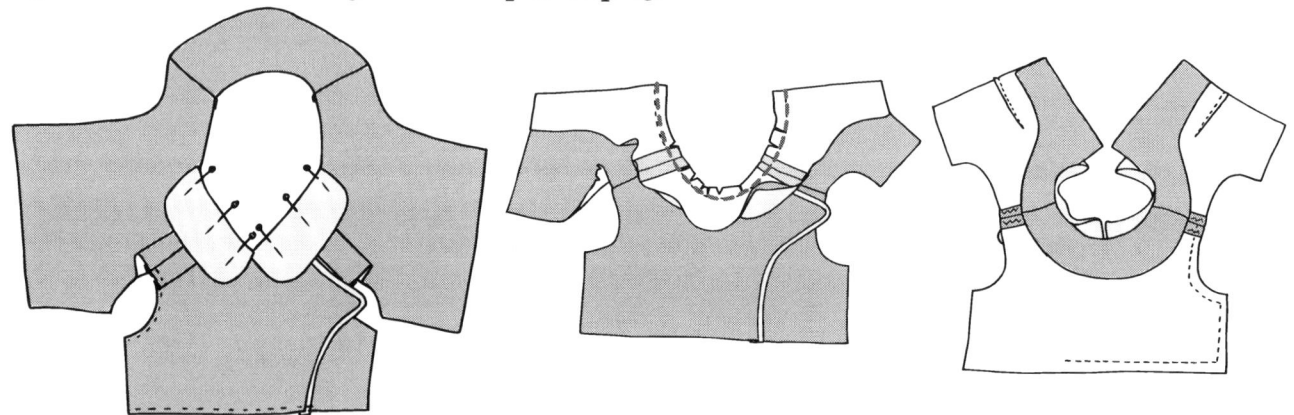

View A Sleeves and Ties

For View B, Skip to Step 16 and For Alternate Long Sleeves, Skip to Step 25

Step 12: Sew two rows of gathering stitches along the top and bottom edges of the sleeves where indicated on the pattern. With the right sides together, pin the lower edge of the sleeve to the sleeve bands, drawing the gathering stitches to fit. Arrange the fullness evenly along the band. Stitch. Press the seam allowances toward the sleeve band being careful not to crush the fullness on the sleeve.

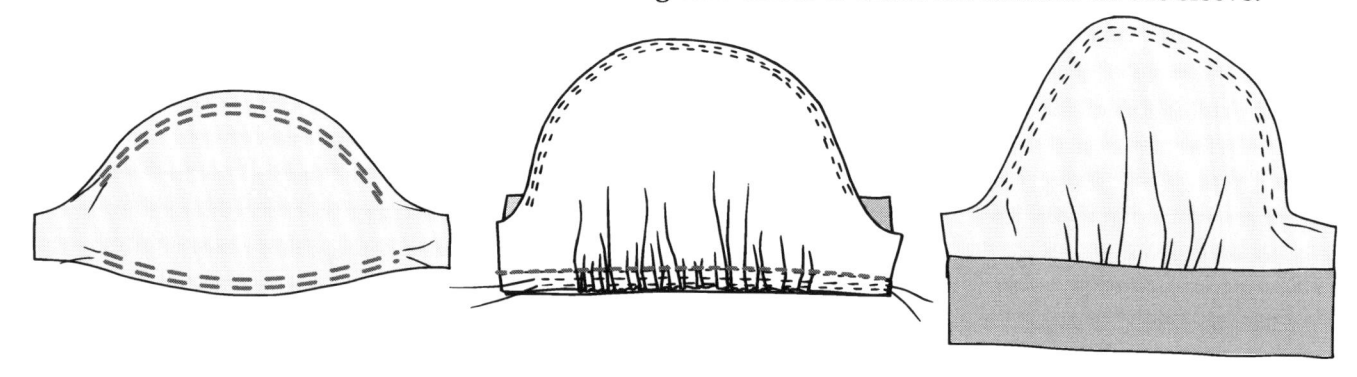

Step 13: With the right sides together and matching the notches, pin the sleeves to the armscyes of the bodice. Draw up the gathering stitches to fit, arranging the fullness evenly along the armscyes. Stitch. Clip the curves and finish the seam allowances, if desired. Press seam allowances toward the bodice.

Step 14: Fold the ties in half along the fold lines, right sides together. Stitch leaving one end open. Clip the corners and trim the seam allowances to 1/8-inch (3 mm). Turn right side out, squaring the corners with a blunt needle. Press, following the seamlines.

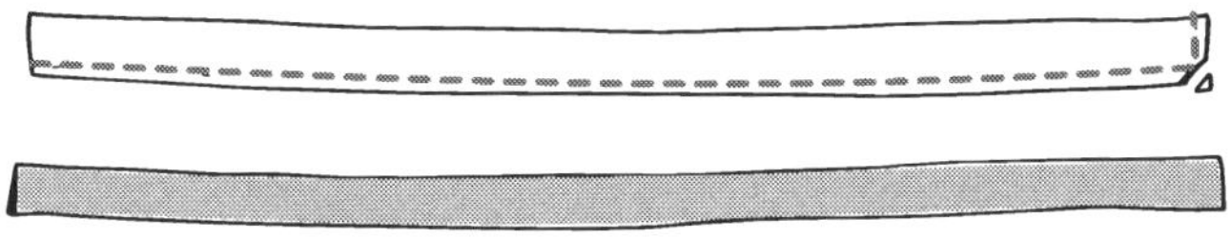

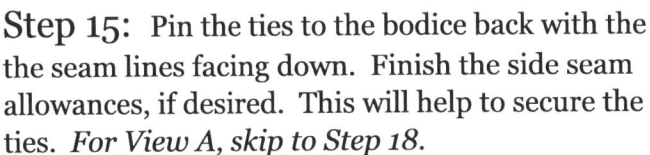

Step 15: Pin the ties to the bodice back with the the seam lines facing down. Finish the side seam allowances, if desired. This will help to secure the ties. *For View A, skip to Step 18.*

View B Sleeves
For View A, Skip to Step 18

Step 16: With the right sides together, pin the sleeve pieces to their corresponding contrasting pieces along the bottom edges. Notch the curves and trim the seam allowances to 1/8-inch (3 mm). Turn right side out and press flat, following the seamline. Pin the back sleeves over the front sleeves, matching the center notches. Secure with two rows of gathering stitches.

Step 17: Pin the bodice overlay out of the way. With the right sides together, pin the sleeves to the armscyes of the bodice, matching the notches. Draw the gathering stitches to fit, arranging the fullness evenly along the armscye. Stitch. Clip the curves and finish the seam allowances, if desired. Press the seam allowances toward the bodice.

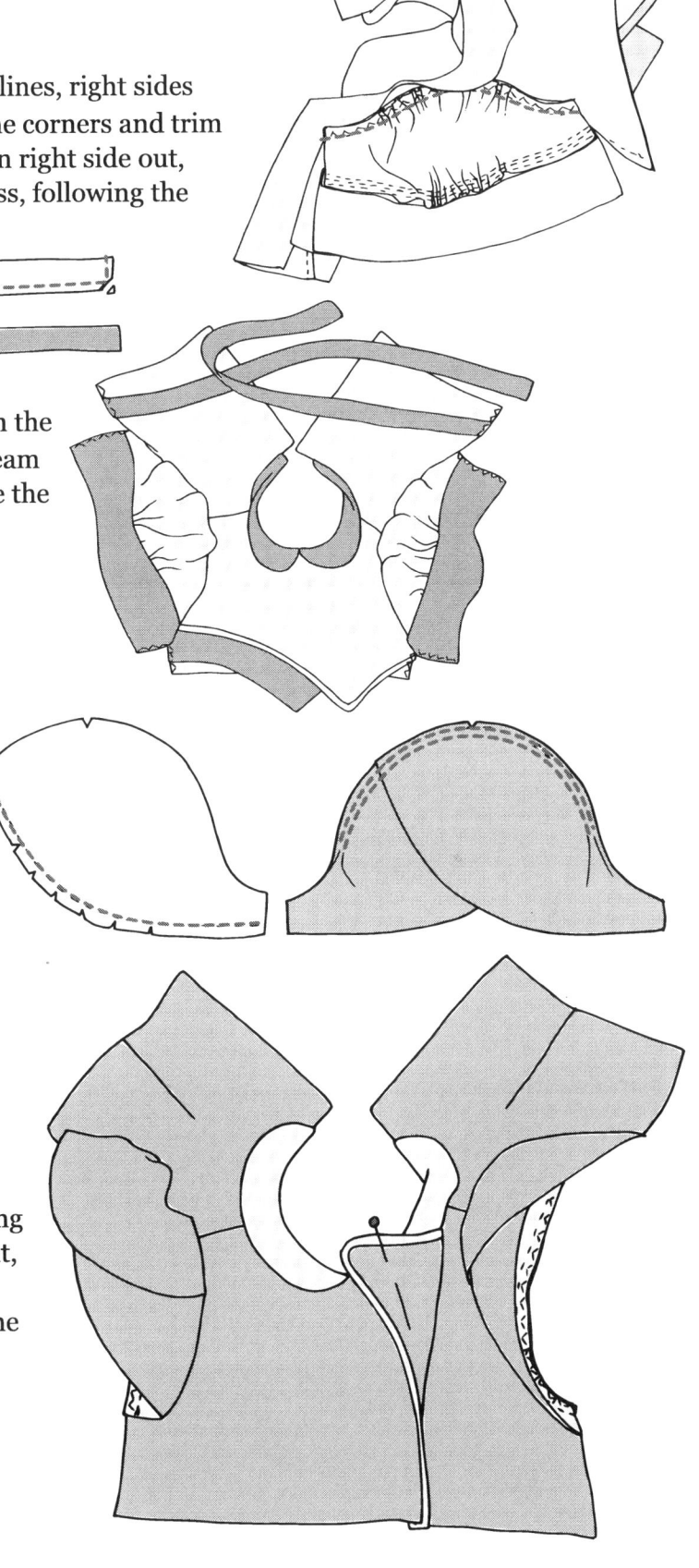

View A & B Bodice

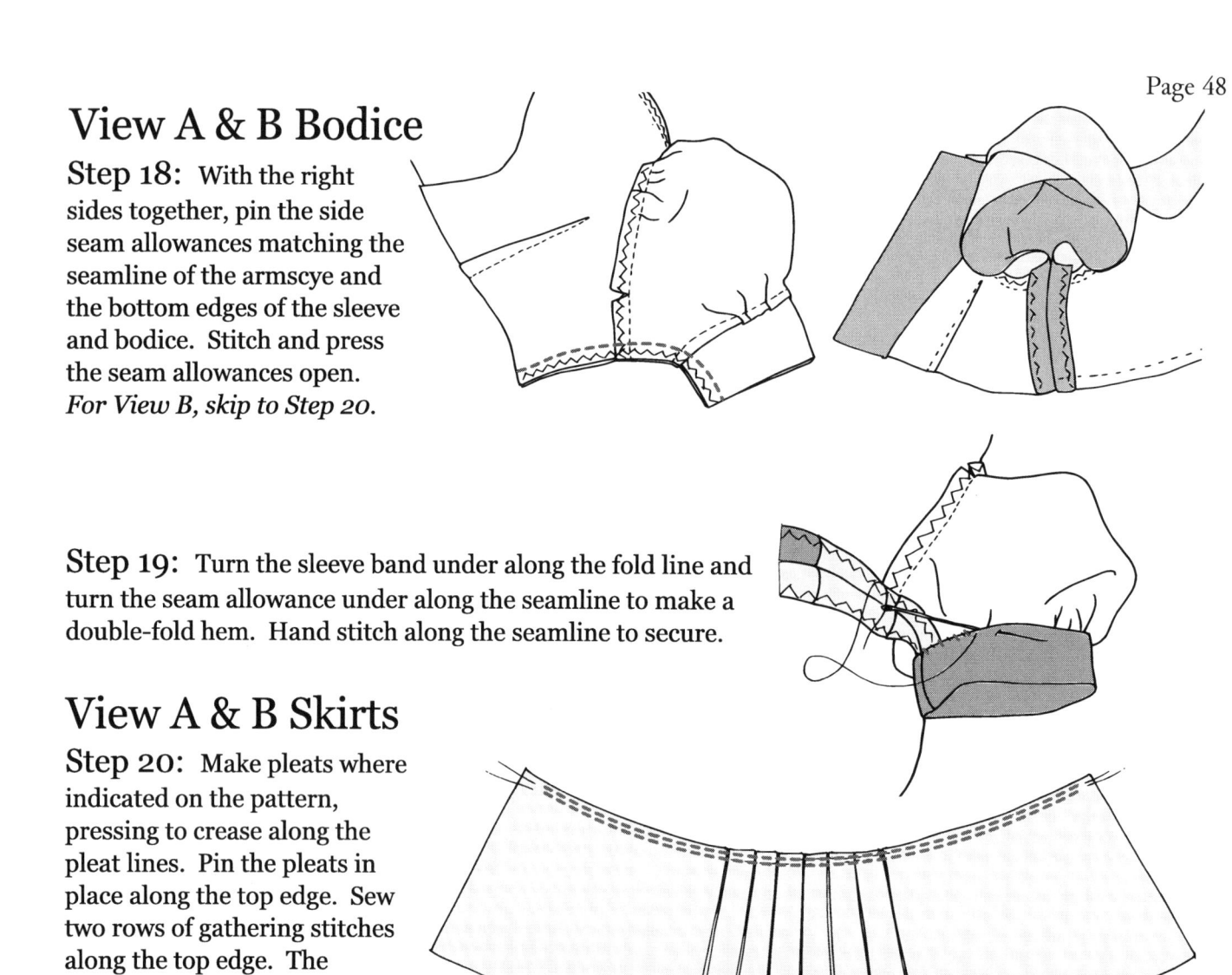

Step 18: With the right sides together, pin the side seam allowances matching the seamline of the armscye and the bottom edges of the sleeve and bodice. Stitch and press the seam allowances open. *For View B, skip to Step 20.*

Step 19: Turn the sleeve band under along the fold line and turn the seam allowance under along the seamline to make a double-fold hem. Hand stitch along the seamline to secure.

View A & B Skirts

Step 20: Make pleats where indicated on the pattern, pressing to crease along the pleat lines. Pin the pleats in place along the top edge. Sew two rows of gathering stitches along the top edge. The stitching hold the pleats in place. If preferred, the pleats can be omitted and gathering used instead.

Step 21: For View A, carefully pin the bodice overlay out of the way. For both views, pin the skirt to the bodice, centering the pleats along the bodice front and drawing up the gathering stitches evenly in back. Stitch. Finish the seam allowance, if desired. Press the seam allowance toward the bodice, being careful not to crush the gathers in the back. Finish the inside edges of the facings.

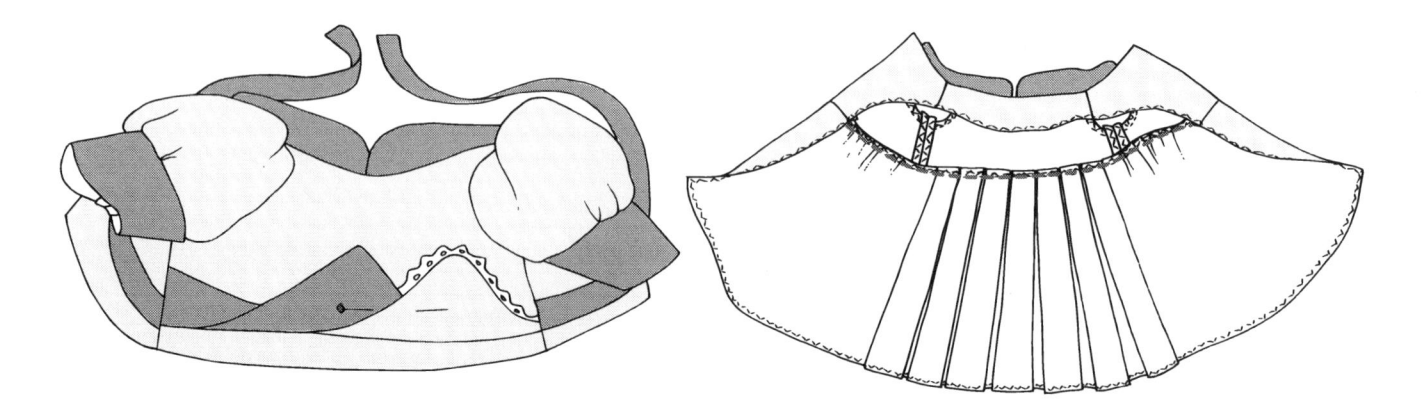

Step 22: With the right sides together, fold the back sides of the skirt over along the facing fold line. Pin in place at the bottom edge. Stitch across the facings at the hemline using a 3/8- inch (9 mm) seam allowance. Finish the bottom edge of the skirt. Turn the facings right side out, squaring the corners with a blunt needle. Press the back facings from the neckline to the hem along the fold line. Turn up a 3/8-inch (9 mm) hem and press to crease. Pin in place. Stitch between the facings. Press the pleats again to freshen the creases. Tack the facings to the bodice at the shoulder and waistline seams.

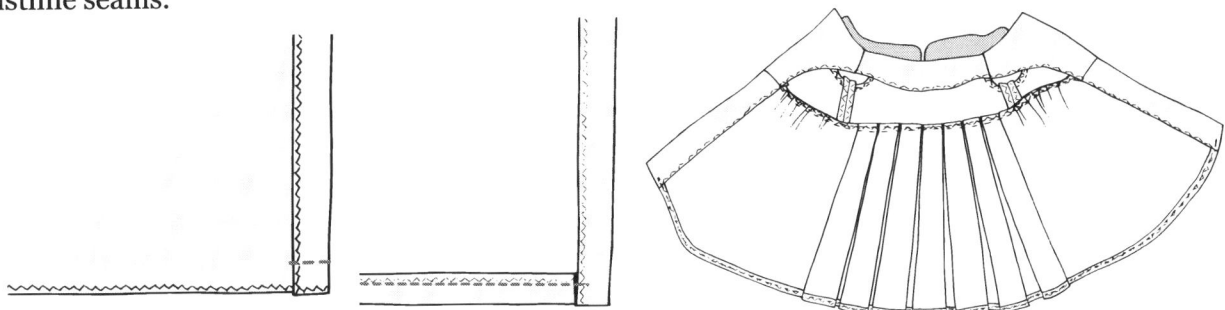

View B Belt

Step 23: With the right sides together, fold the belt in half along the fold line. Stitch, leaving the flat end open. Clip corners and trim the seam allowance to 1/8-inch (3 mm). Turn right side out, squaring the corners with a blunt needle. Press, following the seamline. Topstitch along the edges. Thread the open end of the belt through the center bar of the slider buckle. Turn the raw edge under and handstitch to secure.

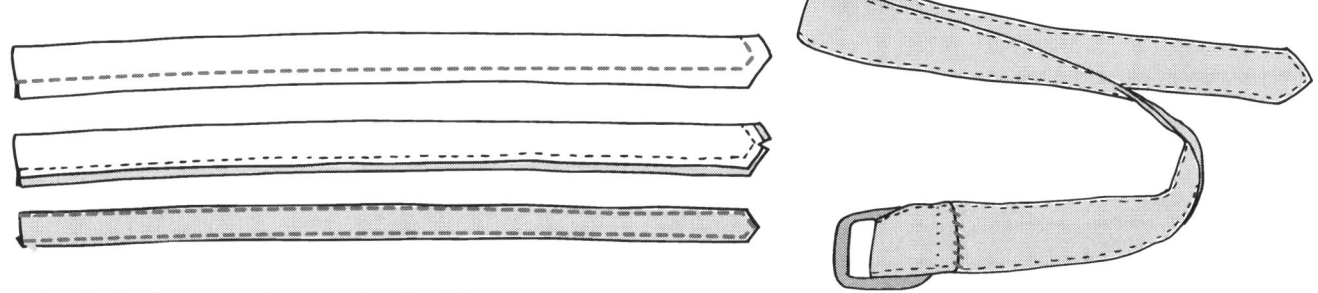

Finishing View A & B

Step 24: Make buttonholes on the proper left side of the bodice back and apply buttons on the proper right side of the bodice back where indicated on the pattern. Attach a decorative bow or buttons to the bodice front overly where indicated on the pattern.

Alternate Long Sleeves

Step 25: Cut each sleeve along the placket cutting line. Spread the cut edges apart. With the right sides together, pin one edge of a placket along each placket line as shown. The seam allowance of the placket line will follow the seam allowance of the placket forming a wide "V" shape. The point of the "V" should fall just inside the placket seam allowance. Stitch in place. Press the seam allowance toward placket and fold opposite edge under to bind the raw edge. Edgestitch along the folded edge to secure.

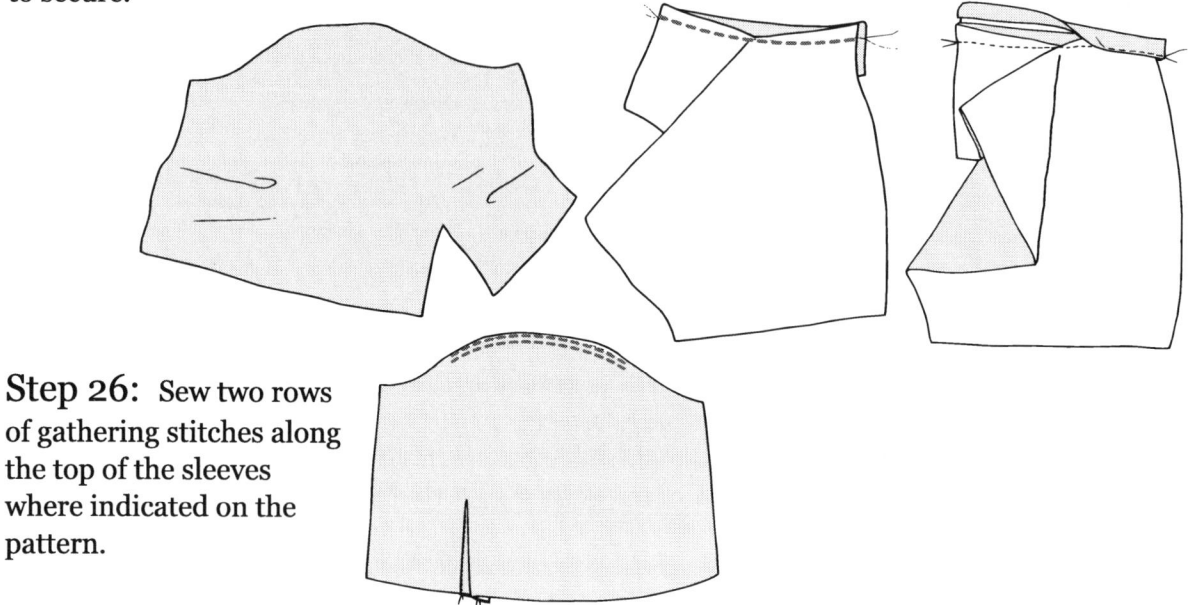

Step 26: Sew two rows of gathering stitches along the top of the sleeves where indicated on the pattern.

Step 27: With the right sides together, pin the sleeves to the armscyes of the bodice, matching the notches. Draw the gathering stitches to fit, arranging the fullness evenly along the armscye. Stitch. Clip the curves and finish the seam allowances, if desired. Press the seam allowances toward the bodice.

Step 28: Sew gathering stitches along the lower edge of the undersleeve.

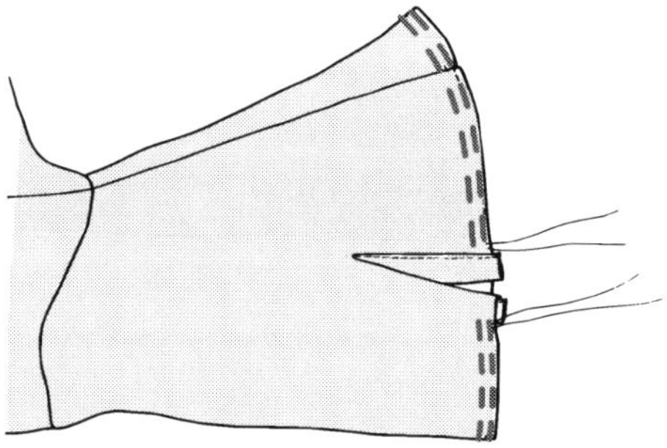

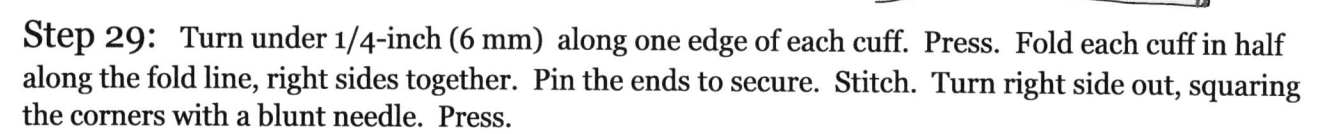

Step 29: Turn under 1/4-inch (6 mm) along one edge of each cuff. Press. Fold each cuff in half along the fold line, right sides together. Pin the ends to secure. Stitch. Turn right side out, squaring the corners with a blunt needle. Press.

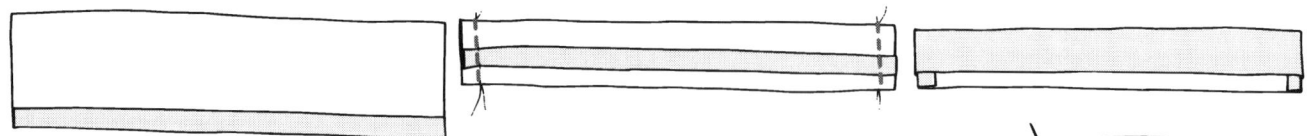

Step 30: Turn the front side of each sleeve placket under and pin in place. With the right sides together, pin the cuff to the sleeve, lining up the placket edges with the edges of the cuff. Draw up the gathering stitches to fit, arranging the fullness evenly along the cuff. Stitch. Turn the cuff over the seam allowance and pin in place along the seamline. Whipstitch along the seamline to secure.

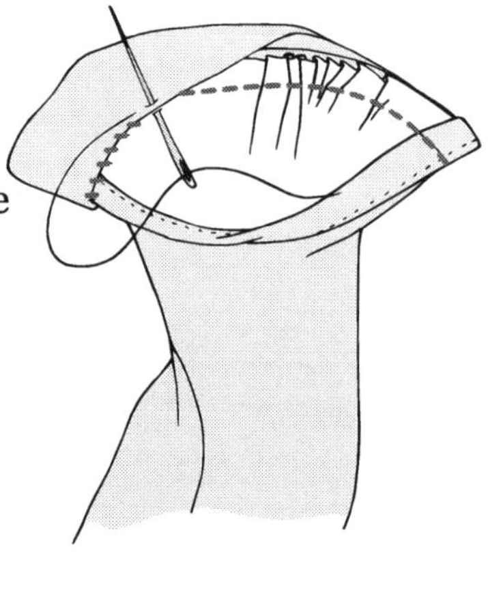

Step 31: Sew a button to the back edge of each sleeve cuff where indicated on the pattern. Make a button loop on the front end, following the instructions below. *Continue on from Step 20.*

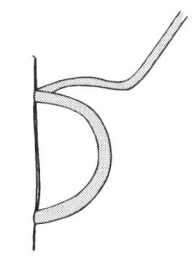

To make the button loop, use a single strand of button thread to make a loop that loosely fits the diameter of the button. Tack the loop in place at each end to secure. Do not cut the thread.

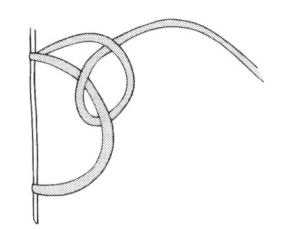

Starting at the end that the thread is attached, make a blanket stitch on the thread loop. Tighten the stitch snugly around the loop.

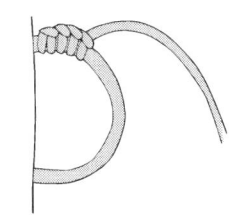

Continue adding stitches until the loop is completely covered.

Tack the end of the thread at the end of the loop and draw it through the fabric to hide. Trim off the extra thread.

Page 52

Bodice Details
Pattern Pieces

Cutting Layout for 45-inch (1.14 m) wide Fabric
20 Pieces

27 ~ View A & B Bodice Front
28 ~ View A & B Bodice Back
29 ~ View A Bodice Front Overlay
30 ~ View A Waist Under-band
31 ~ View A Bodice Overlay Facing
32 ~ View B Bodice Overlay
33 ~ View B Overlay Facing
34 ~ View A & B Collar
35 ~ View A Sleeve
36 ~ View A & B Front Facing
37 ~ View B Sleeve Back
38 ~ View B Sleeve Front
39 ~ View B Belt
40 ~ View A Tie
41 ~ Views A & B Skirt
42 ~ Back Facing Interfacing
43 ~ Alternate Long Sleeve
44 ~ Alternate Long Sleeve Cuff
45 ~ Alternate Long Sleeve Placket
46 ~ View A Sleeve Band

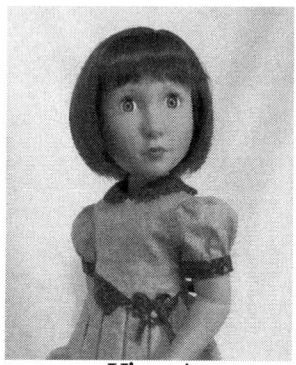

View A Dress
Use pieces: 27, 28, 29, 31, 35, 36, 40, and 41

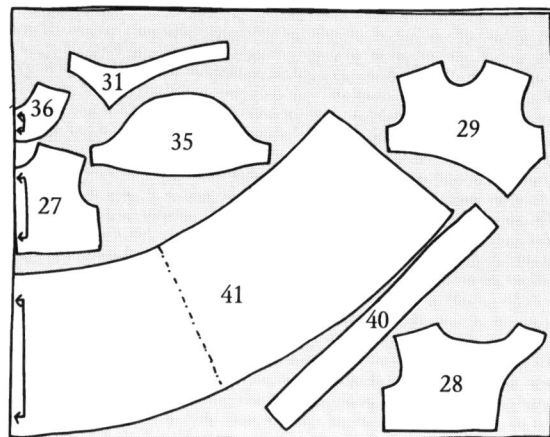

View A Contrast
Use pieces: 30, 34, and 46

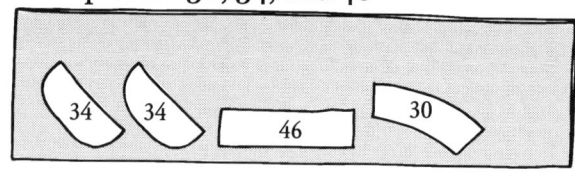

View A

View B Dress
Use pieces: 27, 28, 32, 33, 36, 37, 38, and 41

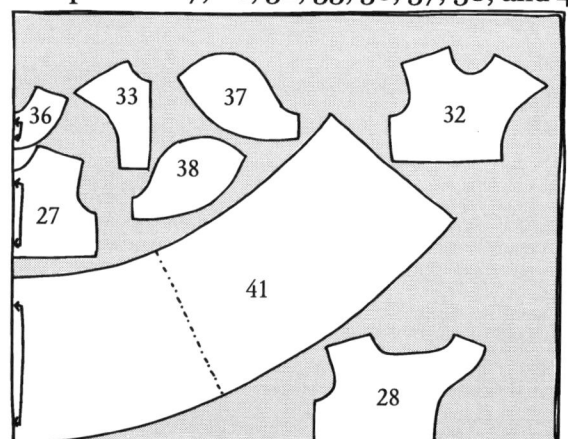

View B Contrast
Use pieces: 34, 37, 38, and 39

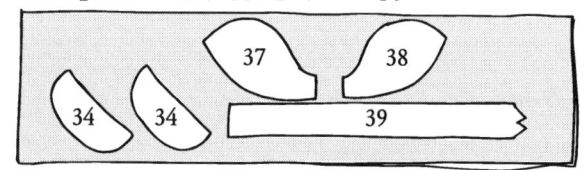

Page 53

Attach Section 2 Here

KeepersDollyDuds Designs
© 2014, Eve Coleman. All Rights Reserved.

3/8-inch Hem Allowed

41
Views A & B
Skirt
(Section 1 of 2)
Cut on Fold
Bodice Details
#KDD14-16

Place on fold

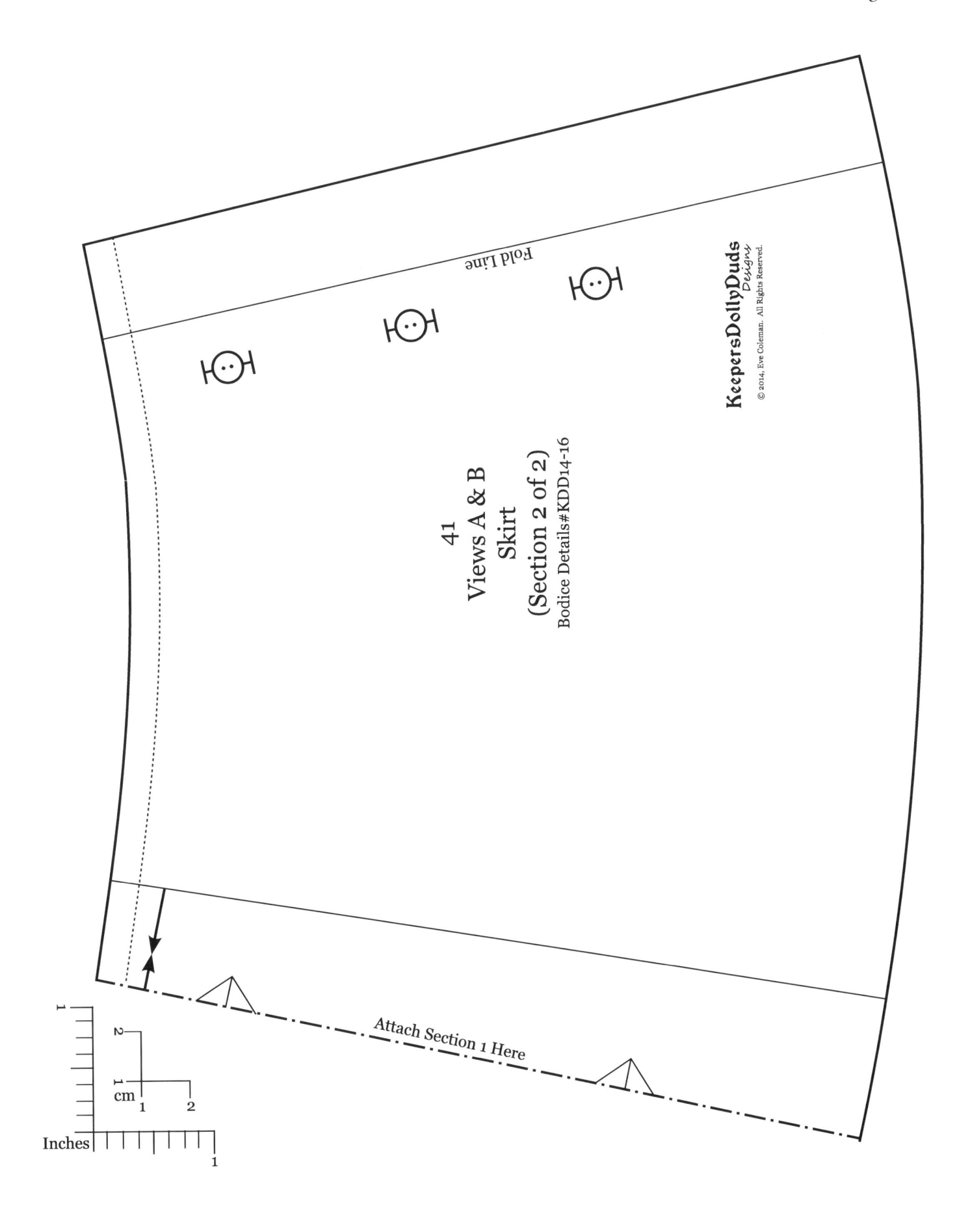

41
Views A & B
Skirt
(Section 2 of 2)
Bodice Details #KDD14-16

Fold Line

KeepersDollyDuds
Designs
© 2014, Eve Coleman. All Rights Reserved.

Attach Section 1 Here

Page 57

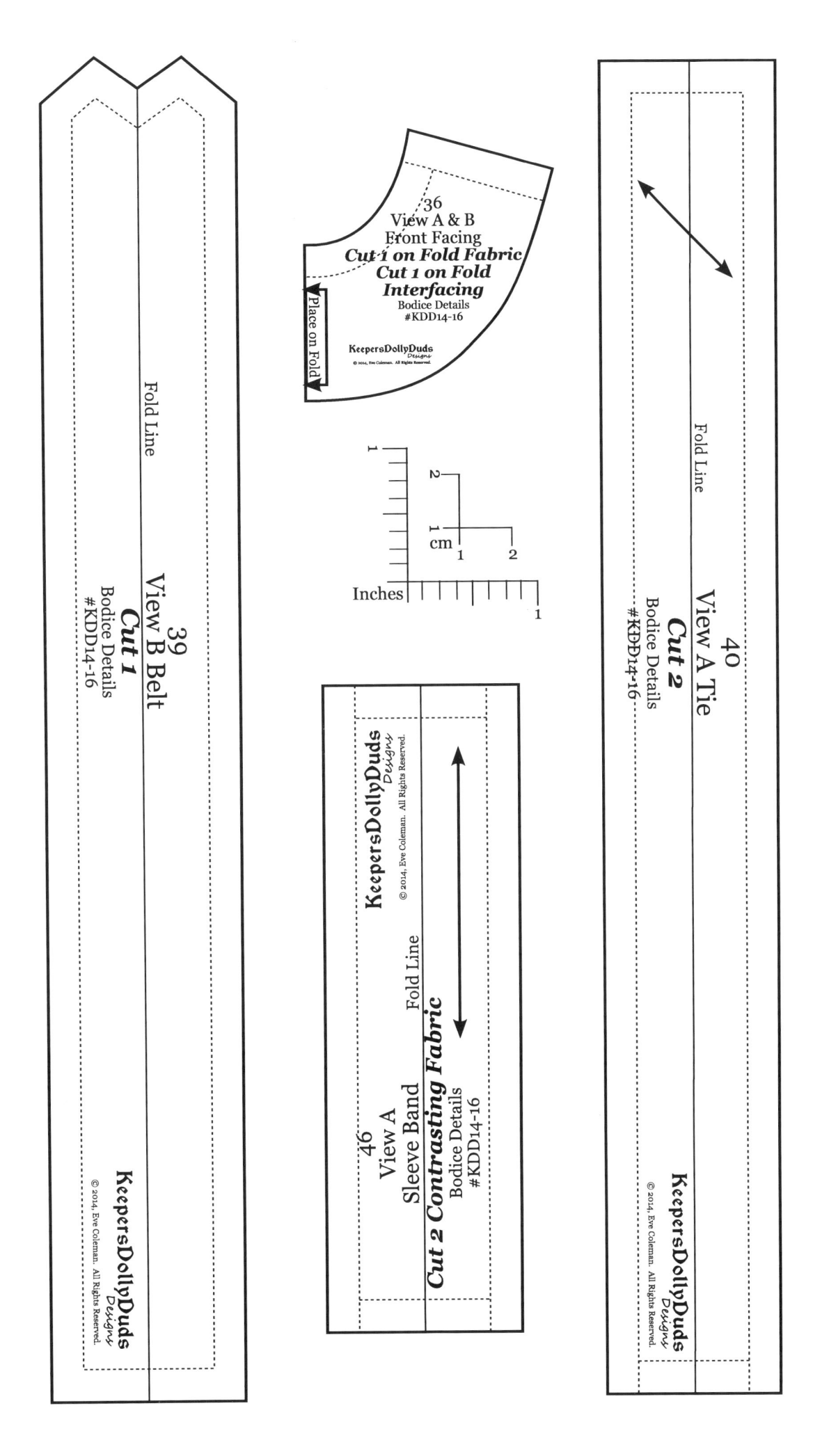

36
View A & B
Front Facing
Cut 1 on Fold Fabric
Cut 1 on Fold
Interfacing
Bodice Details
#KDD14-16

Place on Fold

KeepersDollyDuds
Designs
© 2014, Eve Coleman. All Rights Reserved.

39
View B Belt
Cut 1
Bodice Details
#KDD14-16

Fold Line

KeepersDollyDuds
Designs
© 2014, Eve Coleman. All Rights Reserved.

40
View A Tie
Cut 2
Bodice Details
#KDD14-16

Fold Line

KeepersDollyDuds
Designs
© 2014, Eve Coleman. All Rights Reserved.

46
View A
Sleeve Band
Cut 2 Contrasting Fabric
Bodice Details
#KDD14-16

Fold Line

KeepersDollyDuds
Designs
© 2014, Eve Coleman. All Rights Reserved.

Page 59

31
View A
Bodice Overlay Facing
Cut 1 of Fabric
Cut 1 of Interfacing
Bodice Details
#KDD14-16

29
View A
Bodice Front Overlay
Cut 1 of Fabric
Bodice Details
#KDD14-16

30
View A
Waist Under-band
Cut 2 of Contrasting Fabric
Bodice Details
#KDD14-16

34
View A & B
Collar
Cut 4 of Contrasting Fabric
Bodice Details
#KDD14-16

Optional Lace Line

Page 61

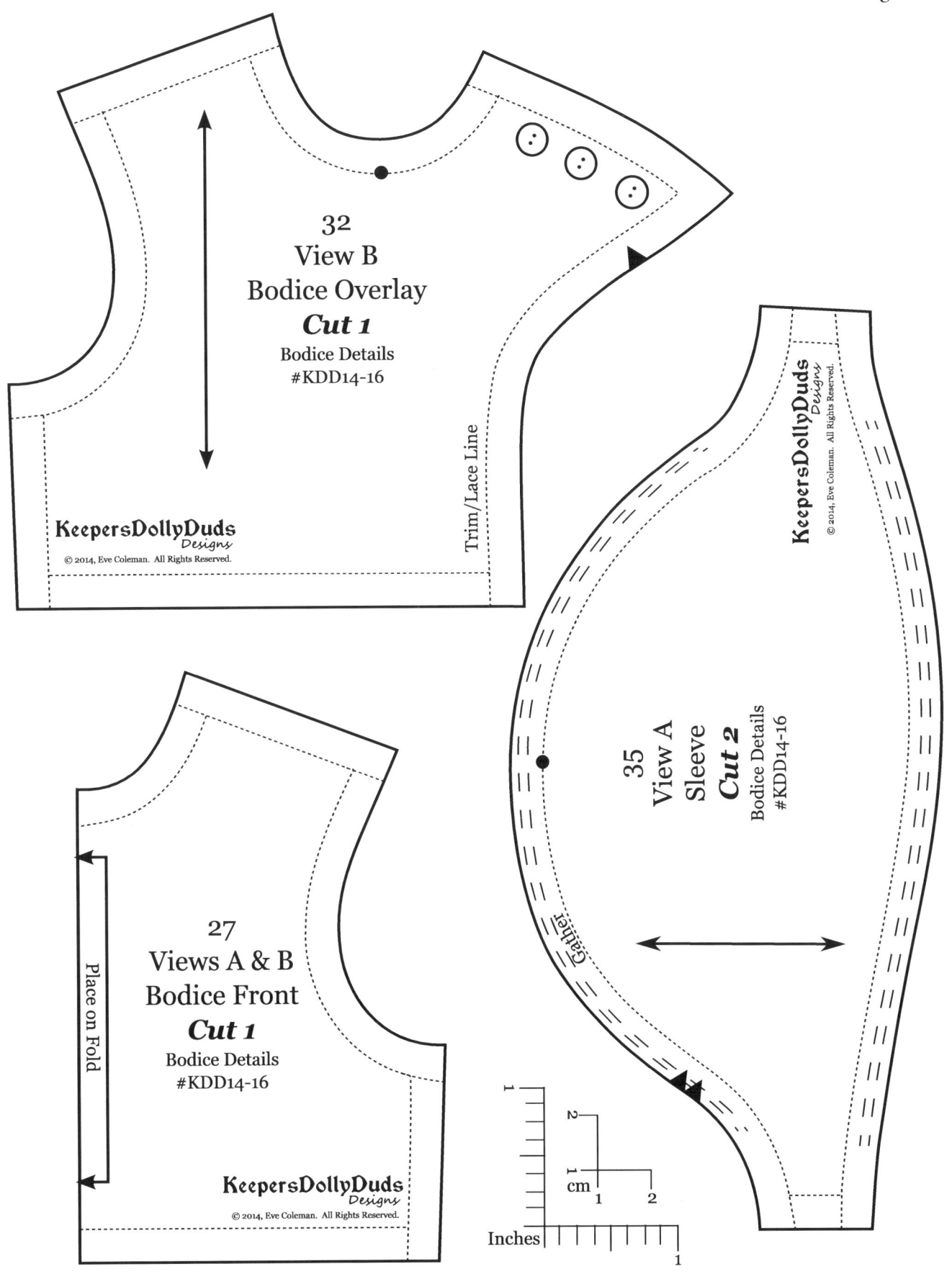

32
View B
Bodice Overlay
Cut 1
Bodice Details
#KDD14-16

Trim/Lace Line

35
View A
Sleeve
Cut 2
Bodice Details
#KDD14-16

Gather

27
Views A & B
Bodice Front
Cut 1
Bodice Details
#KDD14-16

Place on Fold

44
Alternate Long Sleeve Cuff   Fold Line
Cut 2 of Fabric
Bodice Details
#KDD14-16

33
View B
Overlay Facing
Cut 1 of Fabric
Bodice Details
#KDD14-16

43
Alternate Long Sleeve
Cut 2 of Fabric
Bodice Details
#KDD14-16

Gather

45
Fold Line   Alternate Long Sleeve Placket   Fold Line
Cut 2 of Fabric
Bodice Details
#KDD14-16

Inches
cm

Page 63

Page 65

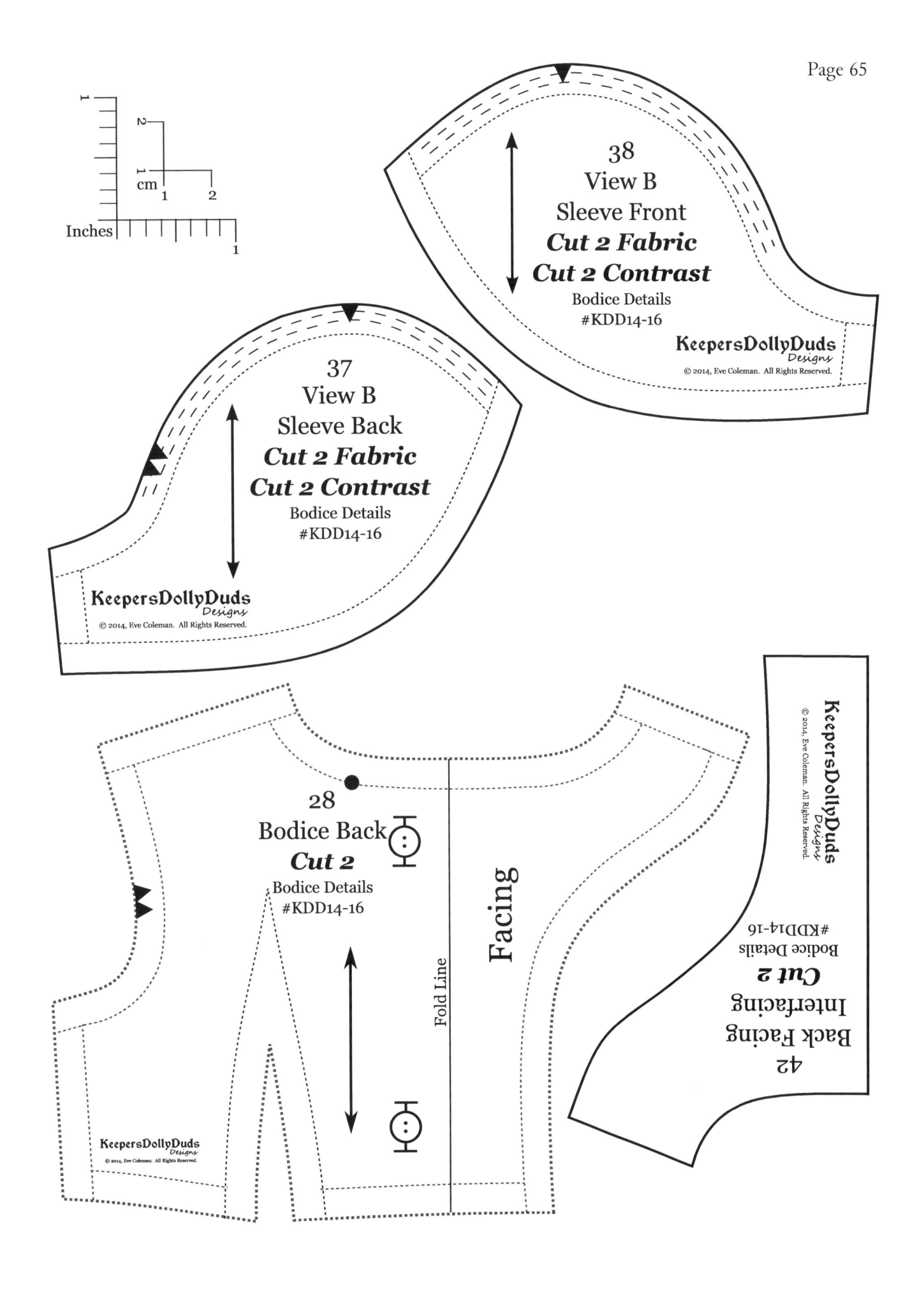

Page 67

Downtown 1920's

Materials List
#KDD-25-16

Suggested Fabrics: *Dress and Dress Contrast* in lightweight cotton or cotton blends, linen, chambray, or twill. Not suitable for knits. *Cloche* in lightweight wool, wool blend, cordouroy, or linen. Not suitable for knits.

Fabric Yardage:

Dress ~ 1/2 yard (0.5 m)
Dress Contrast ~ 1/4 yard (0.25 m)
Cloche ~ 1/4 yard (0.25 m)

Notions:

___Thread
Dress
___eight 1/4-inch (6 mm) buttons
___four 3/8-inch (9 mm) buttons.
___optional, nine inches of 3/8-inch (9mm) wide lace for trimming the bottom edge of the bodice front

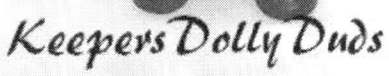

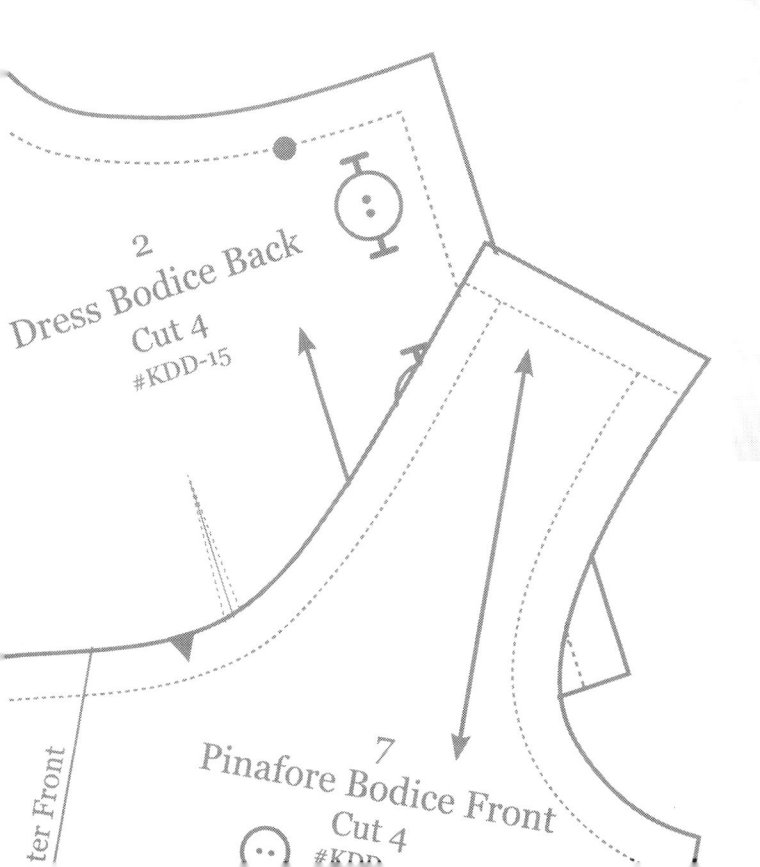

Keepers Dolly Duds

Page 68

Dress Front

Step 1: With the right sides out, fold one of the bias trim pieces in half along the fold line. Press flat. Pin the raw edge of the trim along the bottom edge of the front over-bodice. Lace may be used instead of bias trim if preferred.

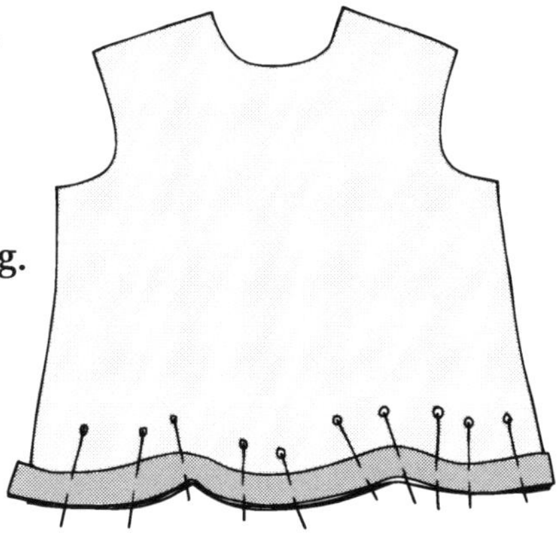

Step 2: Finish the top edge of the over-bodice hem facing.

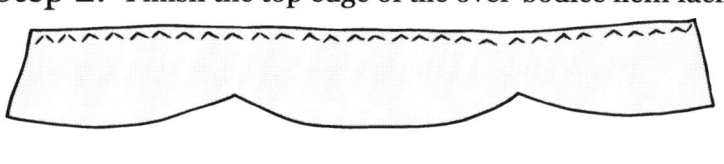

Step 3: With the right sides together, pin the over-bodice hem facing over the over-bodice along the scalloped edge. Stitch. Clip the corners and notch the curves. Turn the hem right side out and press, following the seamline.

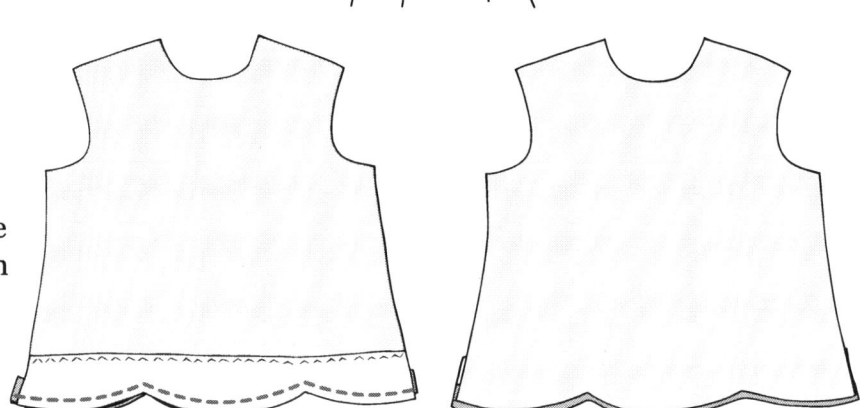

Step 4: With the right sides together and matching the notches, pin the inset pleats to the center front skirting panel and the side front skirting panels. Stitch. Finish the seam allowances, if desired. Press the seam allowances toward the inset pleats.

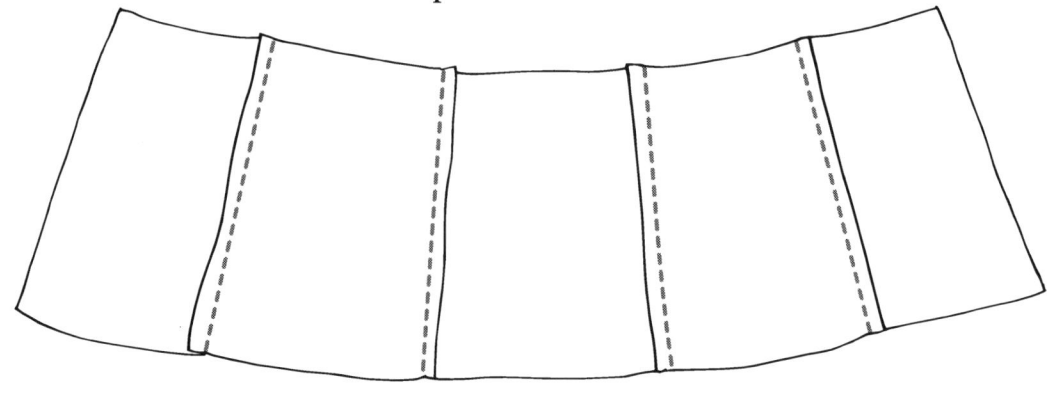

Step 5: Working on the right side of the skirt, fold the pleats over the inset pleat panels where indicated on the pattern. Press pleats down the length of the skirting so that the seamlines meet neatly at the center of the inset pleats when they lay flat. Pin the pleats in place at the top edge.

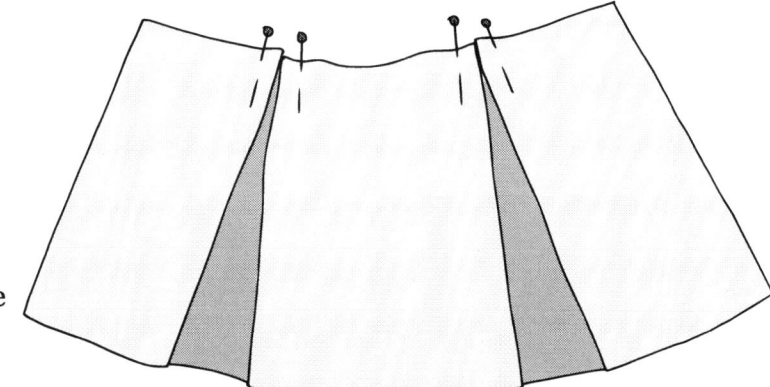

Page 69

Step 6: With the right sides together, pin the top edge of the pleated skirting to the bottom edge of the under-bodice. Stitch. Finish the seam allowance, if desired, and press toward the under-bodice.

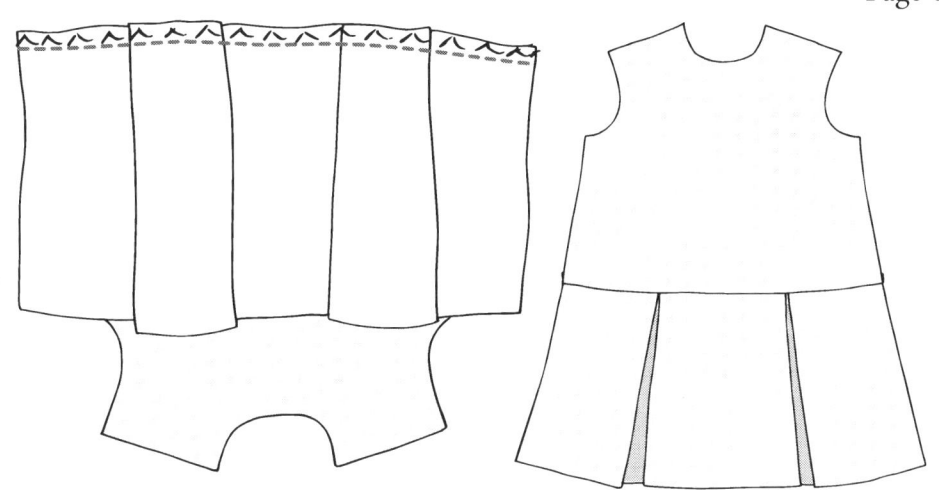

Step 7: With the right sides together, fold each tie along the fold line and pin in place. Stitch, leaving one end open. Clip the corners and trim the seam allowance to 1/8-inch (3 mm). Turn right side out, squaring the corners with a blunt needle. Press, following the seamline.

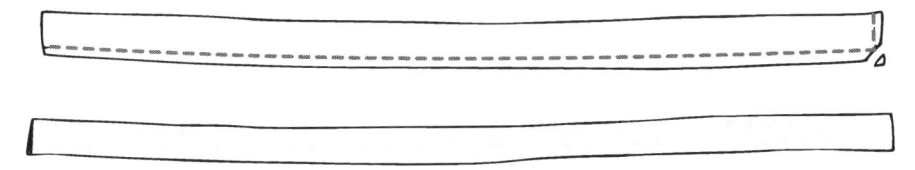

Step 8: With the right sides facing up, pin the over-bodice on top of the underbodice along the sides, armscyes, and shoulders. Pin the ties to the sides where indicated on the pattern. Baste through all layers to secure.

Dress Back

Step 9: Pin the front neck facing to the back facing at the shoulders. Stitch. Press the seam allowances open. Finish the outside edges of the facing, if desired.

Page 70

Step 10: Finish the shoulder seam allowances, if desired. Pin the dress front to the dress back pieces at the shoulders. Stitch. Press the seam allowances toward the back.

Collar

Step 11: With the right sides together, pin two sets of collar pieces along the outside edges. Stitch. Clip the corners and notch the curves. Trim the seam allowances to 1/8-inch (3 mm). Turn right side out, squaring the corners with a blunt needle. Press, following the seam line.

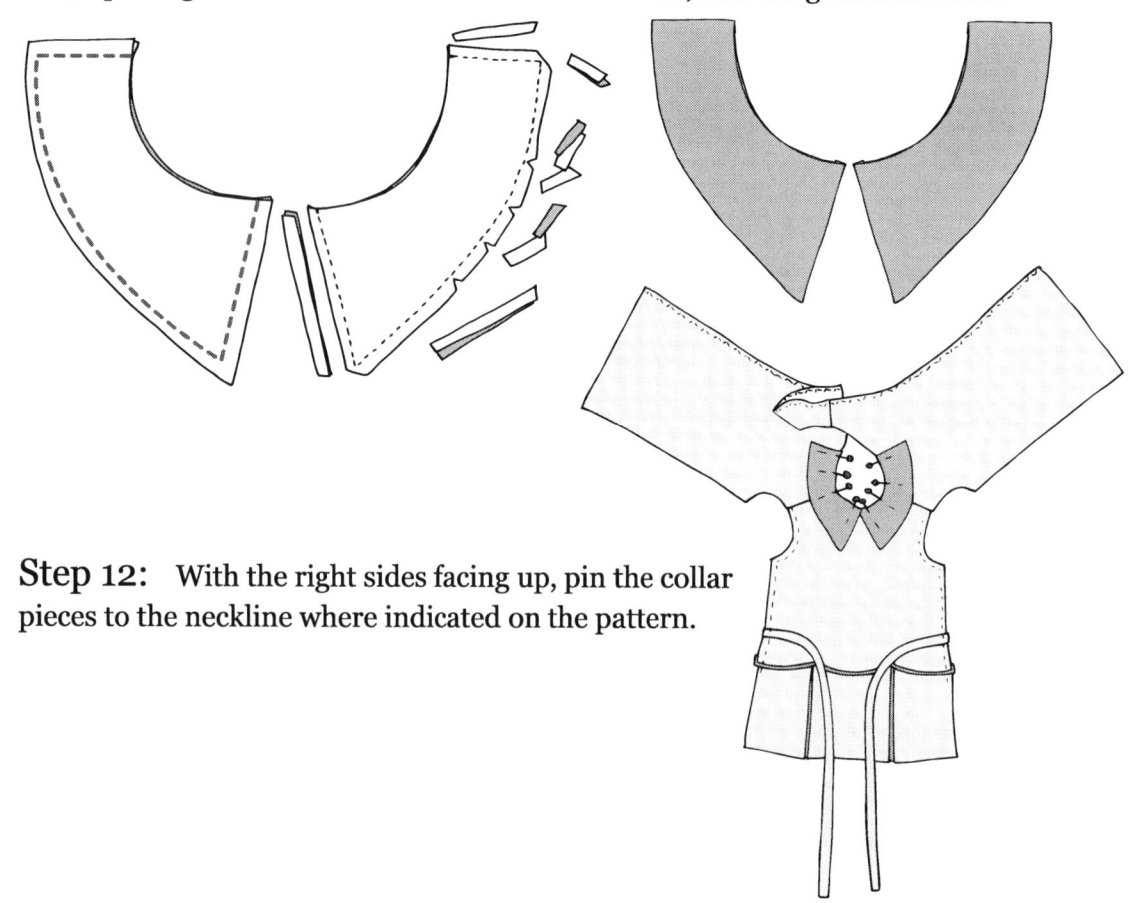

Step 12: With the right sides facing up, pin the collar pieces to the neckline where indicated on the pattern.

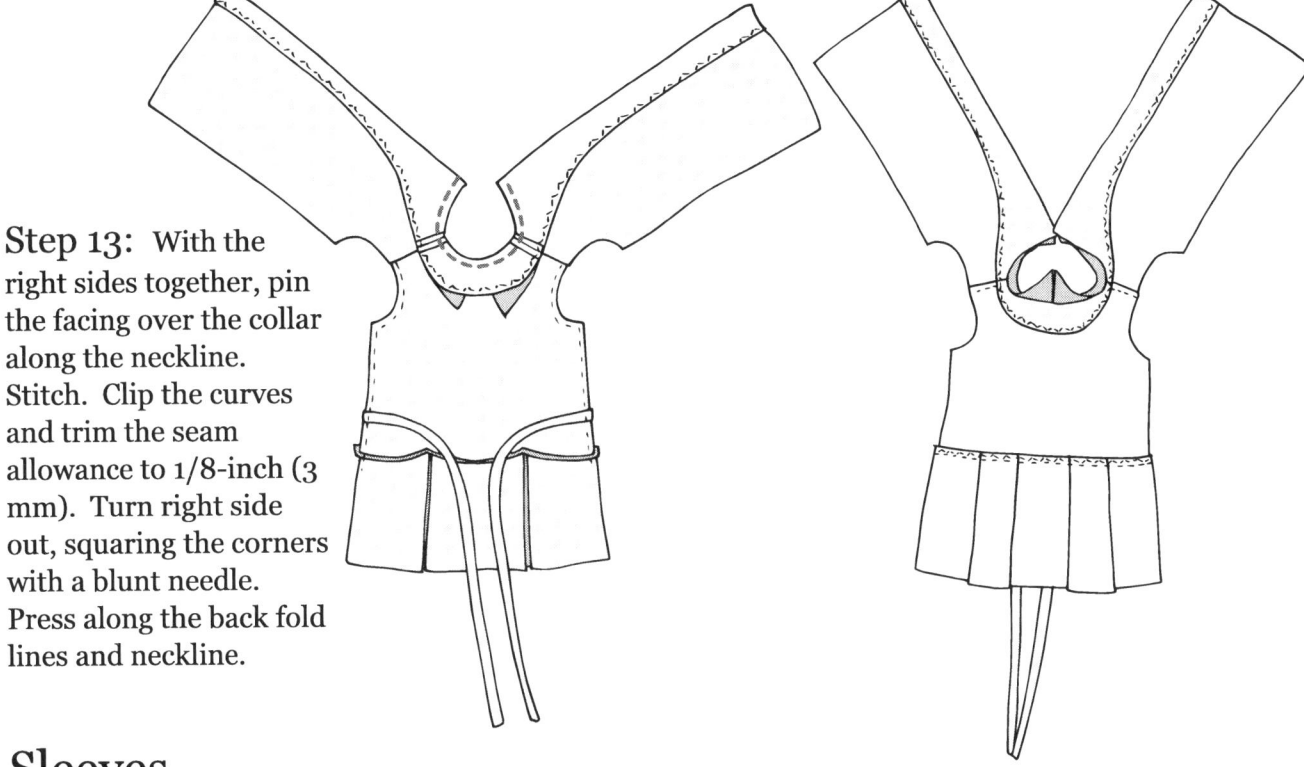

Step 13: With the right sides together, pin the facing over the collar along the neckline. Stitch. Clip the curves and trim the seam allowance to 1/8-inch (3 mm). Turn right side out, squaring the corners with a blunt needle. Press along the back fold lines and neckline.

Sleeves

Step 14: Cut each sleeve along the placket cutting line. Spread the cut edges apart. With the right sides together, pin one edge of a placket along each placket line as shown. The seam allowance of the placket line will follow the seam allowance of the placket forming a wide "V" shape. The point of the "V" should fall just inside the placket seam allowance. Stitch in place. Press the seam allowance toward placket and fold opposite edge under to bind the raw edge. Edgestitch along the folded edge to secure.

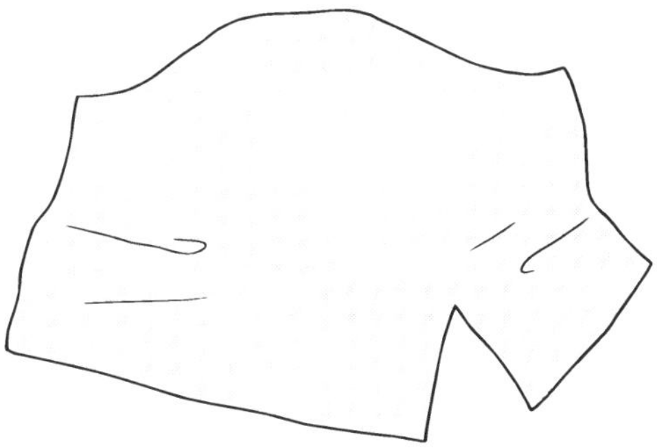

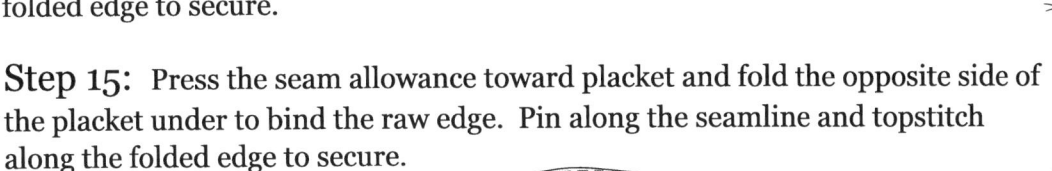

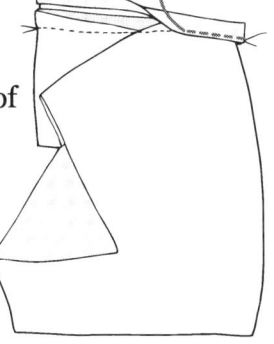

Step 15: Press the seam allowance toward placket and fold the opposite side of the placket under to bind the raw edge. Pin along the seamline and topstitch along the folded edge to secure.

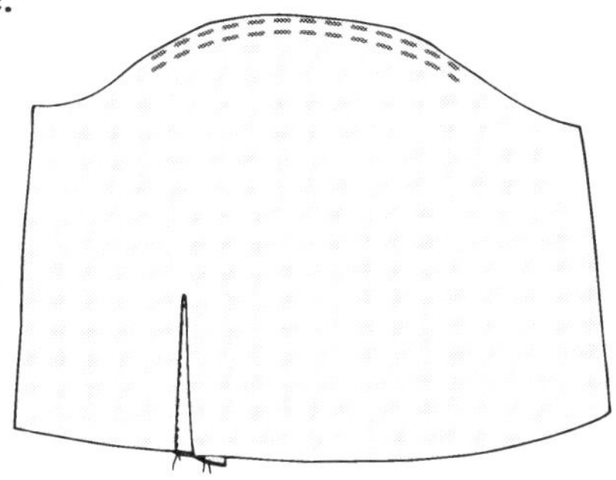

Step 16: Sew gathering stitches along the top edges of the sleeves.

Page 72

Step 17: With the right sides together and matching the notches, pin the sleeves to the armscyes of the bodice. The plackets should be toward the back. Draw up the gathering stitches to ease the fit. Stitch. Finish the armscye seam allowances, if desired, and press toward the sleeves. Finish the side seam allowances, if desired.

Step 18: With the right sides together, pin the sides of the bodice together, aligning the seamlines of the armscyes and the bottom edges of the bodice and sleeves. Stitch. Press the seam allowances open.

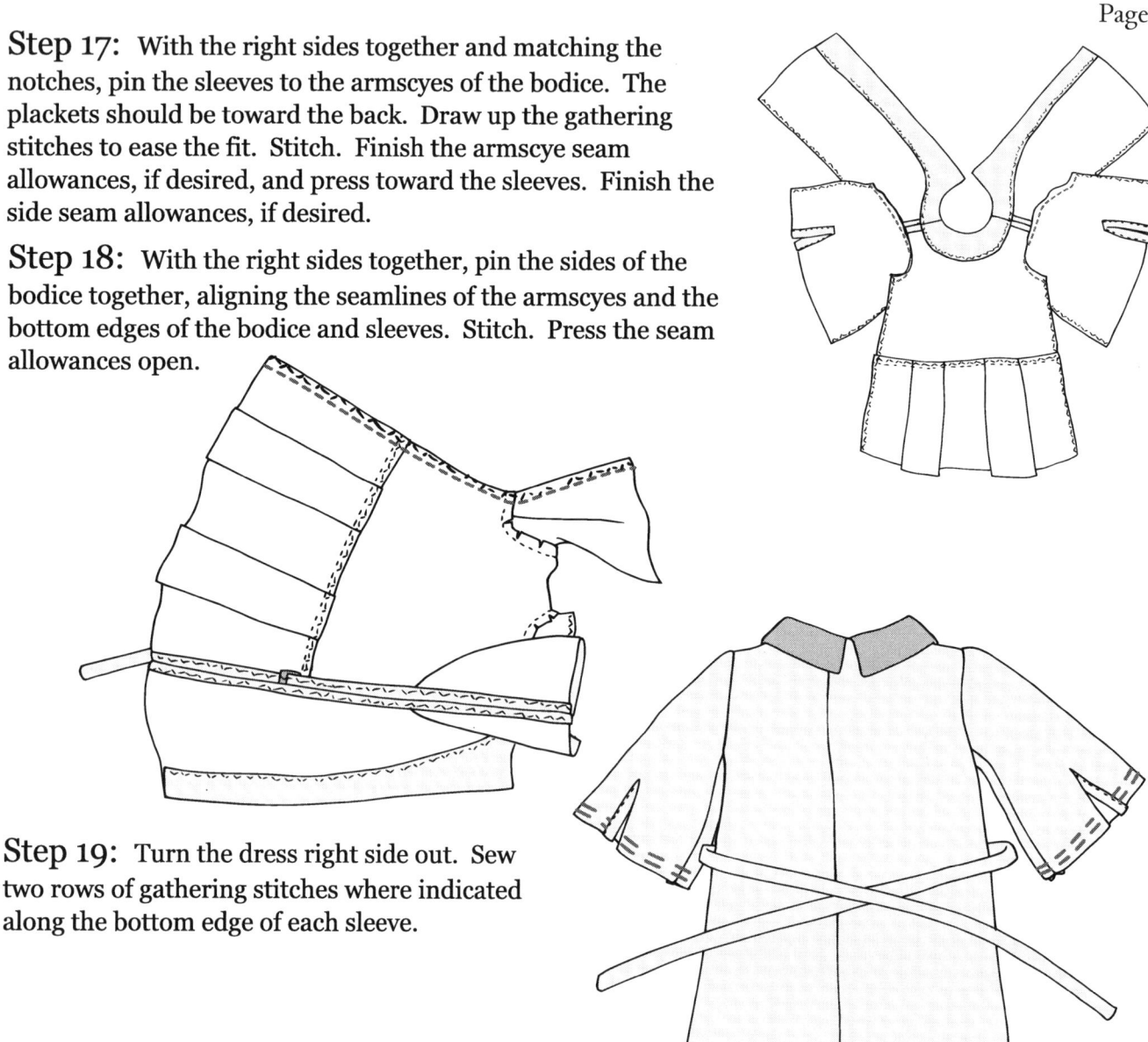

Step 19: Turn the dress right side out. Sew two rows of gathering stitches where indicated along the bottom edge of each sleeve.

Step 20: Turn under 1/4-inch (6 mm) along one edge of each cuff. Press. Fold each cuff in half along the fold line, right sides together. Pin the ends to secure. Stitch. Turn right side out, squaring the corners with a blunt needle. Press.

Step 21: Turn the front side of each sleeve placket under and pin in place. With the right sides together, pin the cuff to the sleeve, lining up the placket edges with the edges of the cuff. Draw up the gathering stitches to fit, arranging the fullness evenly along the cuff. Stitch. Turn the cuff over the seam allowance and pin in place along the seamline. Whipstitch along the seam line to secure.

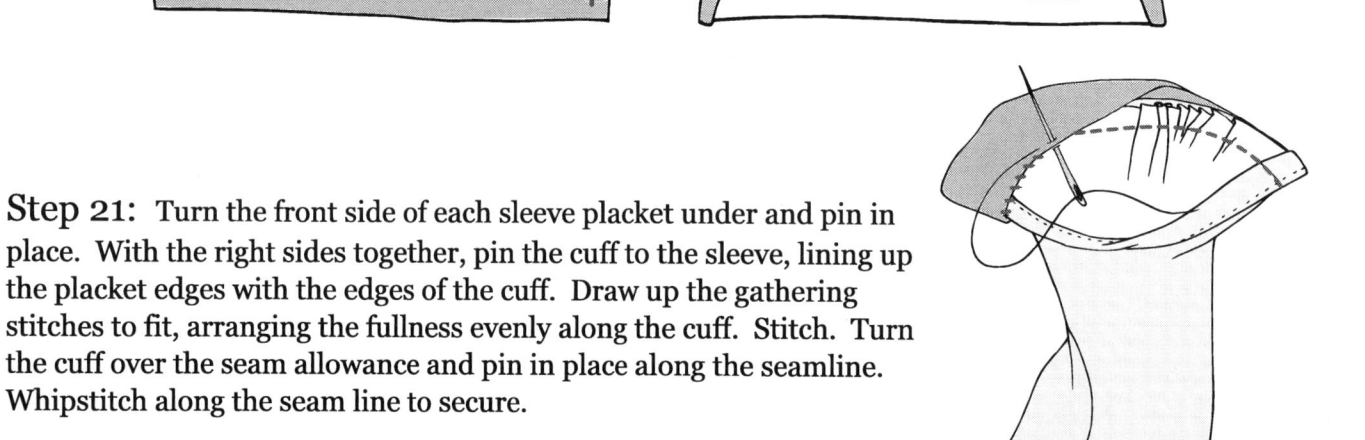

Finishing the Dress

Step 22: With the right sides together, turn each back facing under at the bottom edge along the fold line. Pin in place. Stitch across the facing 1/2-inch (12 mm) from the bottom edge. Finish the bottom edge of the skirting. Turn the facing right side out, squaring the corners with a blunt needle. Press a 1/2- inch (12 mm) hem under along the bottom edge of the skirting and pin in place. Stitch the hem by machine or by hand. Press the pleats after finishing the hem to freshen the creases.

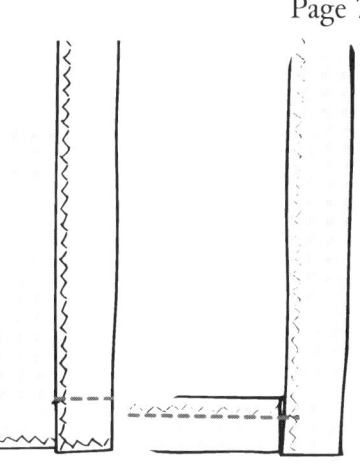

Step 23: Sew buttons to the back ends of the cuffs where indicated on the pattern. Make button loops on the front ends where indicated on the pattern, following the instructions below.

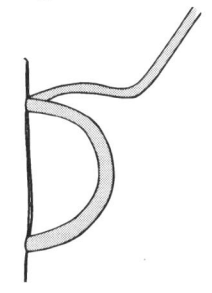

To make the button loop, use a single strand of button thread to make a loop that loosely fits the diameter of the button. Tack the loop in place at each end to secure. Do not cut the thread.

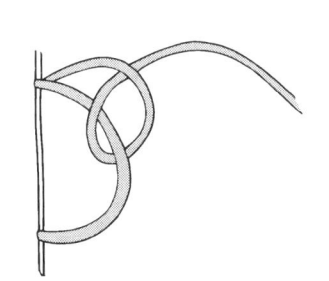

Starting at the end that the thread is attached, make a blanket stitch on the thread loop. Tighten the stitch snugly around the loop.

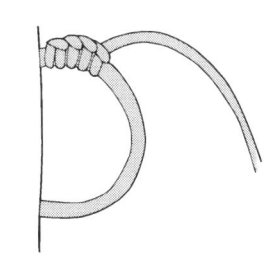

Continue adding stitches until the loop is completely covered.

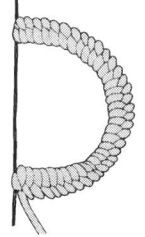

Tack the end of the thread at the end of the loop and draw it through the fabric to hide. Trim off the extra thread.

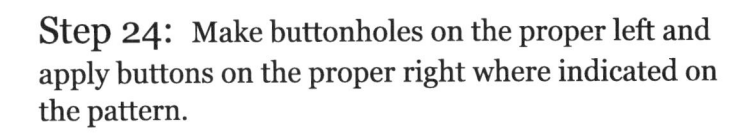

Step 24: Make buttonholes on the proper left and apply buttons on the proper right where indicated on the pattern.

Page 74

Step 25: To make the bow on the front neckline, fold the second bias trim piece in half along the fold line with the right sides together. Using a narrow zigzag stitch, sew a seam 1/4- inch (6 mm) from the *folded* edge. To turn the tube, snip the folded edge up to the seamline about 1/2-inch (12 mm) from the end. Slip a bobby pin onto the cut end of the tube and slide it into the tube through the slit. Push the bobby pin through the tube. Work the end of the tube inside and the rest of the tube should slide through easily. Knot the ends of the tube and trim the excess fabric from the ends to finish. Tie the tube in a bow and tack to the neckline where indicated on the pattern.

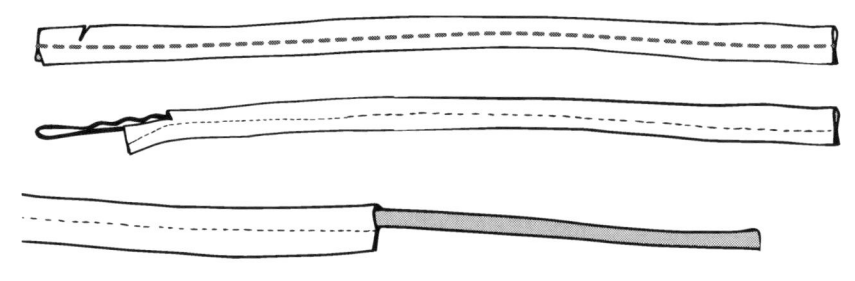

Step 26: Apply decorative buttons to the front over-bodice where indicated on the pattern.

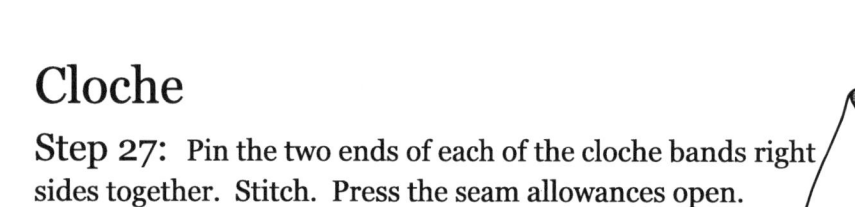

Cloche

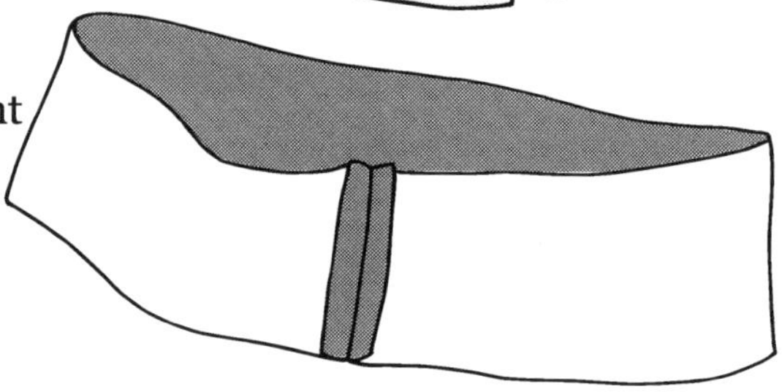

Step 27: Pin the two ends of each of the cloche bands right sides together. Stitch. Press the seam allowances open.

Step 28: Sew two rows of gathering stitches around the cloche crown where indicated on the pattern. Draw up the gathering stitches to fit the cloche band.

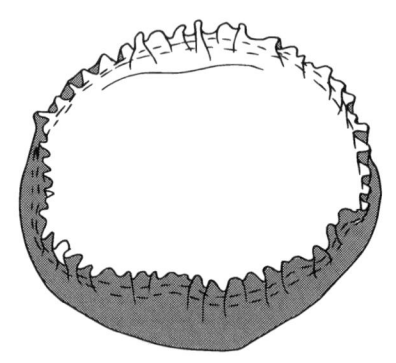

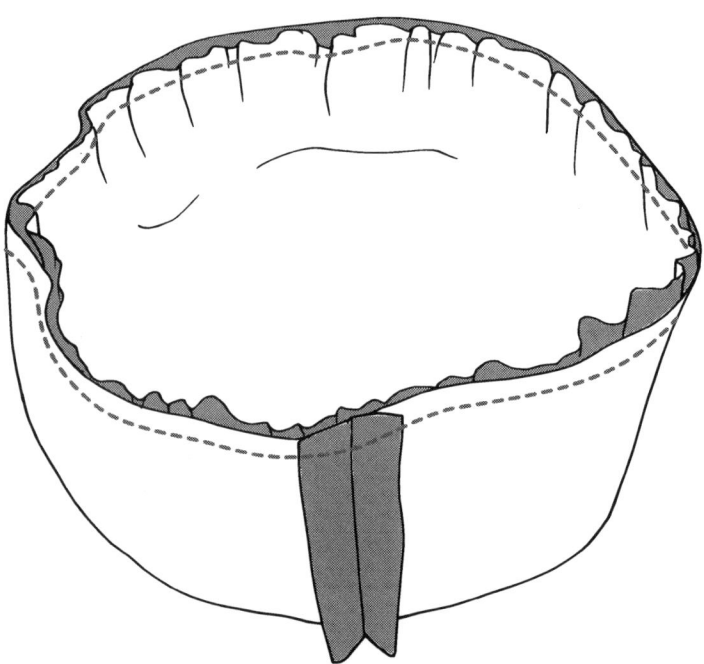

Step 29: With the right sides together and matching the center front and center back dots, pin the cloche band to the cloche crown. Arrange the fullness of the crown evenly along the band. Stitch.

Step 30: With the right sides together, pin the cloche brim pieces along the bottom edge. Stitch. Clip the inside curve and notch the outside curves and trim the seam allowances to 1/8-inch (3 mm). Turn right side out and press, following the seam line.

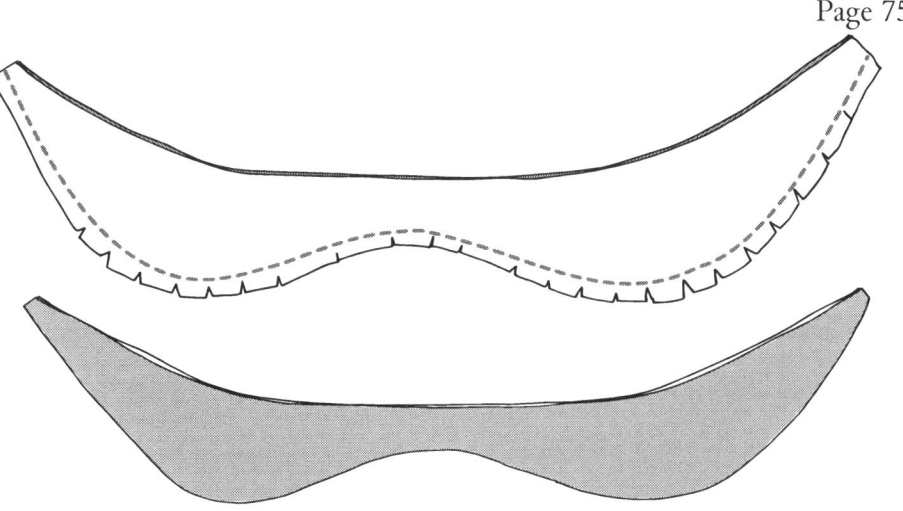

Step 31: Turn the band up from the crown and pin the raw edge of the brim along the bottom edge of the band matching the center front and center back dots.

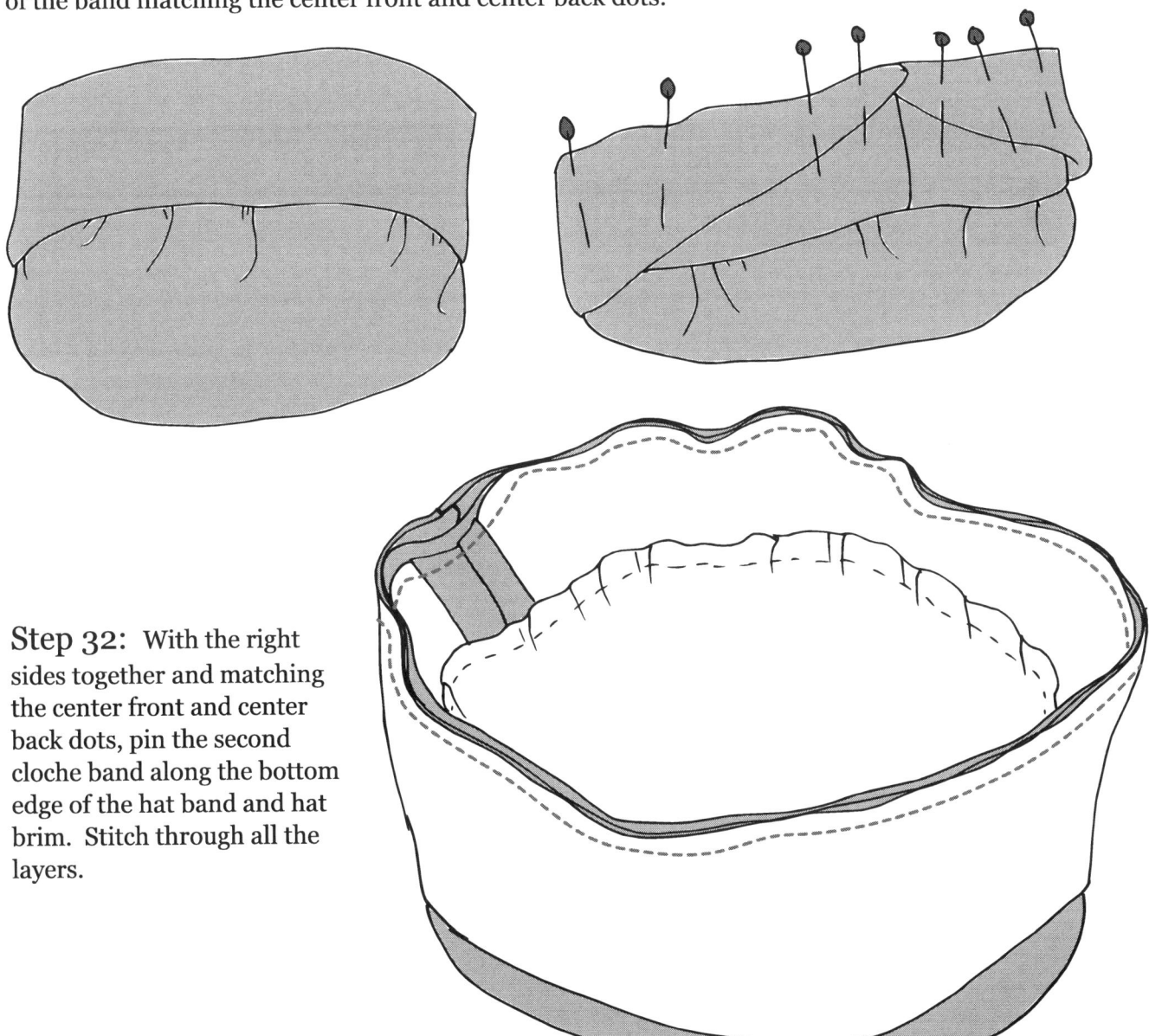

Step 32: With the right sides together and matching the center front and center back dots, pin the second cloche band along the bottom edge of the hat band and hat brim. Stitch through all the layers.

Page 76

Step 33: Turn the second band down and understitch the seam allowance to the band close to the seamline.

Step 34: Turn the second band to the inside of the cloche. Turn the raw edge under and pin along the top seamline. Blindstitch to secure.

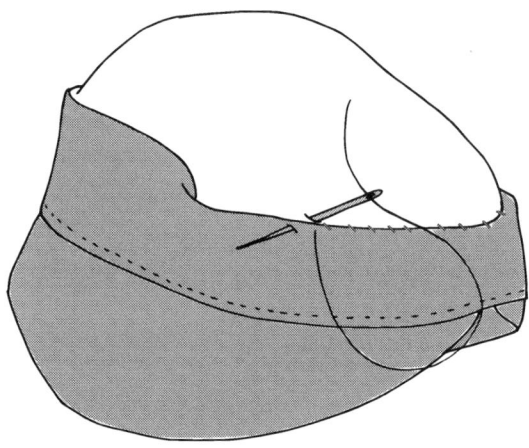

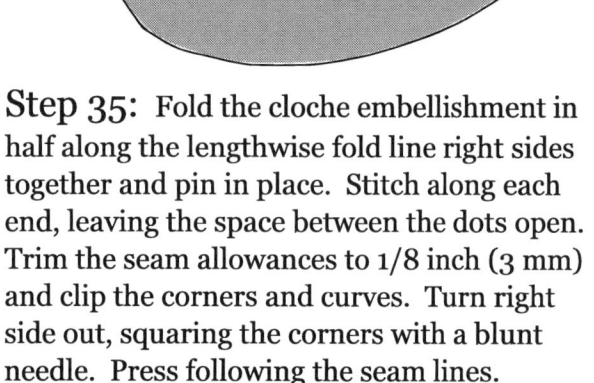

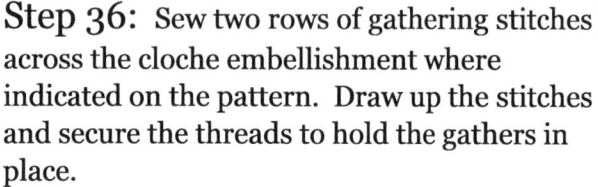

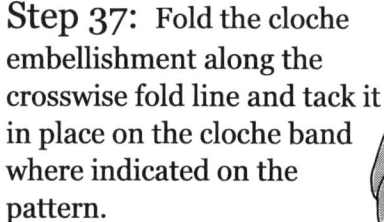

Step 35: Fold the cloche embellishment in half along the lengthwise fold line right sides together and pin in place. Stitch along each end, leaving the space between the dots open. Trim the seam allowances to 1/8 inch (3 mm) and clip the corners and curves. Turn right side out, squaring the corners with a blunt needle. Press following the seam lines. Whipstitch the opening closed.

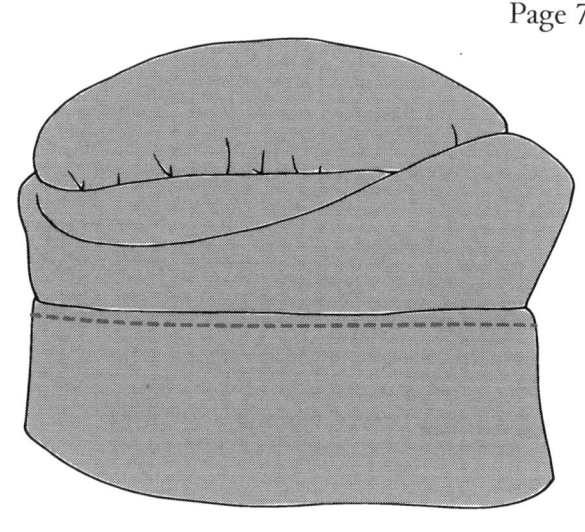

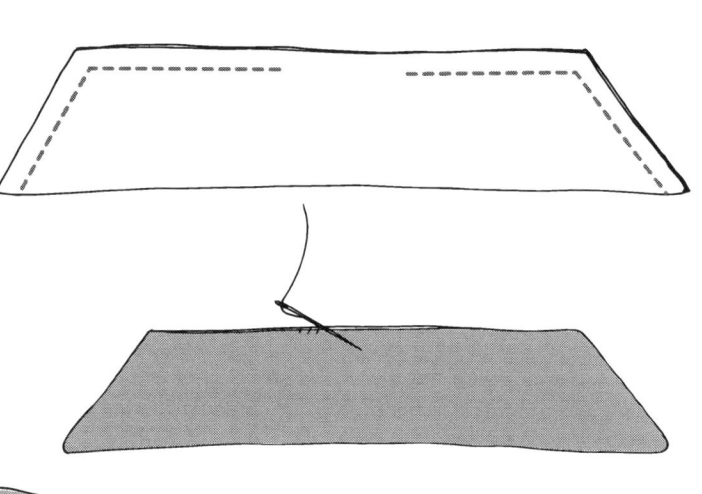

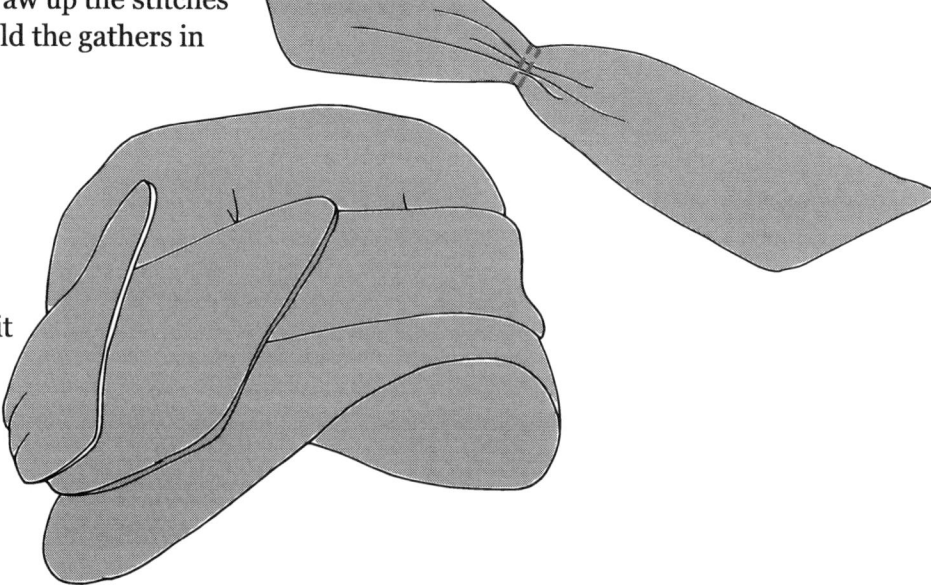

Step 36: Sew two rows of gathering stitches across the cloche embellishment where indicated on the pattern. Draw up the stitches and secure the threads to hold the gathers in place.

Step 37: Fold the cloche embellishment along the crosswise fold line and tack it in place on the cloche band where indicated on the pattern.

Page 77

Downtown 1920's
Pattern Pieces

Cutting Layout for 45-inch (1.14 m) wide Fabric
18 Pieces

47 ~ Front Under-Bodice
48 ~ Center Skirting Panel
49 ~ Inset Pleat
50 ~ Side Skirting
51 ~ Front Over-Bodice
52 ~ Bias Trim
53 ~ Over-Bodice Hem Facing
54 ~ Ties
55 ~ Back
56 ~ Neck Front Facing
57 ~ Collar
58 ~ Sleeve
59 ~ Placket
60 ~ Cuff
61 ~ Cloche Crown
62 ~ Cloche Band
63 ~ Cloche Brim
64 ~ Cloche Embellishment

Dress
Use pieces: 47, 48, 50, 51, 53, 54, 55, 56, 58, and 59

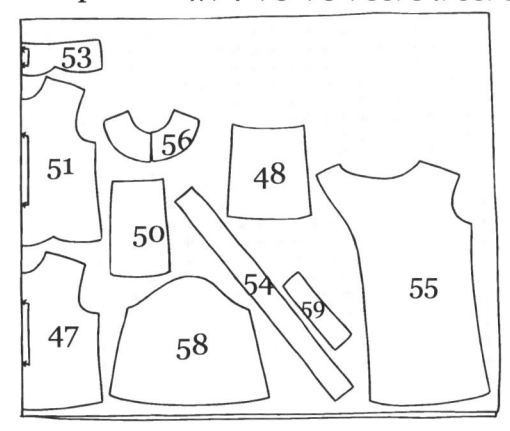

Dress Contrast
Use pieces: 49, 52, 57, and 60

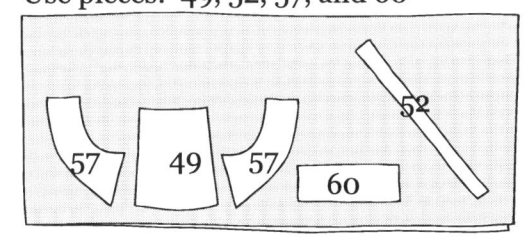

Cloche
Use pieces: 61, 62, 63, and 64

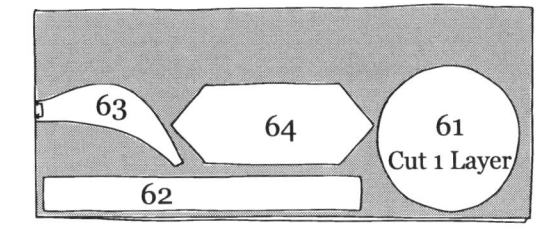

Page 79

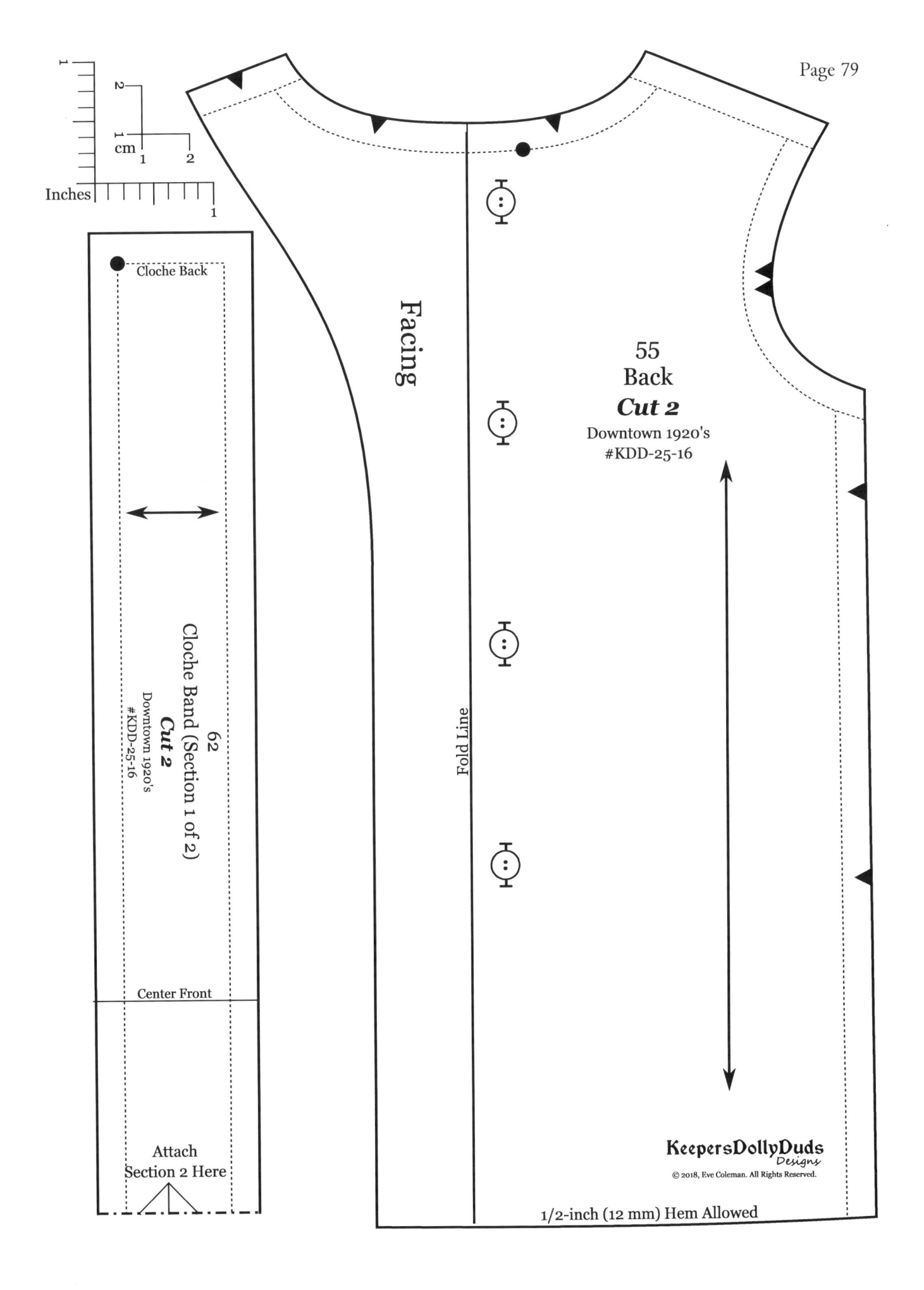

Inches

cm

Cloche Back

62
Cloche Band (Section 1 of 2)
Cut 2
Downtown 1920's
#KDD-25-16

Center Front

Attach Section 2 Here

Facing

55
Back
Cut 2
Downtown 1920's
#KDD-25-16

Fold Line

KeepersDollyDuds Designs
© 2018, Eve Coleman. All Rights Reserved.

1/2-inch (12 mm) Hem Allowed

Page 81

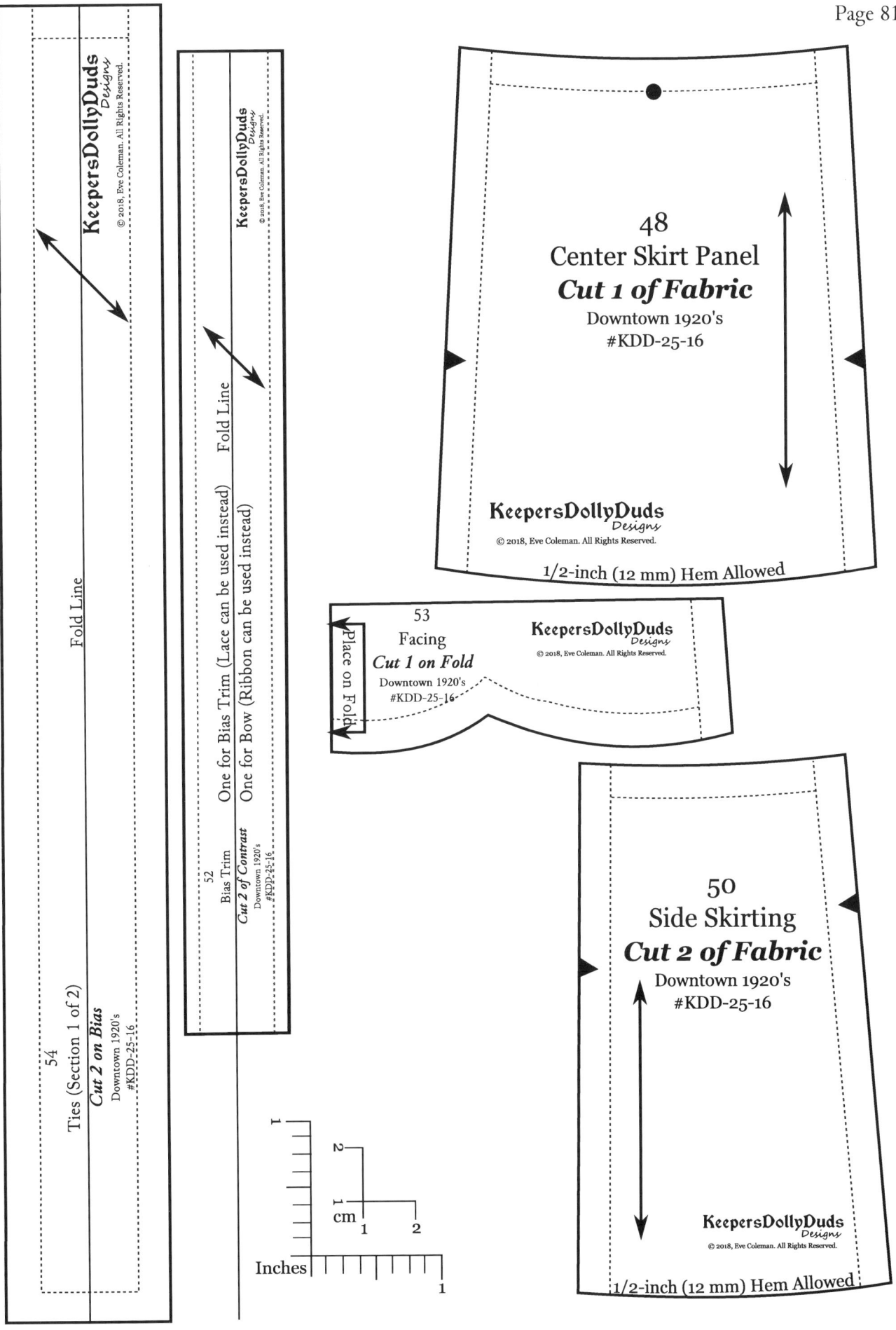

48
Center Skirt Panel
Cut 1 of Fabric
Downtown 1920's
#KDD-25-16

1/2-inch (12 mm) Hem Allowed

53
Facing
Cut 1 on Fold
Downtown 1920's
#KDD-25-16

52
Bias Trim
Cut 2 of Contrast
Downtown 1920's
#KDD-25-16

One for Bias Trim (Lace can be used instead)
One for Bow (Ribbon can be used instead)

54
Ties (Section 1 of 2)
Cut 2 on Bias
Downtown 1920's
#KDD-25-16

50
Side Skirting
Cut 2 of Fabric
Downtown 1920's
#KDD-25-16

1/2-inch (12 mm) Hem Allowed

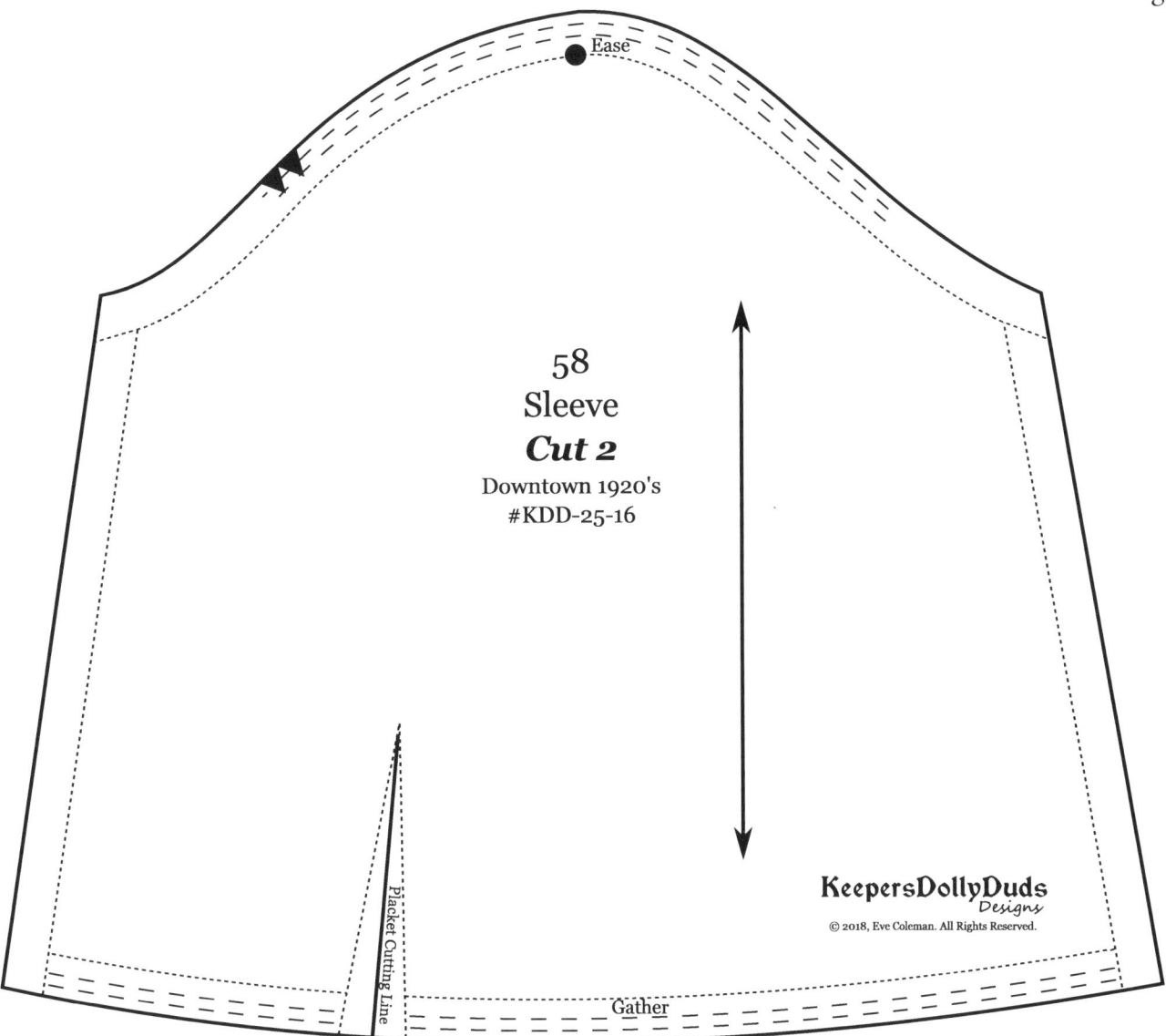

Page 83

58
Sleeve
Cut 2
Downtown 1920's
#KDD-25-16

Ease

Placket Cutting Line

Gather

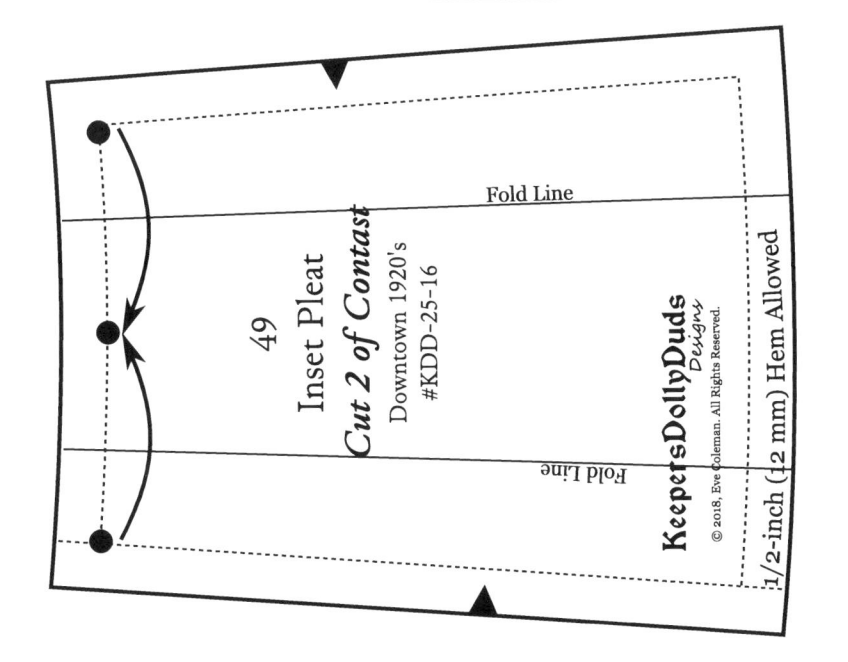

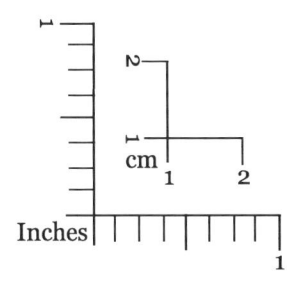

KeepersDollyDuds
Designs
© 2018, Eve Coleman. All Rights Reserved.

49
Inset Pleat
Cut 2 of Contast
Downtown 1920's
#KDD-25-16

Fold Line
Fold Line
1/2-inch (12 mm) Hem Allowed

KeepersDollyDuds
Designs
© 2018, Eve Coleman. All Rights Reserved.

Inches
cm

Page 85

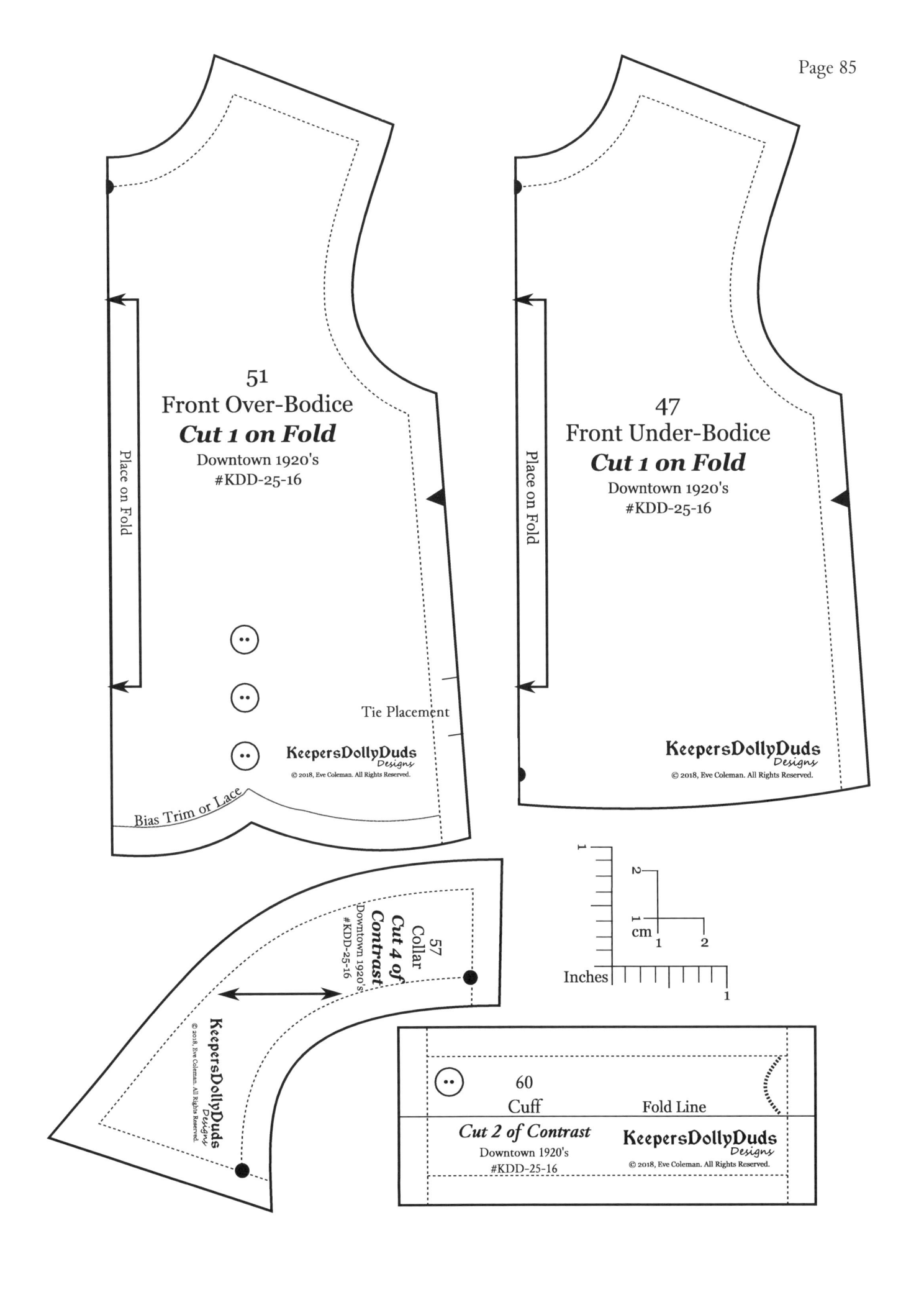

51
Front Over-Bodice
Cut 1 on Fold
Downtown 1920's
#KDD-25-16

Place on Fold

Tie Placement

Bias Trim or Lace

KeepersDollyDuds Designs
© 2018, Eve Coleman. All Rights Reserved.

47
Front Under-Bodice
Cut 1 on Fold
Downtown 1920's
#KDD-25-16

Place on Fold

KeepersDollyDuds Designs
© 2018, Eve Coleman. All Rights Reserved.

57
Collar
Cut 4 of Contrast
Downtown 1920's
#KDD-25-16

KeepersDollyDuds Designs
© 2018, Eve Coleman. All Rights Reserved.

cm
Inches

60
Cuff   Fold Line
Cut 2 of Contrast
Downtown 1920's
#KDD-25-16

KeepersDollyDuds Designs
© 2018, Eve Coleman. All Rights Reserved.

Page 87

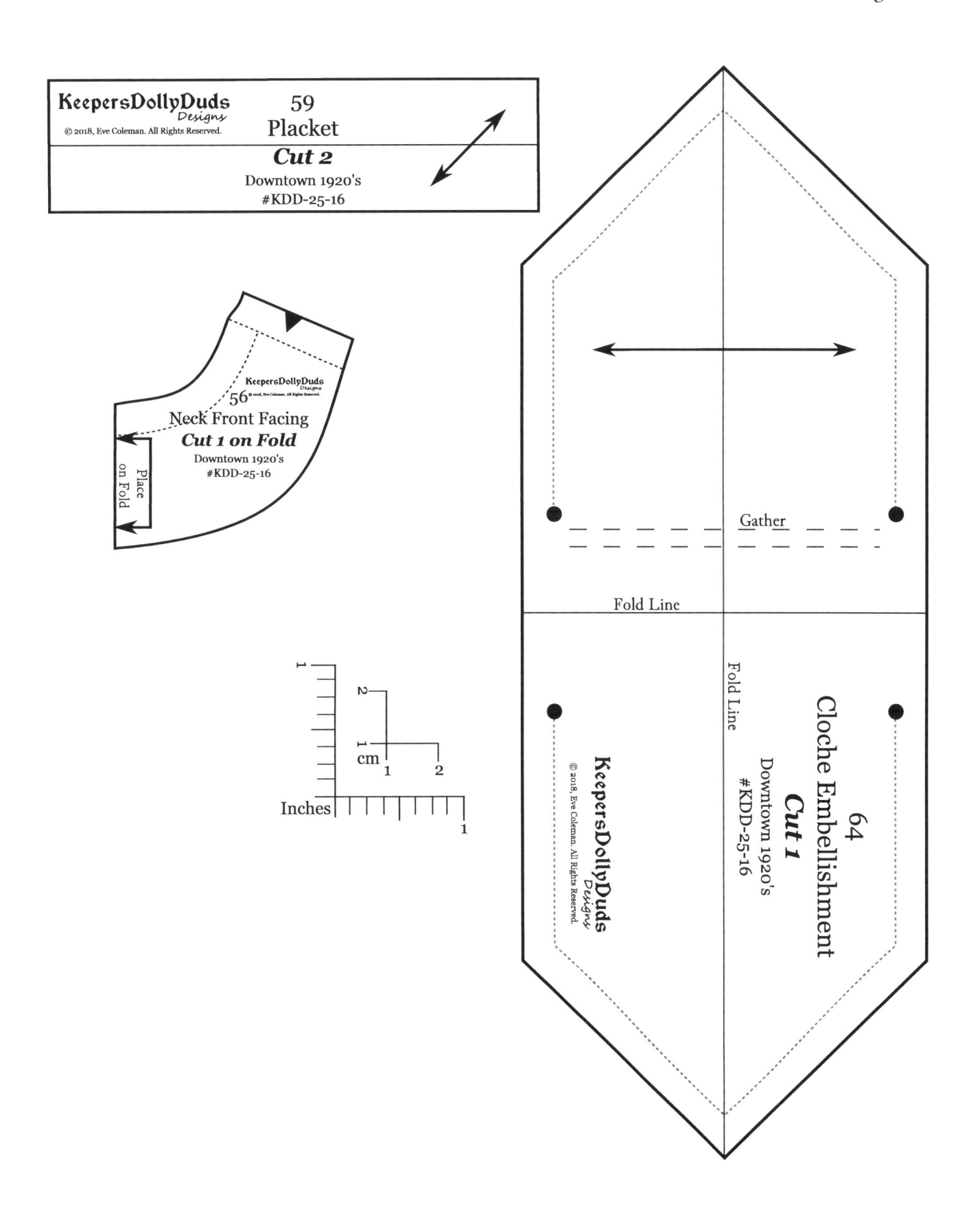

KeepersDollyDuds Designs
© 2018, Eve Coleman. All Rights Reserved.

59
Placket
Cut 2
Downtown 1920's
#KDD-25-16

KeepersDollyDuds Designs
56 © 2018, Eve Coleman. All Rights Reserved.
Neck Front Facing
Cut 1 on Fold
Downtown 1920's
#KDD-25-16

Place on Fold

Gather

Fold Line

Fold Line

64
Cloche Embellishment
Cut 1
Downtown 1920's
#KDD-25-16

KeepersDollyDuds Designs
© 2018, Eve Coleman. All Rights Reserved.

Page 89

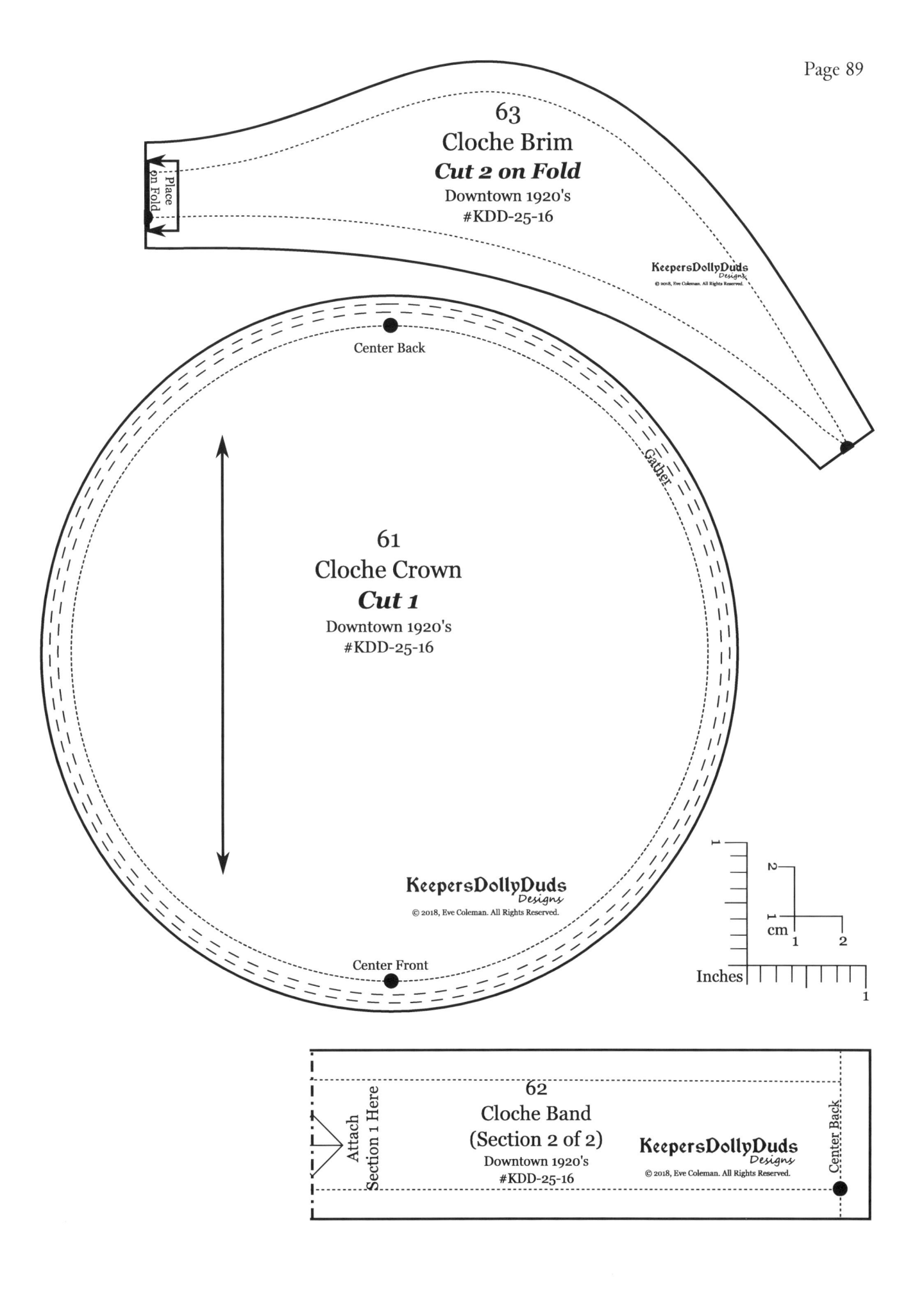

63
Cloche Brim
Cut 2 on Fold
Downtown 1920's
#KDD-25-16

Place on Fold

KeepersDollyDuds Designs
© 2018, Eve Coleman. All Rights Reserved.

Center Back

Gather

61
Cloche Crown
Cut 1
Downtown 1920's
#KDD-25-16

KeepersDollyDuds Designs
© 2018, Eve Coleman. All Rights Reserved.

Center Front

cm
Inches

Attach Section 1 Here

62
Cloche Band
(Section 2 of 2)
Downtown 1920's
#KDD-25-16

KeepersDollyDuds Designs
© 2018, Eve Coleman. All Rights Reserved.

Center Back

Victorian Christmas Caroler

Materials List
#KDD-07-16

Suggested Fabrics: *Coat and Bonnet* in lightweight woven fabric such as wool flannel, linen, twill, cotton, or lightweight cordouroy. Not suitable for knits. *Lining* in lightweight woven fabric such as flannel, muslin, silk, or lining fabric. Not suitable for knits.

Fabric Yardage:
Coat and Bonnet ~ 1 yard (1 m) 45-inch wide fabric
Lining ~ 3/4 yard (0.75 m) 45-inch wide fabric

Notions:
__Thread
Coat and Bonnet
__6-inch by 12-inch (15 cm x 30 cm) piece of lightweight fusible interfacing
__3 yards (3 m) 3/8-inch (9 mm) wide trim (gimp, bias tape, braid etc.) Note: 1/2 yard of fabric will be needed to make bias tape trim.
__1 yard (1 m) 3/8-inch (9 mm) wide lace for the collar and outside bonnet (optional)
__12-inches of 1-inch (2.5 cm) wide pre-ruffled lace or trim for the inside of the bonnet brim
__five 3/8-inch (9 mm) buttons
__two snap closures

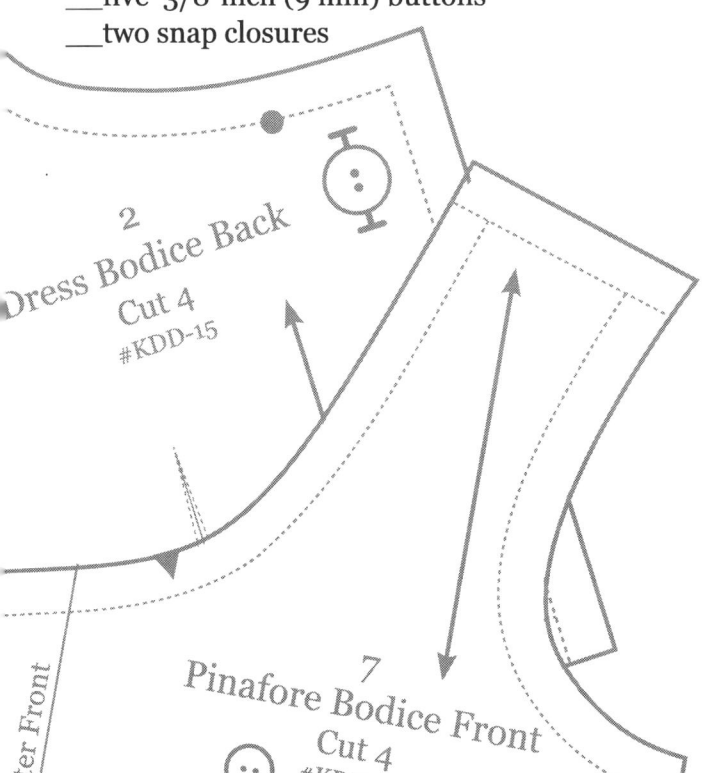

Page 92

Caroler's Coat

Step 1: If desired, finish the side seam allowances of the the coat front piece and the front seam allowance of each coat side front piece. With the right sides together, pin each coat side front to the coat front, matching the notches. Clip the curves and press the seam allowances open.

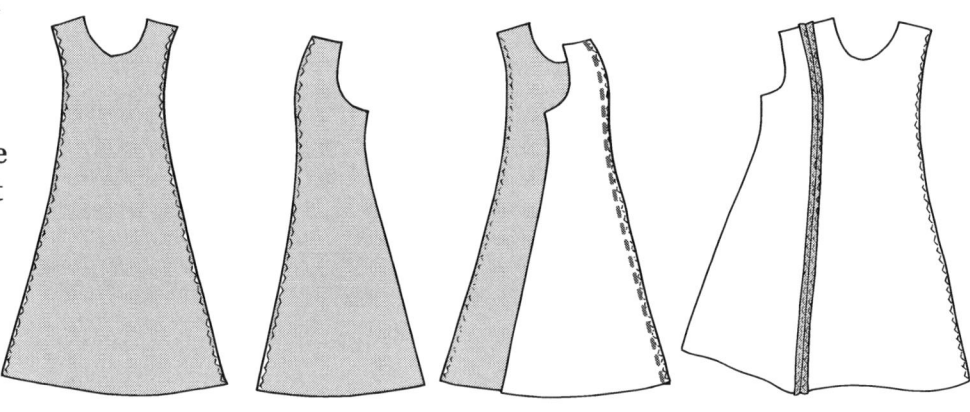

Step 2: If desired, finish the side seam allowances of the coat back piece and the back seam allowances of the coat side back pieces. With the right sides together, pin each coat side back piece to the coat back, matching the notches. Stitch. Clip the curves and press the seam allowances open.

Step 3: Apply trim where indictated along the front and back of the coat, being careful the front and back ends meet at the sides.

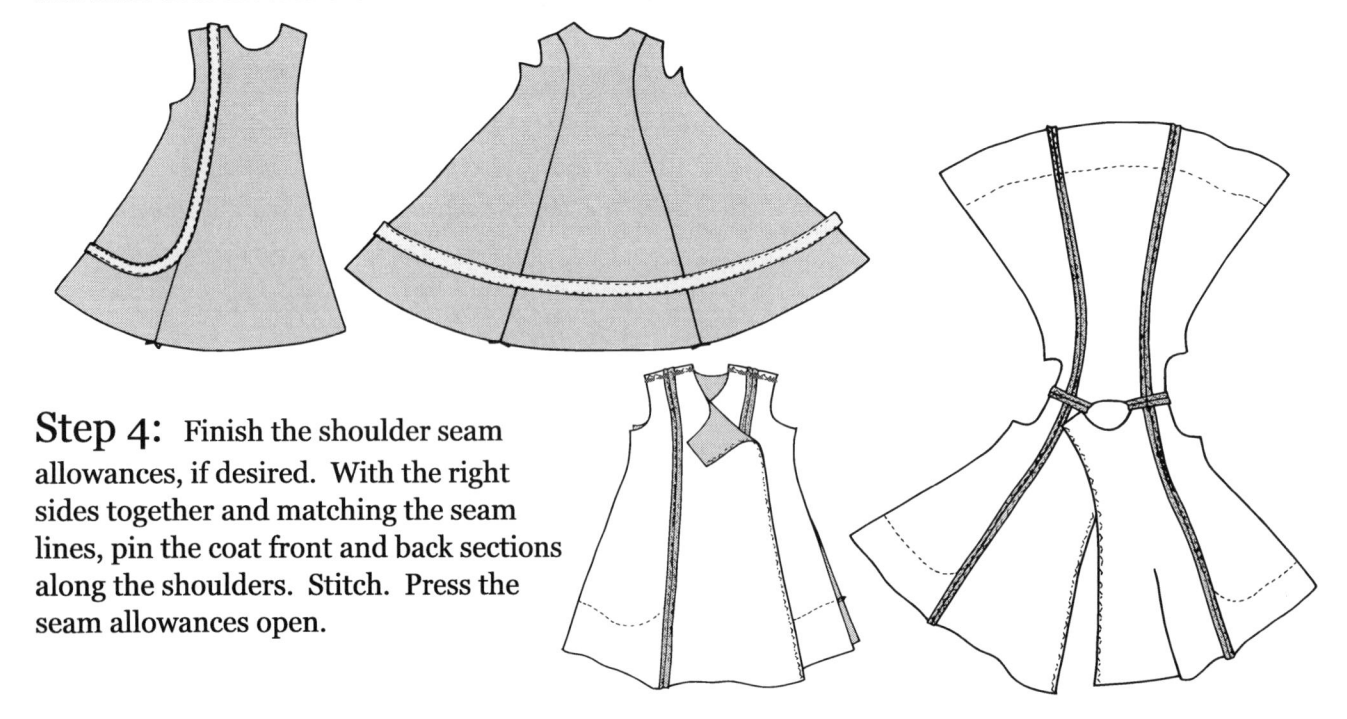

Step 4: Finish the shoulder seam allowances, if desired. With the right sides together and matching the seam lines, pin the coat front and back sections along the shoulders. Stitch. Press the seam allowances open.

Step 5: Apply trim to the sleeves where indicated on the pattern. Sew two rows of gathering stitches along the top edge of each sleeve where indicated on the pattern.

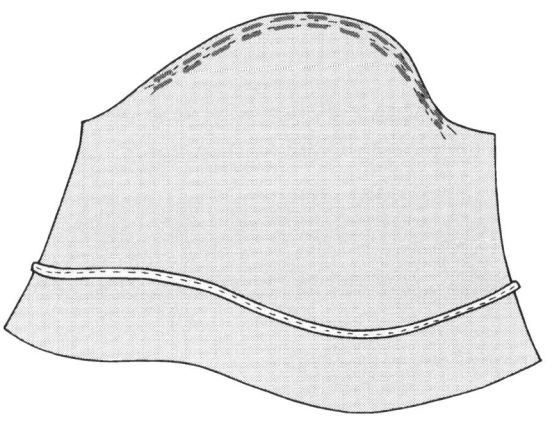

Step 6: With the right sides together and matching the notches, pin each sleeve to the coat at the armscye. Draw the gathering stitches to ease the fit in the armscye. Stitch with a double-stitch to strengthen the seam. Clip the curves and finish the seam allowances if desired. Press the seam allowances toward the coat. Finish the side seam allowances if desired. ***If making an unlined coat, skip to Step 12 and follow the instructions using only the facings.***

Coat Lining

Step 7: With the right sides together and matching the notches, pin the back facing to the center back lining. Stitch. Press the seam allowance down.

Step 8: With the right sides together and matching the notches, pin a coat side back lining to each side of the coat center back lining. Stitch and finish the seam allowances, if desired. Press the seam allowances toward the sides. Finish the shoulder seam allowances, if desired.

Step 9: Finish the bottom edge of the side front lining. Turn under a 1/2-inch (12 mm) hem and press to crease.

Step 10: With the right sides together and matching the notches, pin the side front lining to the bodice front. Making sure the hem remains turned, match the lower edge of the lining to the dot on the coat front. Stitch. Press the seam allowance toward the lining. Finish the shoulder seam allowances if desired.

Step 11: With the rights sides together pin the back lining and facing to the front lining and facing at the shoulders, matching the seamlines. Stitch and press the seam allowances open.

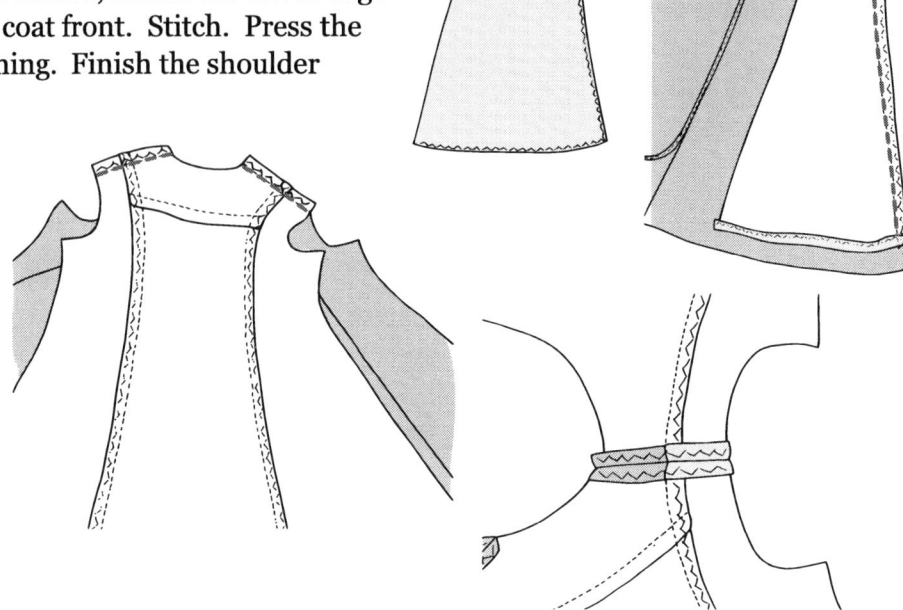

Step 12: Stay-stitch the top edge of the sleeve facings. Clip the curves up to the seamline, and pin to the bottom edge of the sleeve lining, easing the facings along the curves. Stitch. Press the seam allowance toward the sleeve lining. Sew two rows of gathing stitches on the upper edge of the sleeve lining where indicated on the pattern. *If a lining is not being used, finish the top edge of the sleeve facings instead of attaching them to the sleeve lining and skip to Step 14.*

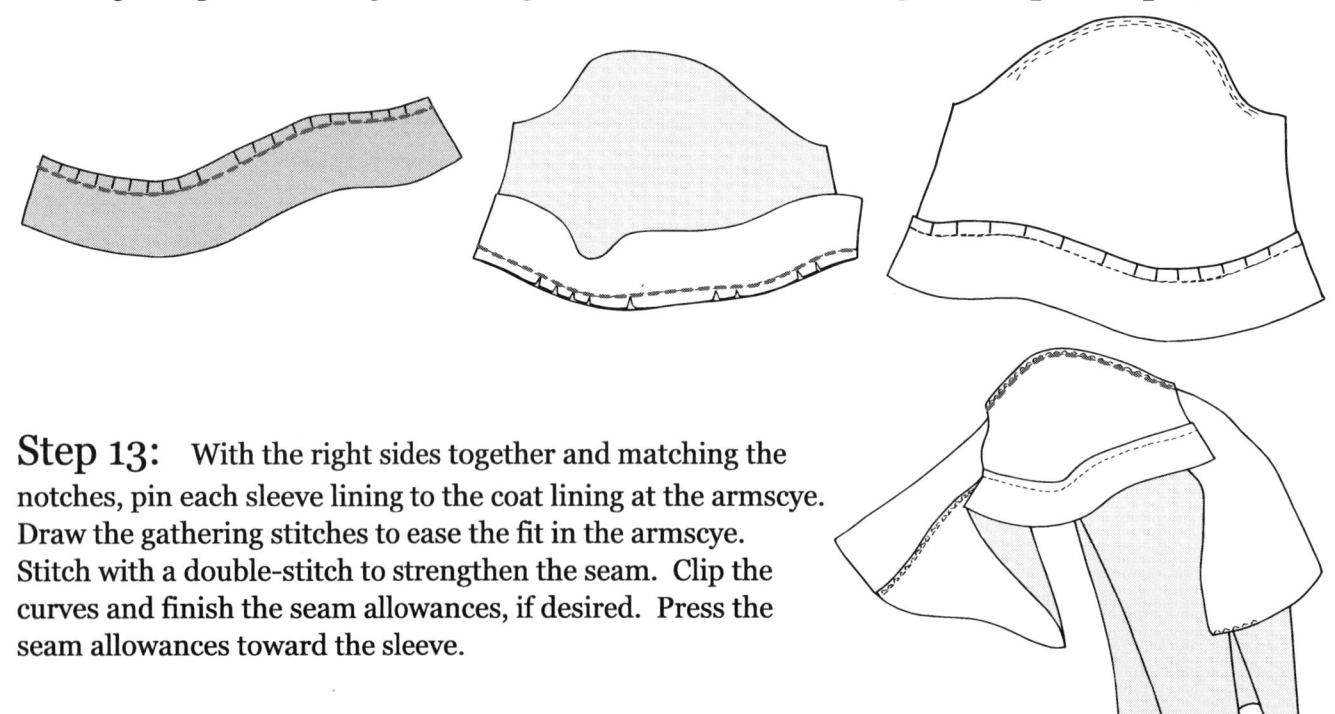

Step 13: With the right sides together and matching the notches, pin each sleeve lining to the coat lining at the armscye. Draw the gathering stitches to ease the fit in the armscye. Stitch with a double-stitch to strengthen the seam. Clip the curves and finish the seam allowances, if desired. Press the seam allowances toward the sleeve.

Step 14: Finish the side seam allowances and bottom edge of the back lining, if desired. ***If lining isn't being used, pin the sleeve facings directly to the coat sleeve, matching the notches. With the facings down, finish the side seams of the coat from the sleeve facings to the hemline of the coat. Press the seam allowances open. Continue following the instructions***

Step 15: Pin the sides of the lining together, being careful to match the seams of the facings and underarms. Stitch. Press the seam allowances open. Repeat this procedure for the side seams of the coat.

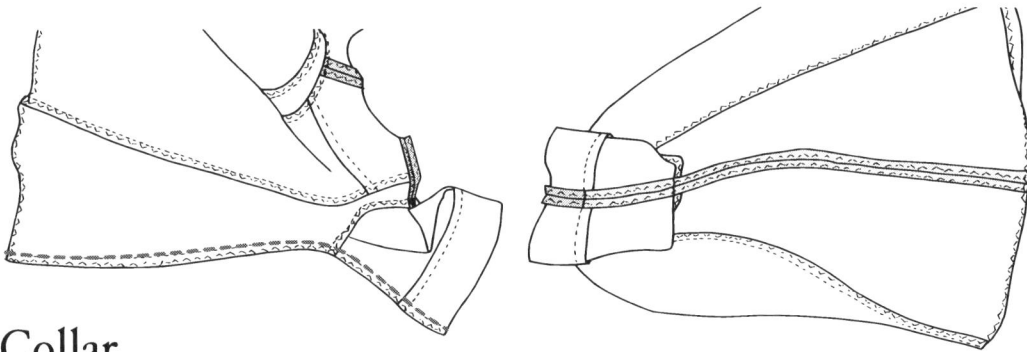

Collar

Step 16: Baste lace to one of the collar pieces just inside the seam allowance with the decorative edge of the lace facing the the collar.

Step 17: Pin the collar pieces right sides together along the outer edge. Stitch. Notch the curves and trim the seam allowance to 1/8-inch (3 mm). Turn right side out and press, following the seamlines.

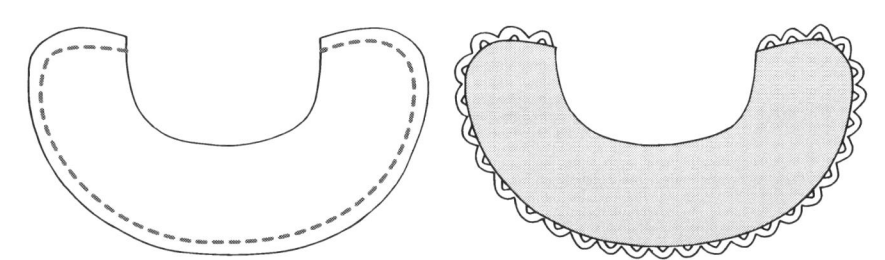

Step 18: Pin the collar to neckline of the coat, matching the notches and dots.

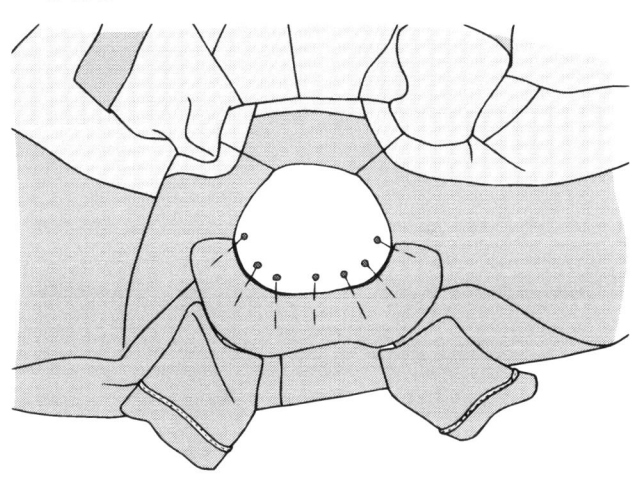

Coat Facings

Step 19: Turn the coat and lining inside out. With the right sides together, being careful not to twist the sleeves, pin the sleeve facings to the lower edge of the corresponding sleeve. Stitch. Clip the curves. ***If lining isn't being used, turn the facing under the sleeve. Press and hand stitch directly to the coat along the top edge of the facing.***

Step 20: With the right sides together, pin the coat facing over the collar, along the neckline. Stitch. Clip the curves.

Step 21: Fold the coat front along the fold line, right sides together. Pin along the bottom edge of the coat front and sew using a 1/2 inch (12 mm) seam allowance.

Step 22: Clip the corners on the front of the coat. Turn the coat right side out. Press the neckline, lower sleeve, front facing.

Finishing the Coat

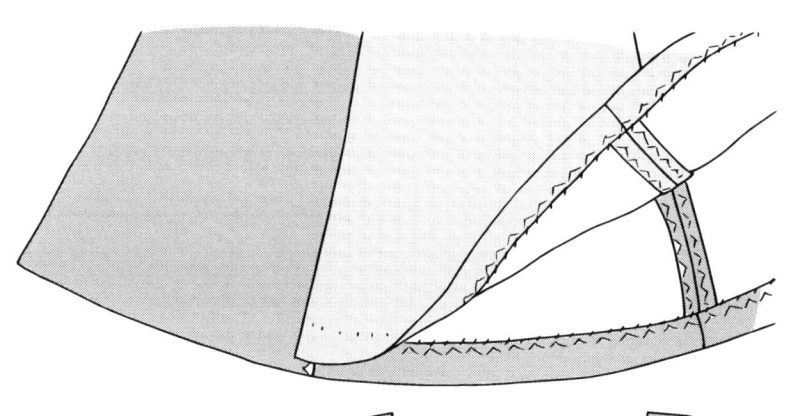

Step 23: Turn under a 1/2-inch (12 mm) hem on the coat, easing the fabric around the curve and pin in place. Stitch and press. Repeat for the the lining. Make buttonholes on the proper right and attach buttons on the proper left and at the neckline for the pelerine where indicated on the pattern.

Pelerine

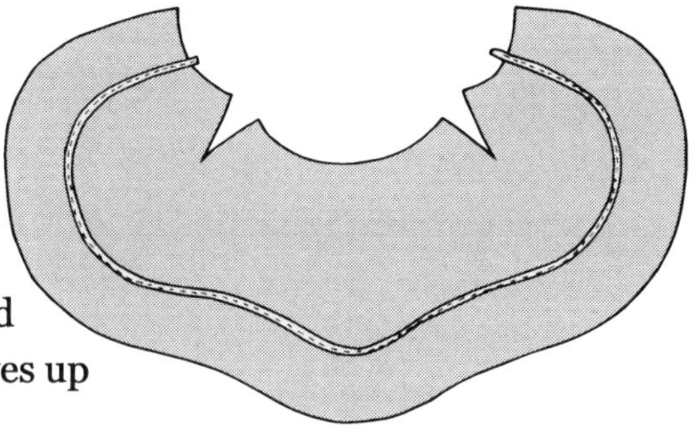

Step 24: Sew trim to the outer layer of the pelerine where indicated on the pattern.

Step 25: Sew the darts at the shoulders of the pelerine and lining. Press open. Stay-stitch the necklines and clip the curves up to the seamline.

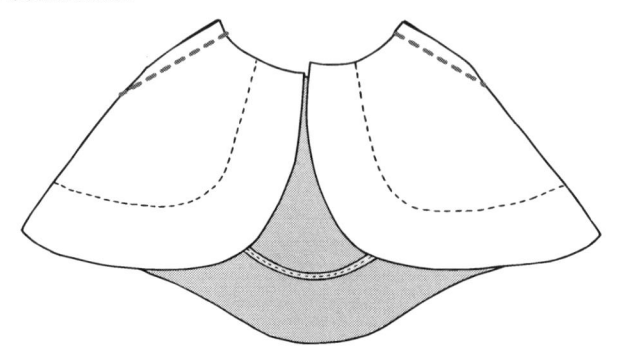

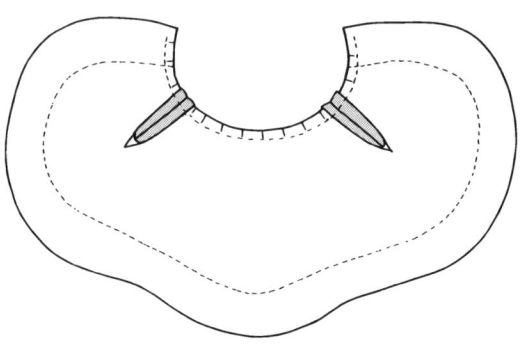

Page 97

Step 26: With the right sides together, pin the pelerine and lining along the outeside edges. Starting at one of the dots at the neck line, stitch around the outer edge of the pelerine to the second dot, leaving the center of the neckline open.

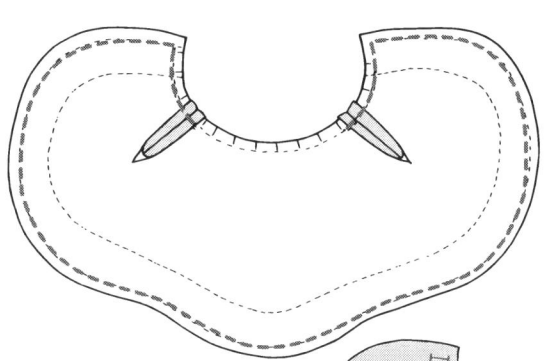

Step 27: Turn the pelerine right side out and press, following the seam line. Turn the raw edges of the neckline inside and blind stitch the neck opening shut. Make buttonholes on each side of the Pelerine where indicated on the pattern. Attach the pelerine to the coat using the buttons under the collar.

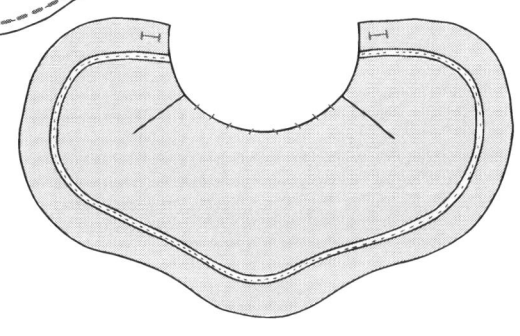

Bonnet

Step 28: Apply fusible interfacing to the wrong side of the outer brim and crown fabric following the manufacturer's instructions. Sew trim to the right side of of the brim where indicated on the pattern. Stay-stitch the back edge of the brim and clip the curve up to the stay-stitching.

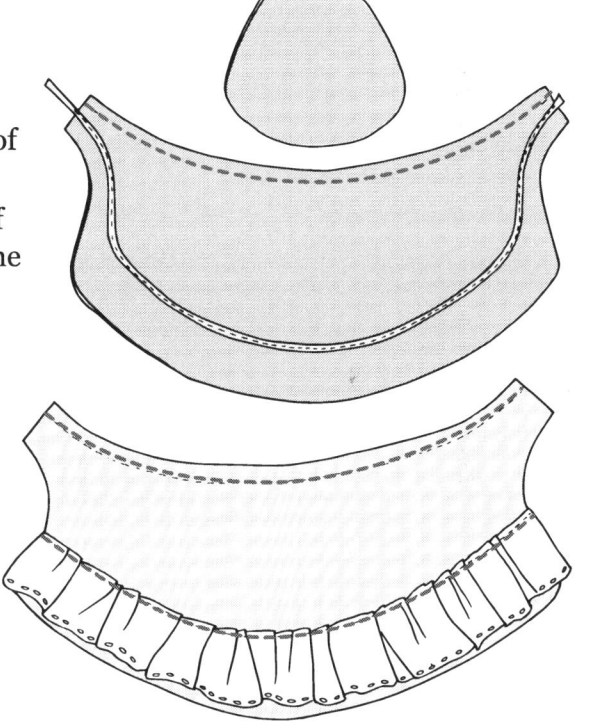

Step 29: Sew gathered lace to the brim lining where indicated on the pattern. Stay-stitch the back edge of the brim. Clip the curve up to the stay-stitching.

Step 30: With right sides together and matching the notches, pin the back sides of the brim. Stitch. Press the seam allowances open. Repeat with the lining.

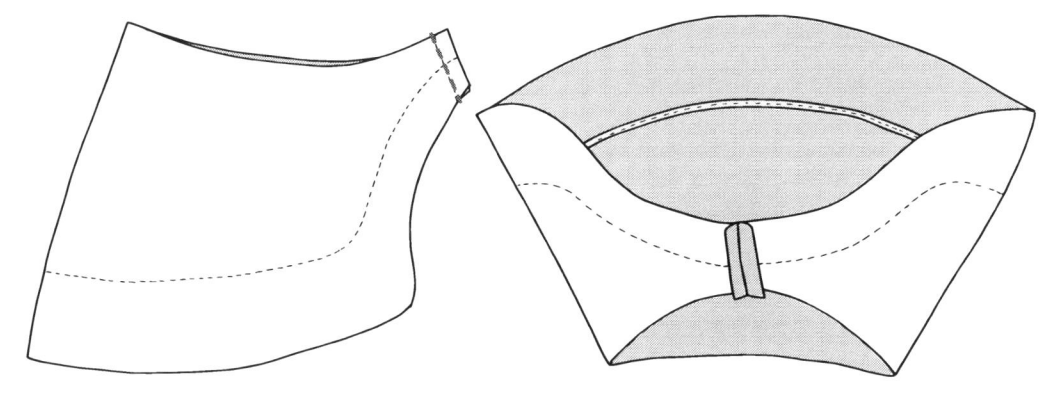

Step 31: With the right sides together and matching the notches, pin the crown to the back of the brim. Ease the edge of the brim around the curves. Stitch. Press the seam allowance toward the brim. Repeat for the brim lining.

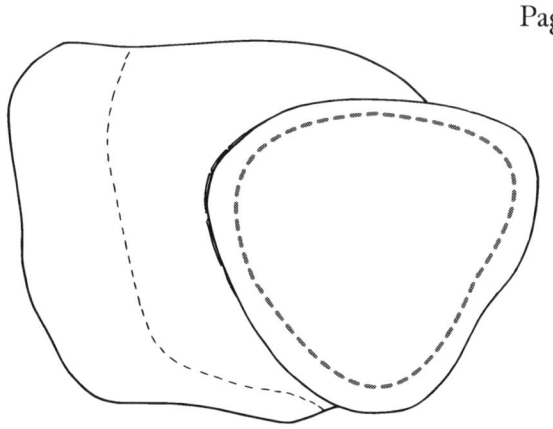

Step 32: Fold the bonnet ties along the foldline right sides together. Pin along the length of the tie, leaving the top end open. Stitch. Clip the corners and trim the seam allowances to 1/8-inch (3 mm). Turn right side out, squaring the corners with a blunt needle. Press, following the seamlines.

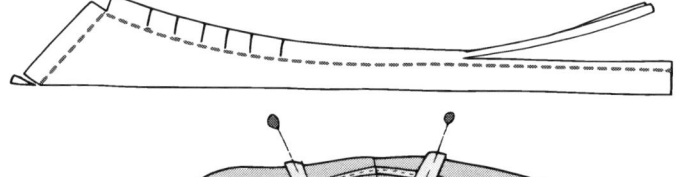

Step 33: Pin the bonnet ties to the bonnet at the dots. Stay-stitch the back edge of the brim and lining between the dots, tacking the bonnet ties in the process.

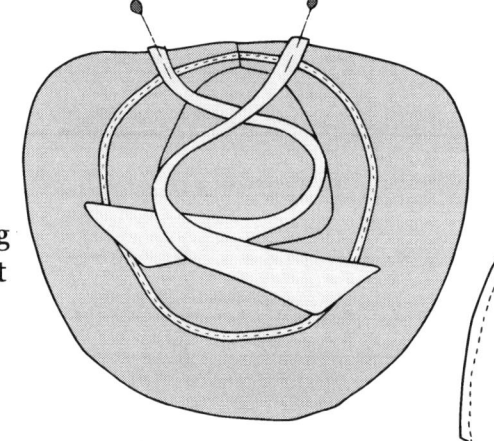

Step 34: With the right sides together, pin the bonnet lining to the bonnet brim, making sure the lace and the ties are tucked inside out of the way of the seamline. Starting at one of the ties, stitch around the brim, past the other tie, leaving the back edge of the bonnet open. Clip and notch the curves where necessary.

Step 35: Turn the bonnet right side out, and press the brim, following the seamline. Turn the seam allowances at the back of the bonnet under along the stay-stitching and blindstitch to close. Turn the bonnet inside out, and pin the lining and bonnet together along the seamline of the crown. Tack the lining to the bonnet along the seam line of the crown. Turn the bonnet right side out. Press.

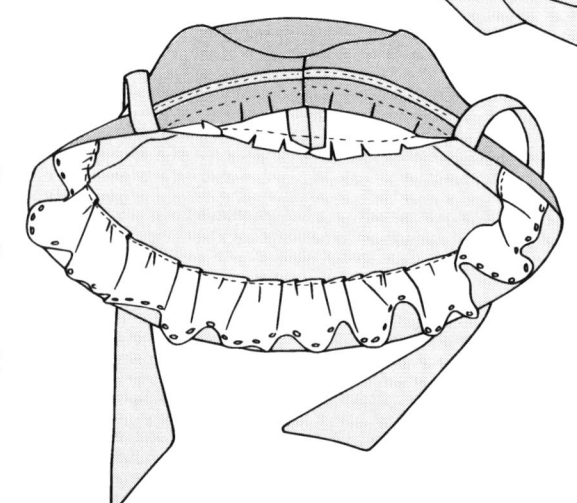

Page 98

Page 99

Victorian Christmas Caroler
Pattern Pieces

Cutting Layout for 45-inch (1.14 m) wide Fabric
14 Pieces

- 65 ~ Coat Front
- 66 ~ Coat Side Front
- 67 ~ Coat Center Back
- 68 ~ Coat Side Back
- 69 ~ Coat Sleeve
- 70 ~ Collar
- 71 ~ Coat Center Back Lining
- 72 ~ Coat Back Neck Facing
- 73 ~ Sleeve Lining
- 74 ~ Sleeve Facing
- 75 ~ Pelerine
- 76 ~ Bonnet Brim
- 77 ~ Bonnet Crown
- 78 ~ Bonnet Tie

Coat, Pelerine, and Bonnet
Use pieces: 65, 66, 67, 68, 69, 70, 72, 74, 75, 76, and 77

Bonnet Interfacing
Use piece: 76

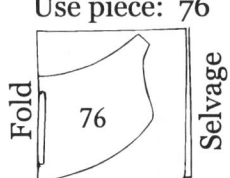

Bias Trim
To make bias tape trim, cut 1-inch (2.5 cm) wide strips of fabric on the bias. Sew together to make 3 yards (3 m). Press the raw edges under 1/4-inch (6 mm) to make 1/2-inch (12 mm) wide trim.

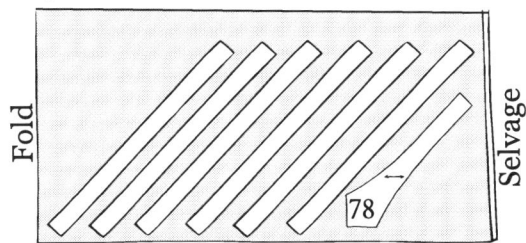

Note: Ties are made with the contrast fabric and can be cut either from the lining fabric OR the Bias Trim fabric

Coat, Pelerine, and Bonnet Lining
Use pieces: 66, 68, 71, 73, 75, 76, 77, and 78

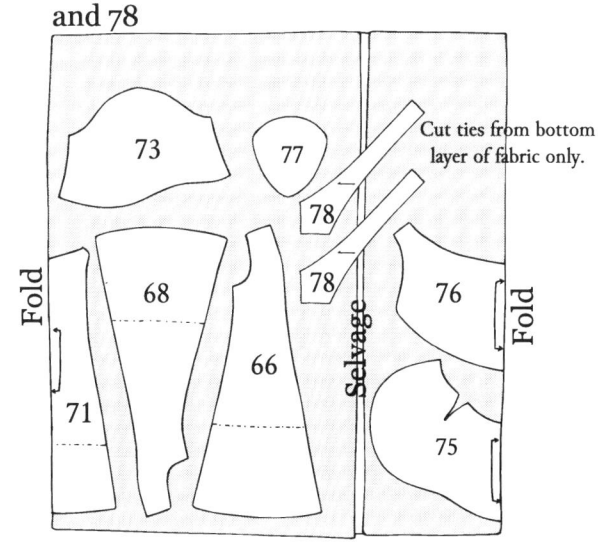

Cut ties from bottom layer of fabric only.

Page 101

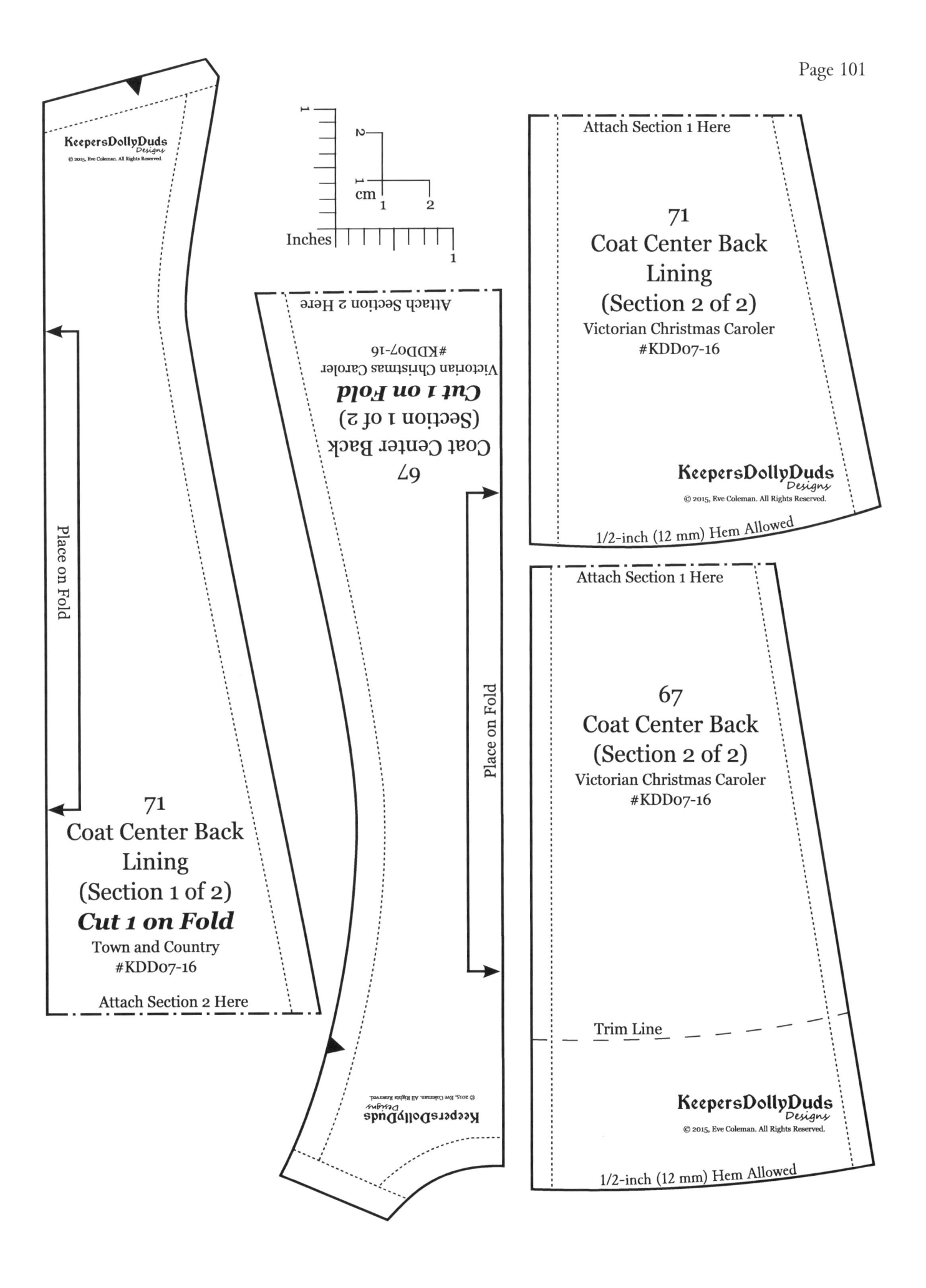

71
Coat Center Back Lining
(Section 2 of 2)
Victorian Christmas Caroler
#KDD07-16

Attach Section 1 Here

1/2-inch (12 mm) Hem Allowed

KeepersDollyDuds Designs
© 2015, Eve Coleman. All Rights Reserved.

67
Coat Center Back
(Section 1 of 2)
Cut 1 on Fold
Victorian Christmas Caroler
#KDD07-16

Attach Section 2 Here

Place on Fold

71
Coat Center Back Lining
(Section 1 of 2)
Cut 1 on Fold
Town and Country
#KDD07-16

Attach Section 2 Here

Place on Fold

KeepersDollyDuds Designs
© 2015, Eve Coleman. All Rights Reserved.

67
Coat Center Back
(Section 2 of 2)
Victorian Christmas Caroler
#KDD07-16

Attach Section 1 Here

Trim Line

1/2-inch (12 mm) Hem Allowed

KeepersDollyDuds Designs
© 2015, Eve Coleman. All Rights Reserved.

Page 103

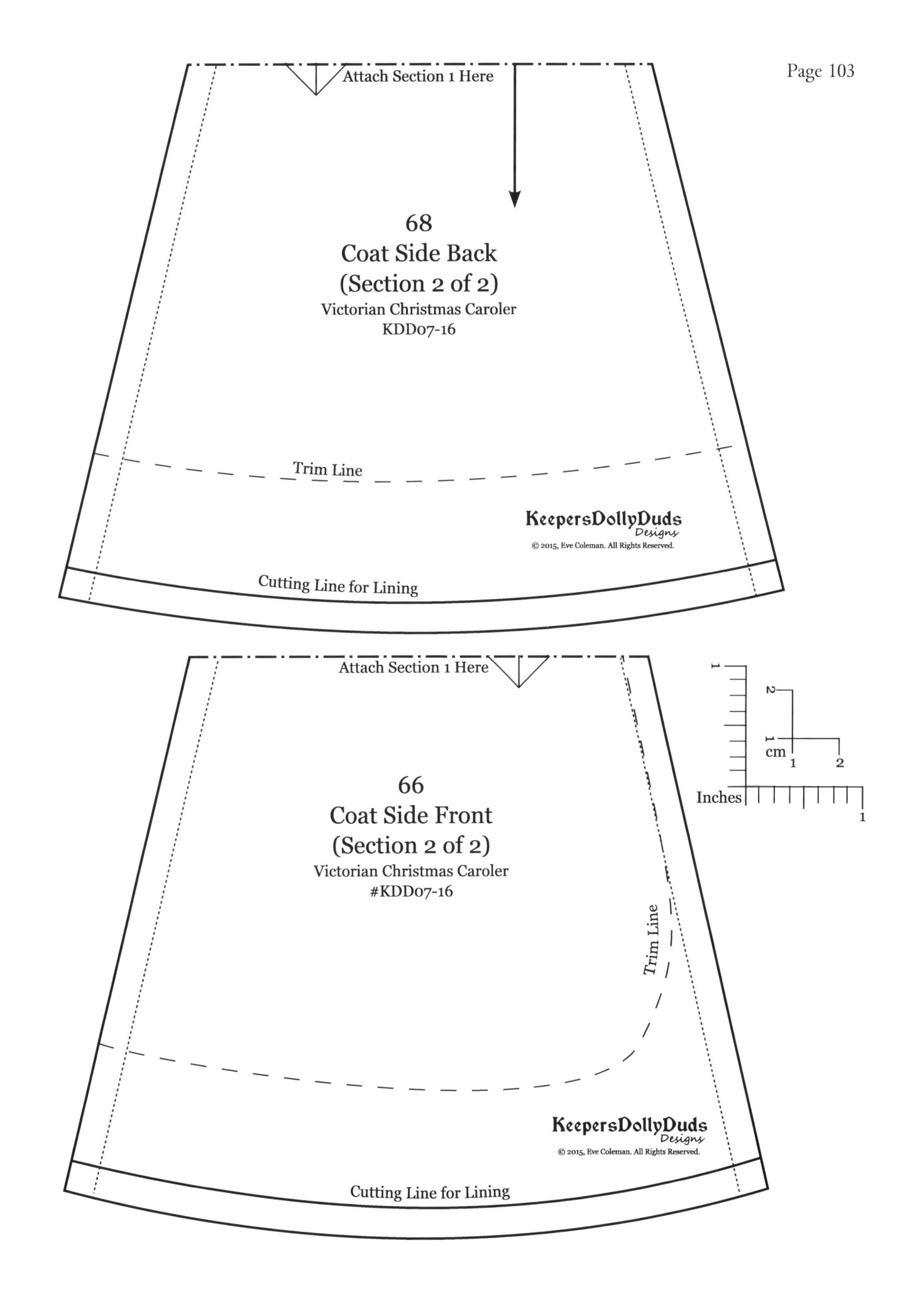

Attach Section 1 Here

**68
Coat Side Back
(Section 2 of 2)**
Victorian Christmas Caroler
KDD07-16

Trim Line

KeepersDollyDuds Designs
© 2015, Eve Coleman. All Rights Reserved.

Cutting Line for Lining

Attach Section 1 Here

**66
Coat Side Front
(Section 2 of 2)**
Victorian Christmas Caroler
#KDD07-16

Trim Line

KeepersDollyDuds Designs
© 2015, Eve Coleman. All Rights Reserved.

Cutting Line for Lining

Page 105

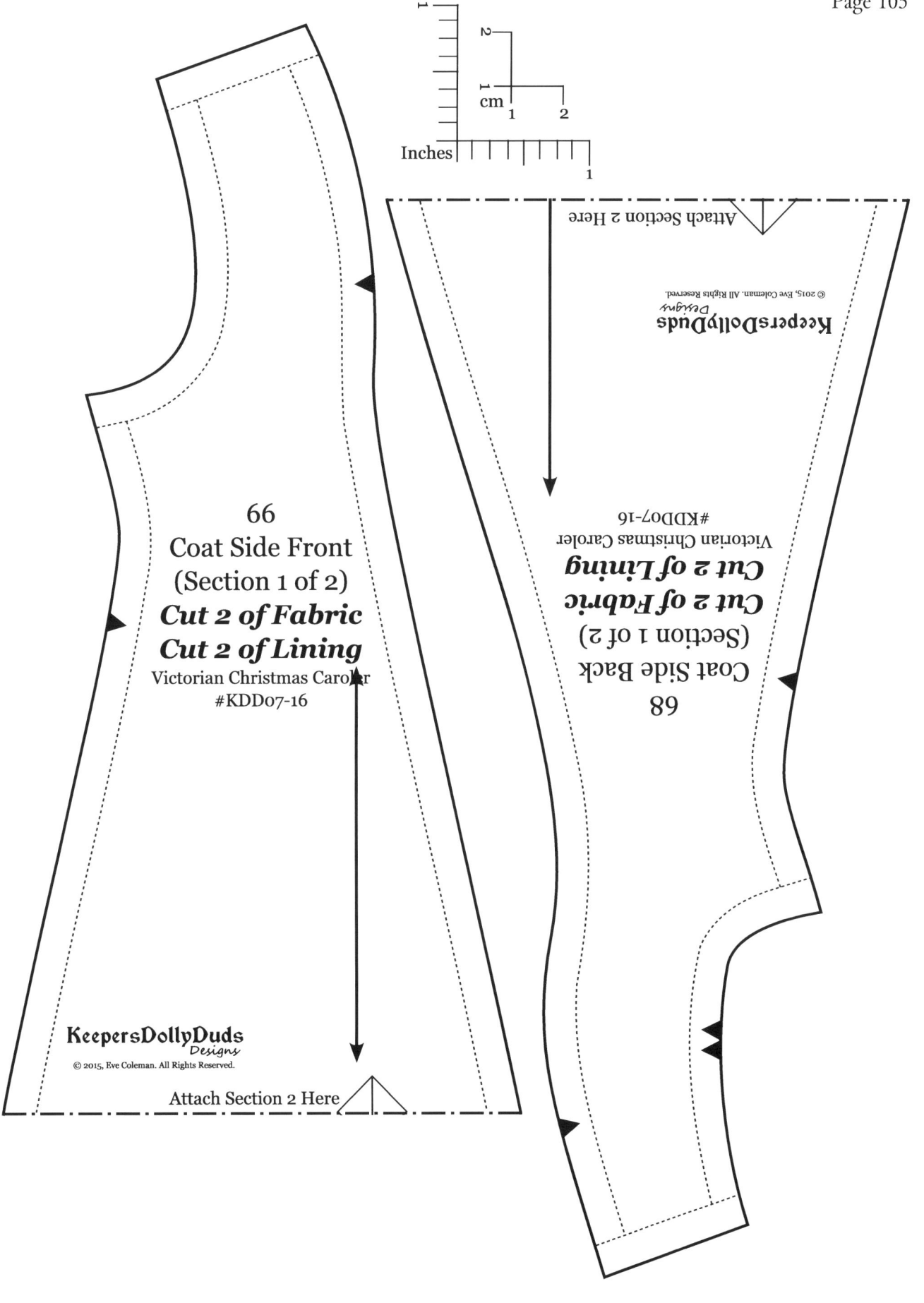

66
Coat Side Front
(Section 1 of 2)
Cut 2 of Fabric
Cut 2 of Lining
Victorian Christmas Caroler
#KDD07-16

KeepersDollyDuds Designs
© 2015, Eve Coleman. All Rights Reserved.

Attach Section 2 Here

68
Coat Side Back
(Section 1 of 2)
Cut 2 of Fabric
Cut 2 of Lining
Victorian Christmas Caroler
#KDD07-16

KeepersDollyDuds Designs
© 2015, Eve Coleman. All Rights Reserved.

Attach Section 2 Here

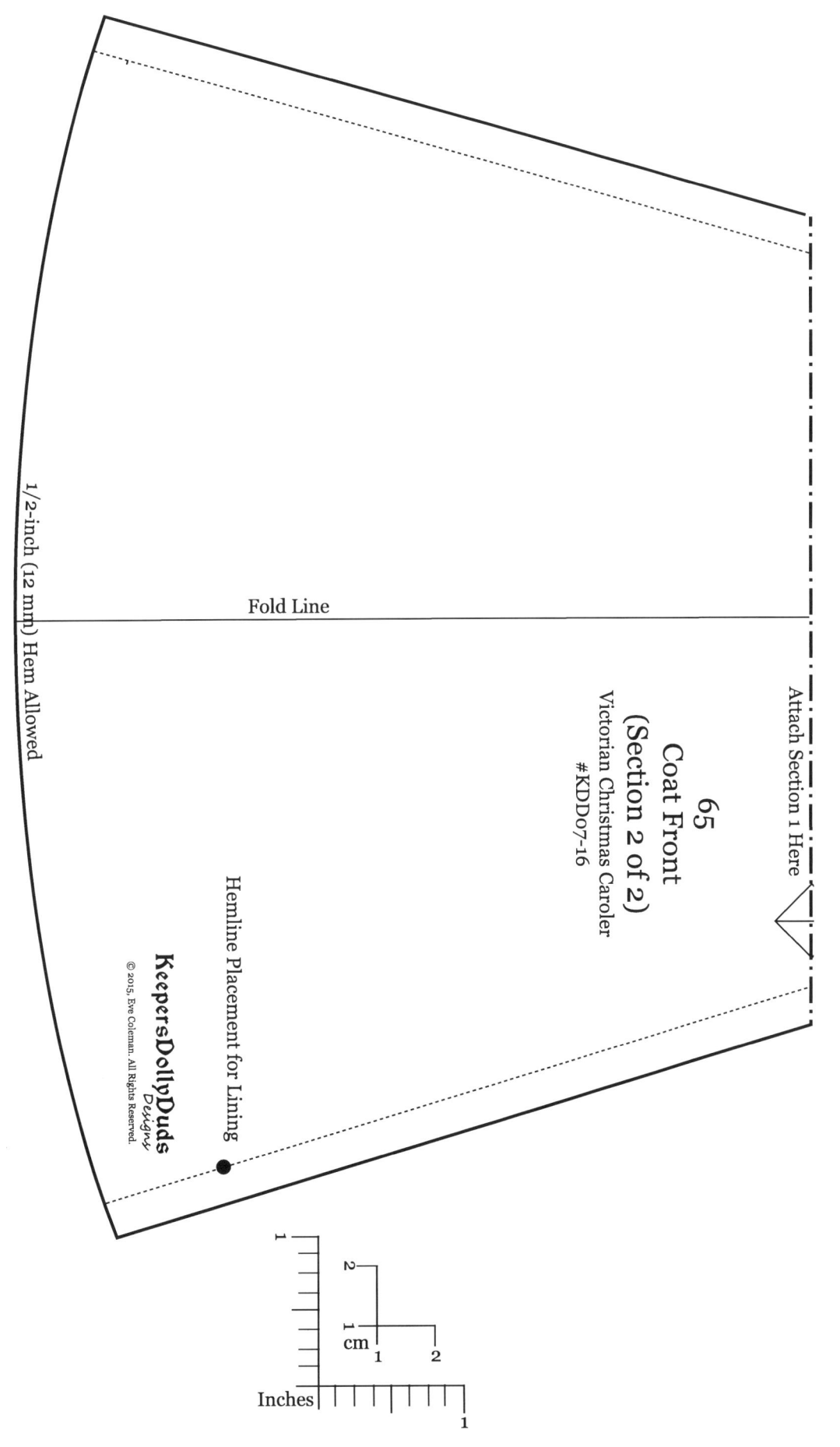

1/2-inch (12 mm) Hem Allowed

Fold Line

**65
Coat Front
(Section 2 of 2)**
Victorian Christmas Caroler
#KDD07-16

Attach Section 1 Here

Hemline Placement for Lining

KeepersDollyDuds *Designs*
© 2015, Eve Coleman. All Rights Reserved.

Page 109

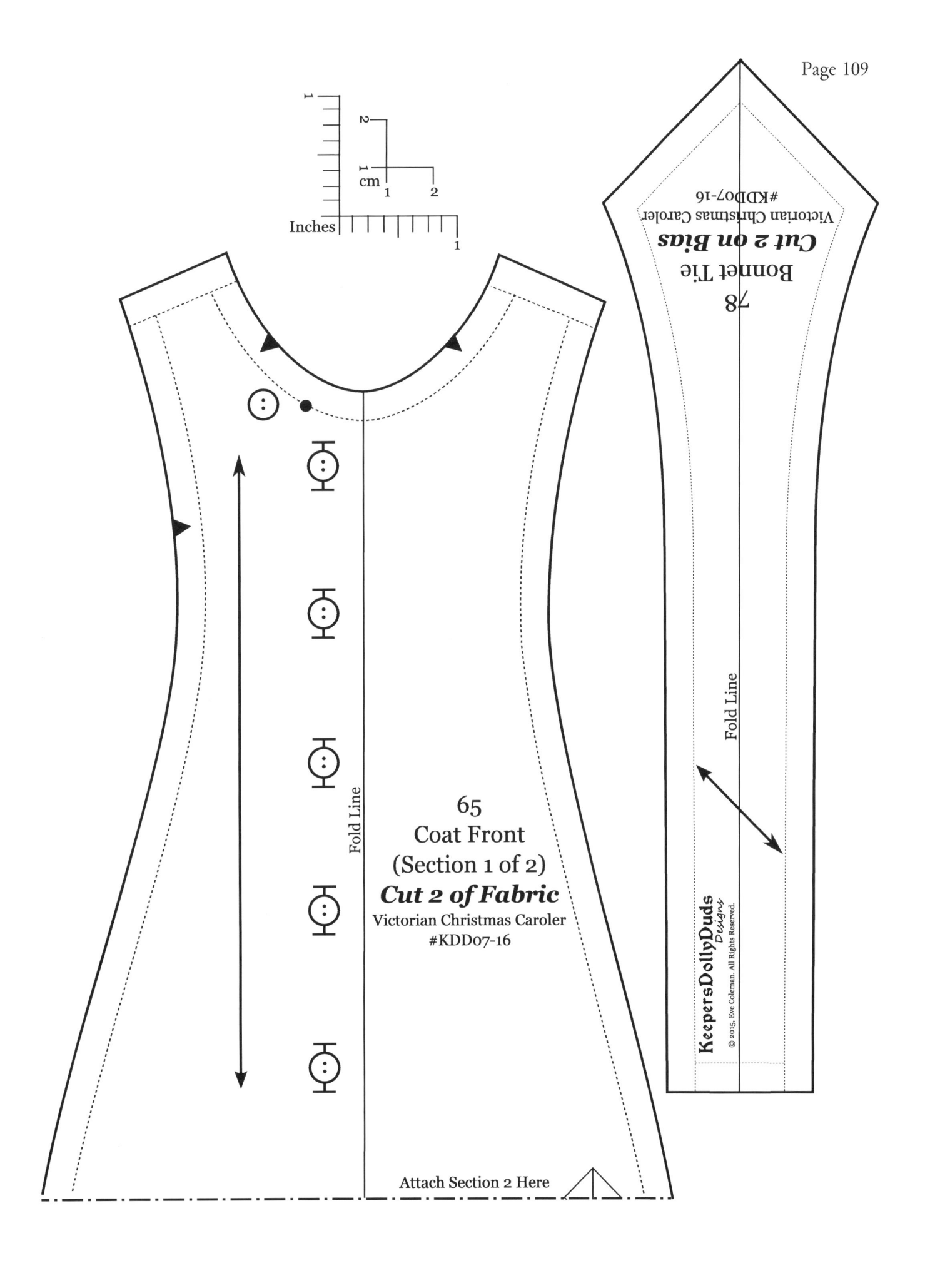

65
Coat Front
(Section 1 of 2)
Cut 2 of Fabric
Victorian Christmas Caroler
#KDD07-16

Fold Line

Attach Section 2 Here

78
Bonnet Tie
Cut 2 on Bias
Victorian Christmas Caroler
#KDD07-16

Fold Line

KeepersDollyDuds Designs
© 2015, Eve Coleman. All Rights Reserved.

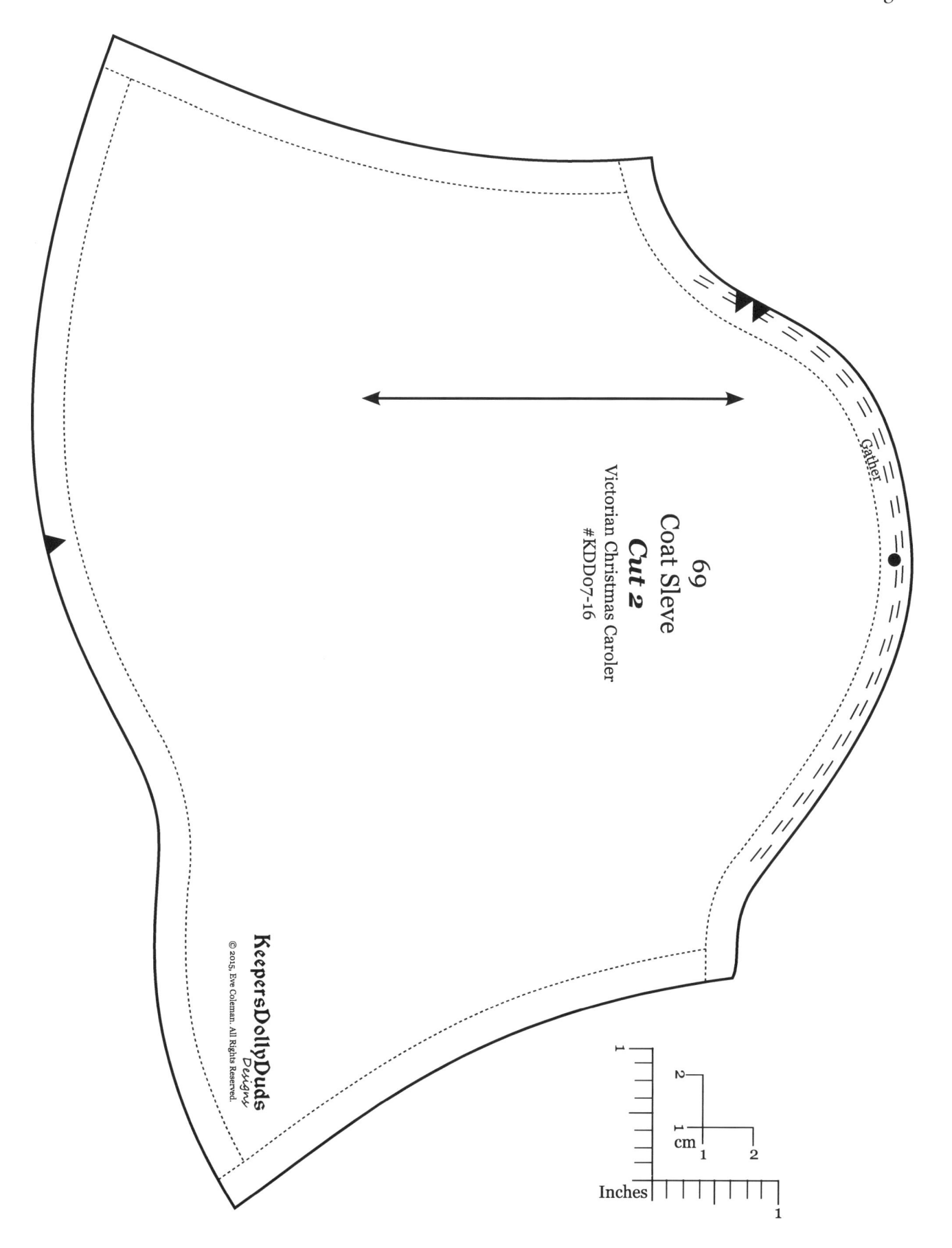

69
Coat Sleve
Cut 2
Victorian Christmas Caroler
#KDD07-16

KeepersDollyDuds
Designs
© 2015, Eve Coleman. All Rights Reserved.

Gather

Page 113

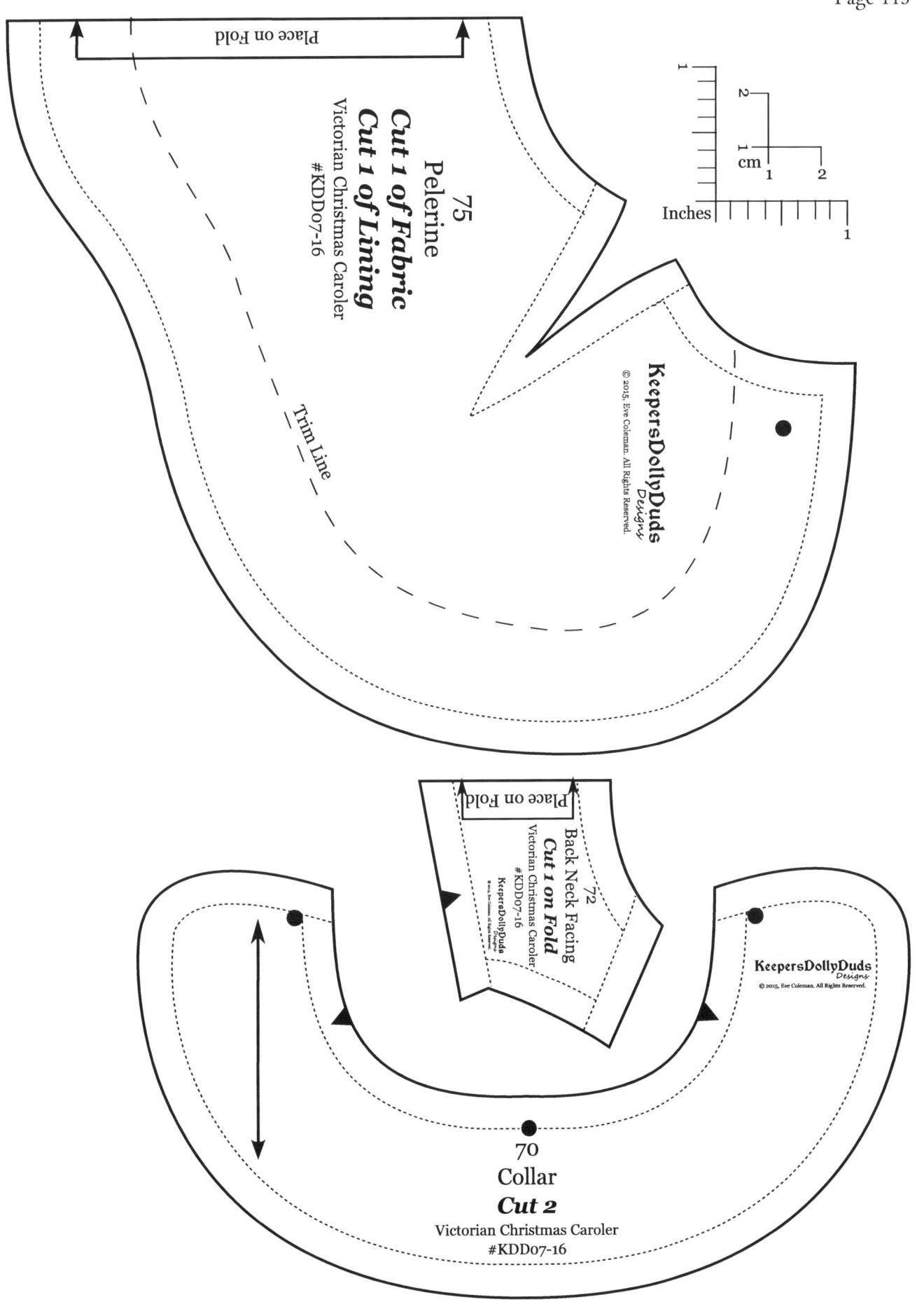

75
Pelerine
Cut 1 of Fabric
Cut 1 of Lining
Victorian Christmas Caroler
#KDD07-16

Place on Fold

Trim Line

KeepersDollyDuds
Designs
© 2015, Eve Coleman. All Rights Reserved.

72
Back Neck Facing
Cut 1 on Fold
Victorian Christmas Caroler
#KDD07-16

Place on Fold

KeepersDollyDuds
Designs
© 2015, Eve Coleman. All Rights Reserved.

70
Collar
Cut 2
Victorian Christmas Caroler
#KDD07-16

Page 115

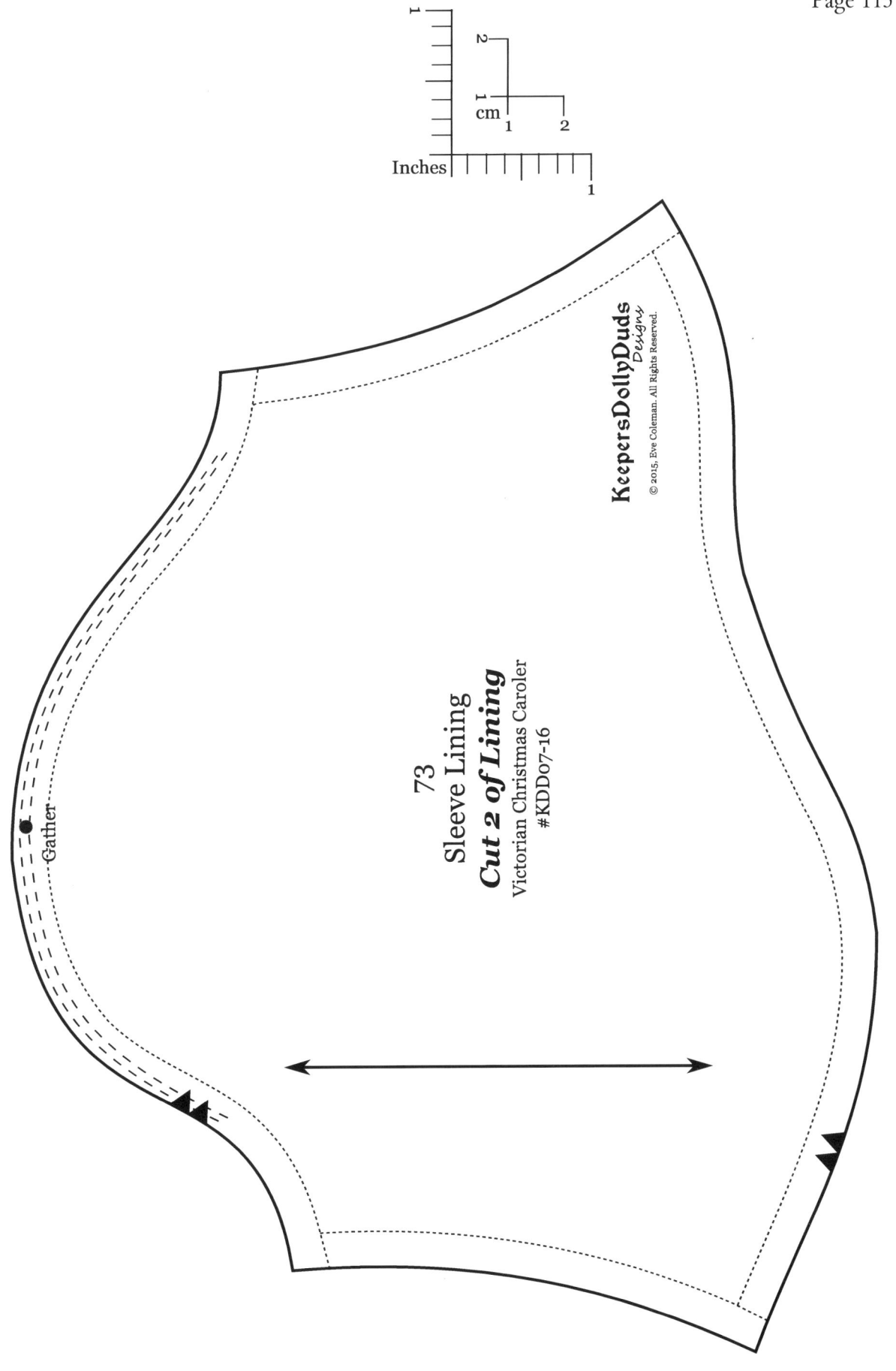

73
Sleeve Lining
Cut 2 of Lining
Victorian Christmas Caroler
#KDD07-16

KeepersDollyDuds
Designs
© 2015, Eve Coleman. All Rights Reserved.

Gather

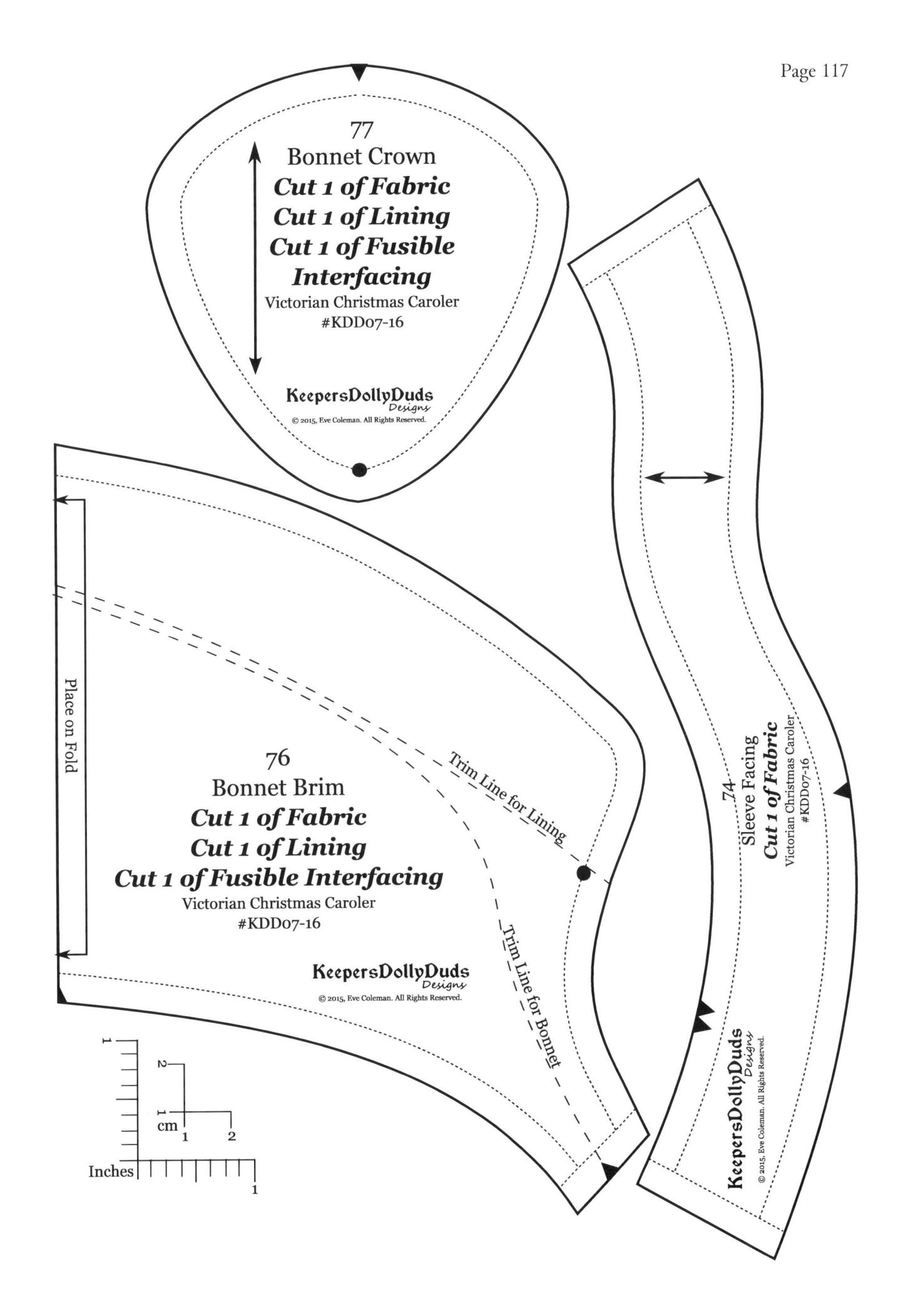

77
Bonnet Crown
Cut 1 of Fabric
Cut 1 of Lining
Cut 1 of Fusible Interfacing
Victorian Christmas Caroler
#KDD07-16

KeepersDollyDuds Designs
© 2015, Eve Coleman. All Rights Reserved.

76
Bonnet Brim
Cut 1 of Fabric
Cut 1 of Lining
Cut 1 of Fusible Interfacing
Victorian Christmas Caroler
#KDD07-16

Place on Fold

Trim Line for Lining

Trim Line for Bonnet

KeepersDollyDuds Designs
© 2015, Eve Coleman. All Rights Reserved.

74
Sleeve Facing
Cut 1 of Fabric
Victorian Christmas Caroler
#KDD07-16

KeepersDollyDuds Designs
© 2015, Eve Coleman. All Rights Reserved.

Page 119

Regency Pinafore Dress and Fichu

Materials List
#KDD-15-16

Suggested Fabrics: ***Dress and Pinafore*** in lightweight fabric such as cotton, cotton blends, linen, or silk. Not suitable for knits. ***Fichu*** in semi-sheer cotton batiste, cotton voile, silk voile, dotted Swiss, or handkerchief linen. Not suitable for knits

Fabric Yardage:
Pinafore ~ 1/3 yard (0.33 m)
Dress ~ 1/3 yard (0.33 m)
Fichu ~ 1/6 yard (0.15 m)
Ruffle, sleeve (plus fichu if desired) ~ 1/2 yard (0.5 m)

Notions:
__Thread
Dress
__2/3 yard (0.6 m) 1/2-inch (12 mm) wide lace
__three small snaps OR 3-inches of
   1/2-inch (12 mm) wide hook and loop tape
   OR three 3/8-inch (9 mm) buttons
Pinafore
__ 2/3 yard (0.6 m) 1/2-inch (12 mm) wide lace
__four 1/4-inch (6 mm) decorative buttons
__four small snaps

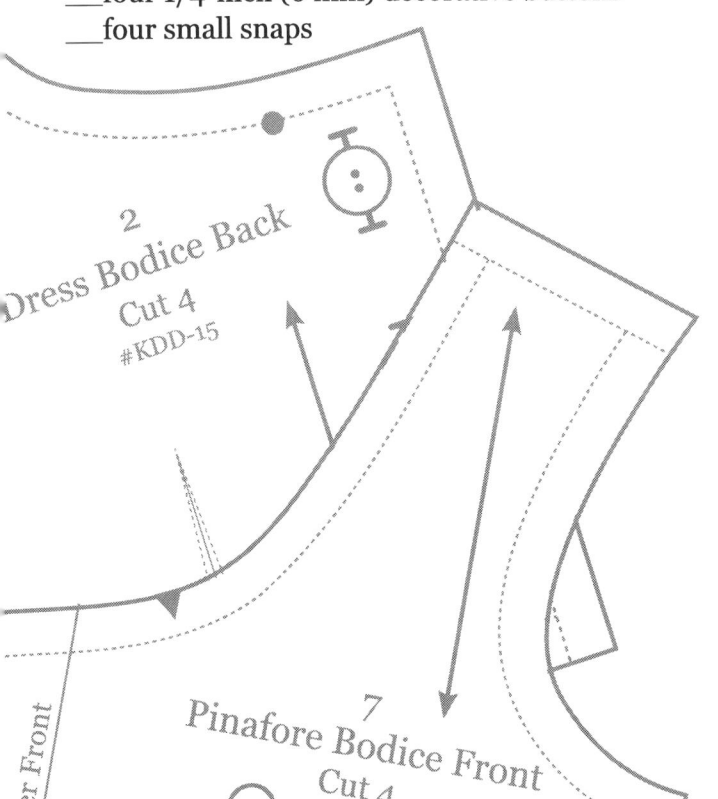

Regency Dress Bodice

Step 1: Sew darts where indicated on the pattern on the bodice back. Press toward center back. Finish the shoulder seam allowances, if desired.

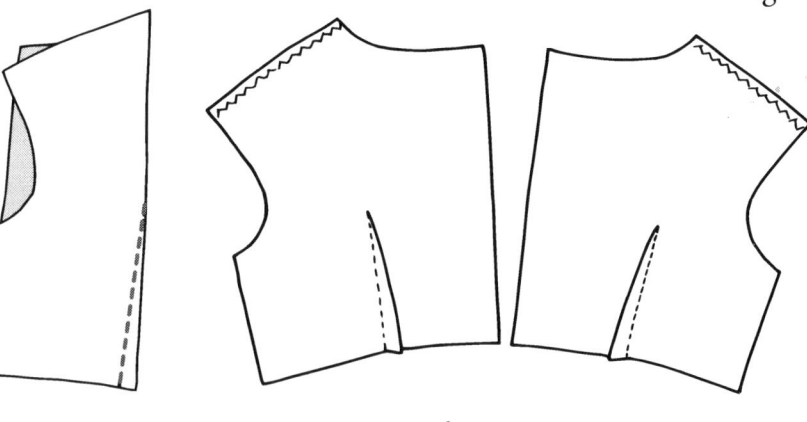

Step 2: With the right sides together, pin the bodice front to the bodice backs along the shoulders. Stitch. Press the seam allowances open. Repeat for the bodice lining.

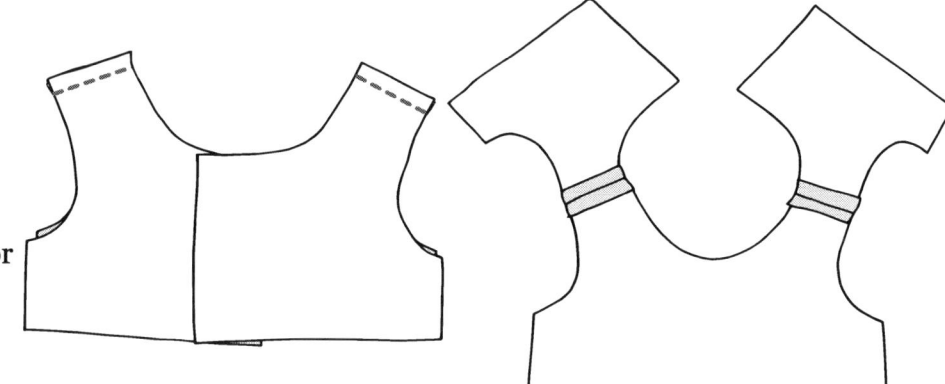

Step 3: Fold the neck ruffle in half along the fold line, right side out. Press. Sew two rows of gathering stitches along the raw edge.

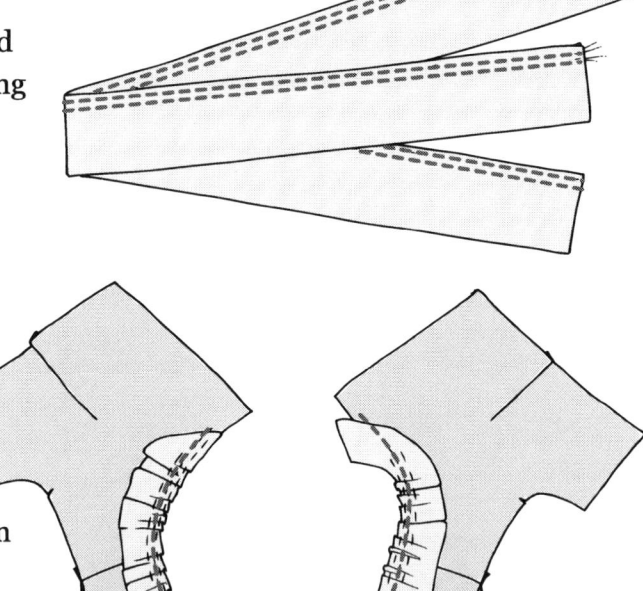

Step 4: Pin the neck ruffle to the bodice between the dots on the back neckline. Draw up the gathering stitches to fit, arranging the fullness evenly around the neckline. Turn the ends of the ruffle inside the seam allowance. Baste to secure.

Regency Dress Sleeves

Step 5: Mark the placement lines for the sleeve trim on the right side of each sleeve. Apply trim along the marked lines.

Step 6: With the right sides together, pin the top edge of the lace to the bottom edge of each sleeve. Stitch. Finish the seam allowances, if desired. Press the seam allowance toward the sleeve. Topstitch along the bottom edge of the sleeves to secure the seam allowance. Sew two rows of gathering stitches along the top of each sleeve where indicated on the pattern.

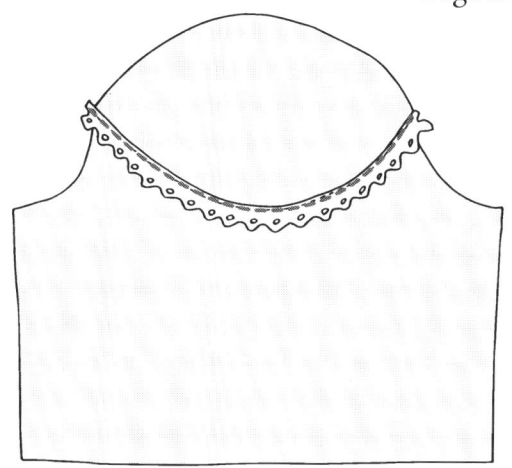

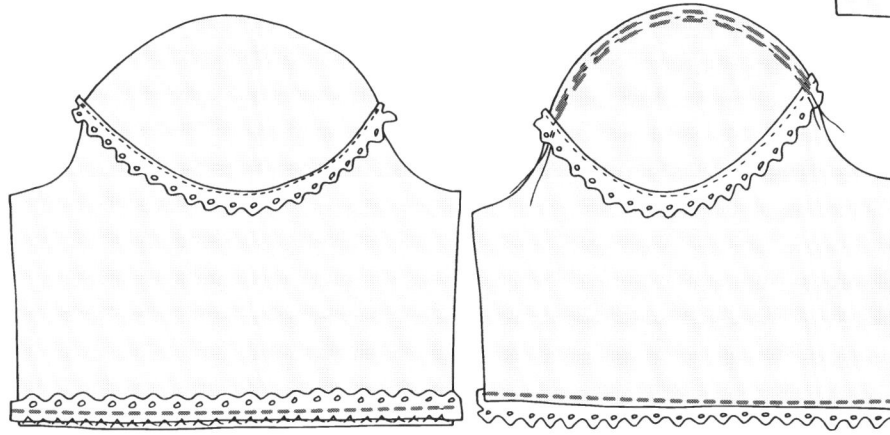

Step 7: With the right sides together and matching the notches, pin the sleeves to the armscyes of the dress bodice. Draw up the gathering stitches to fit, arranging the fullness evenly along the armscyes. Stitch. Clip the curves and finish the seam allowances, if desired. Press the seam allowances toward the bodice. Finish the side seam allowances, if desired.

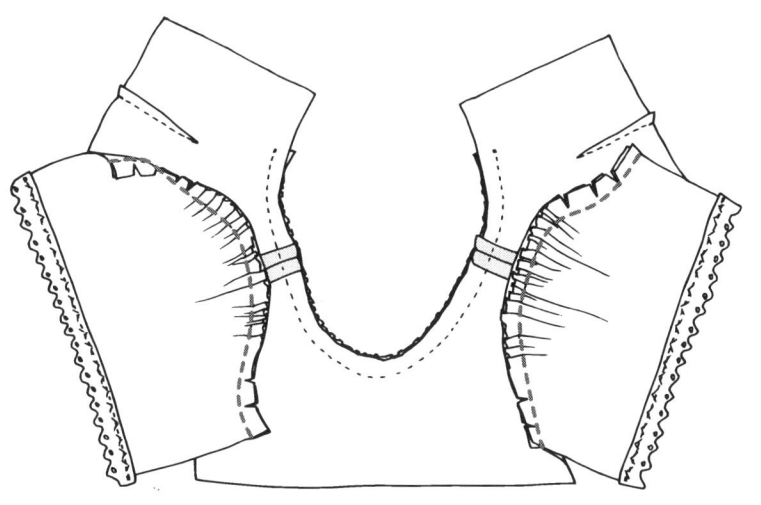

Step 8: Pin the sides right sides together, matching the seamlines of the armscyes and the bottom edges of the sleeves and bodice. Stitch. Press the seam allowances open.

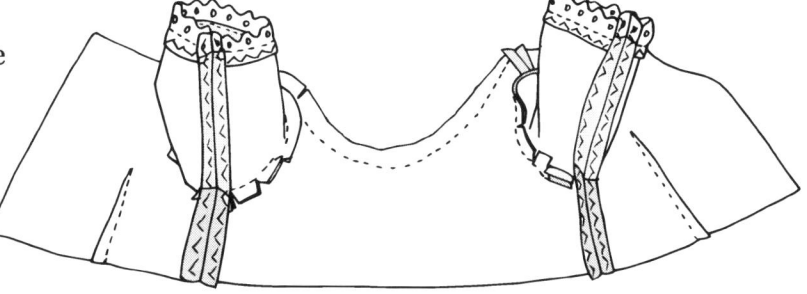

Regency Bodice Lining

Step 9: Stay-stitch along the armscyes of the bodice lining. Clip the curves and press the seam allowances toward the bodice along the stay-stitching.

Step 10: Pin the sides of the bodice lining right sides together. Stitch. Press the seam allowances open.

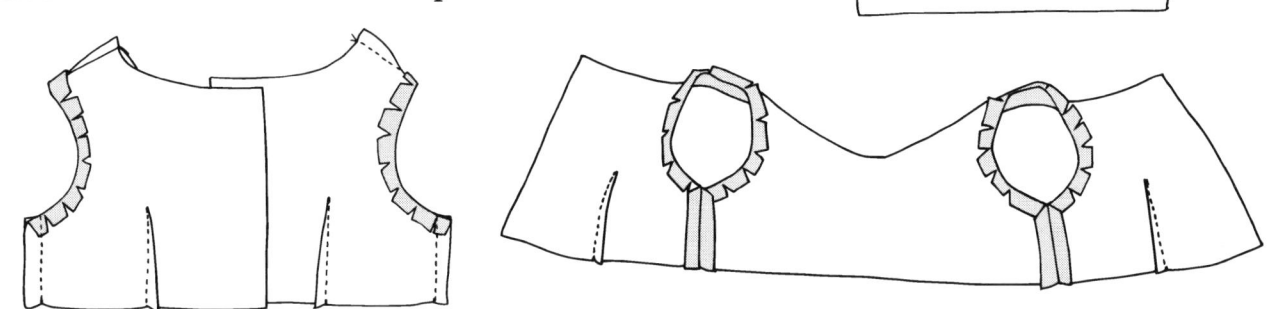

Step 11: With the right sides together, pin the bodice lining to the bodice along the back edges and neckline. Pull the sleeves of the bodice through the armscyes of the lining to help the bodice lay flat. Stitch. Clip the corners and curves. Turn the bodice right side out, squaring the corners with a blunt needle. Press, following the seamlines.

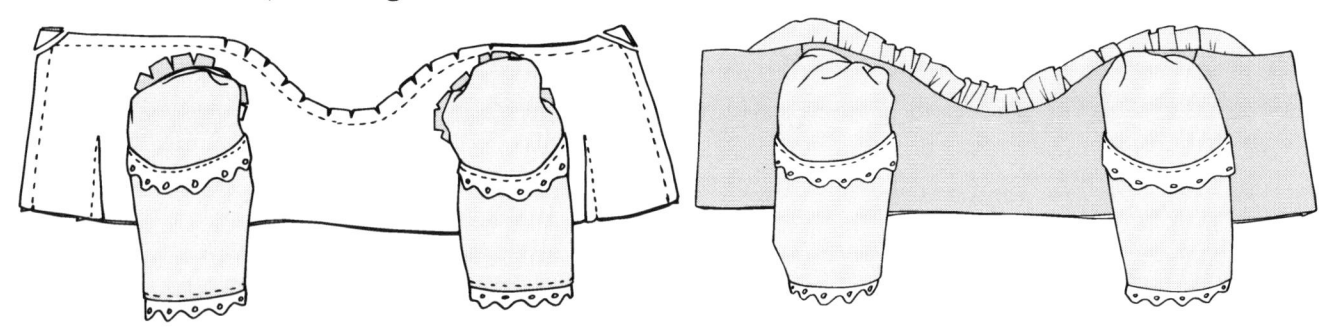

Regency Dress Skirting

Step 12: Finish the back and side seam allowances of the dress front and dress back skirting. Pin the skirting front and backs right sides together, matching the notches. Stitch. Press the seam allowances open.

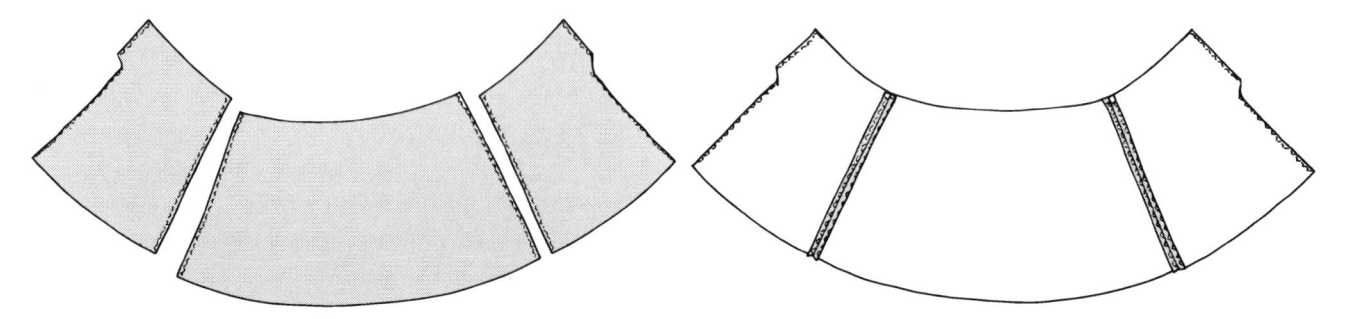

Step 13: Turn the skirt plackets under 1/4-inch (6 mm). Press. Topstitch 1/8-inch (3 mm) from the folded edge to secure. Sew two rows of gathering stitches along the top edge of the skirting where indicated on the pattern. Turn the plackets under 3/4-inch (9 mm), the fold line should line up with the back seamline. Pin to secure.

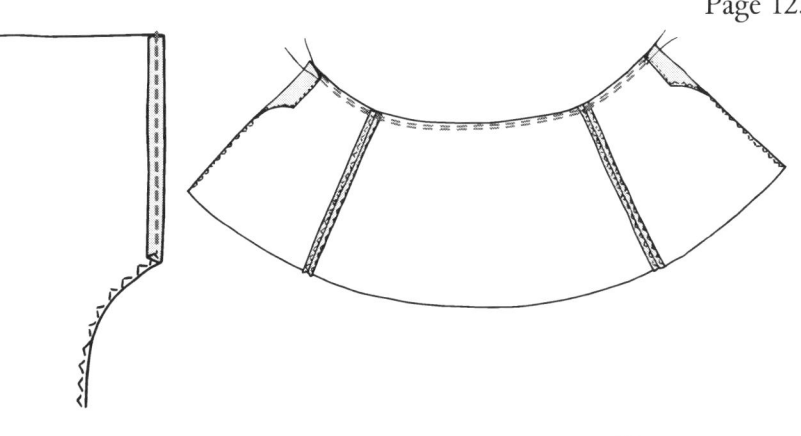

Step 14: With the right sides together, pin the dress skirting to the dress bodice between the back edges of the bodice, matching the center front notches. Do not pin the skirting to the lining. Draw up the gathering stitches and arrange the fullness evenly along the bodice. Stitch, being careful not to catch the lining in the seam. Press the seam allowance toward the bodice, being careful not to crush the gathers.

Step 15: Turn the bottom seam allowance of the bodice lining under and pin along the waistline seam. Hand stitch to secure. Turn the seam allowances of each bodice lining armscye under and pin along the seam lines of the bodice armscyes. Hand stitch to secure. Pin the back edges of the skirting right sides together. Stitch from the dot to the bottom edge. Press the seam allowance open.

Finishing the Dress

Step 16: Finish the bottom edge of the skirting. Turn under a 3/8-inch (9 mm) hem. Press and pin in place. Hand or machine stitch to secure. If preferred, finish the bottom edge of the skirt with a double-fold hem.

Step 17: Make buttonholes on the proper left side of the bodice and attach buttons on the proper right of the bodice where indicated on the pattern. Snaps or hook and loop tape can be used as closures if preferred.

Regency Pinafore

Step 18: Sew darts on the pinafore back where indicated on the pattern. Press the darts toward the center back. Repeat for the pinafore back lining, only press the darts in the opposite direction to reduce bulk.

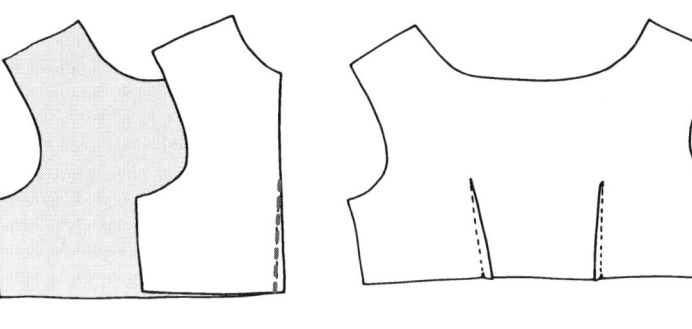

Step 19: With the right sides together, pin the pinafore front and back pieces along the shoulders. Stitch. Press the seam allowances open. Repeat for the pinafore lining.

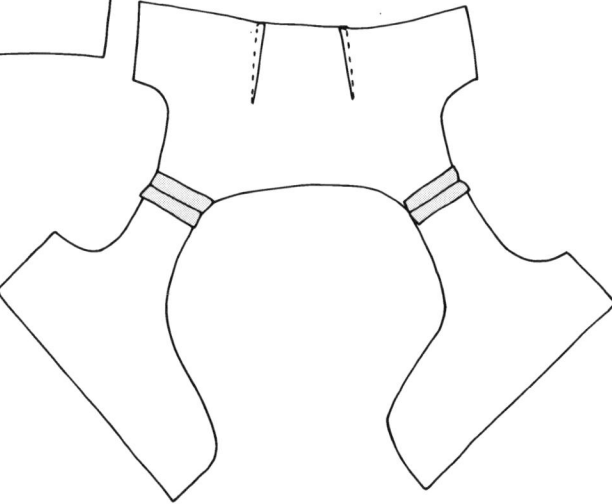

Step 20: With the decorative edge facing the bodice, pin lace to the neckline of the pinafore bodice. Pin the bodice lining over the bodice along the neckline and armscyes, right sides together. Stitch. Clip the curves and trim the seam allowances to 1/8-inch (3 mm). Turn right side out by pulling the bodice fronts through the shoulders. Press, following the seamlines.

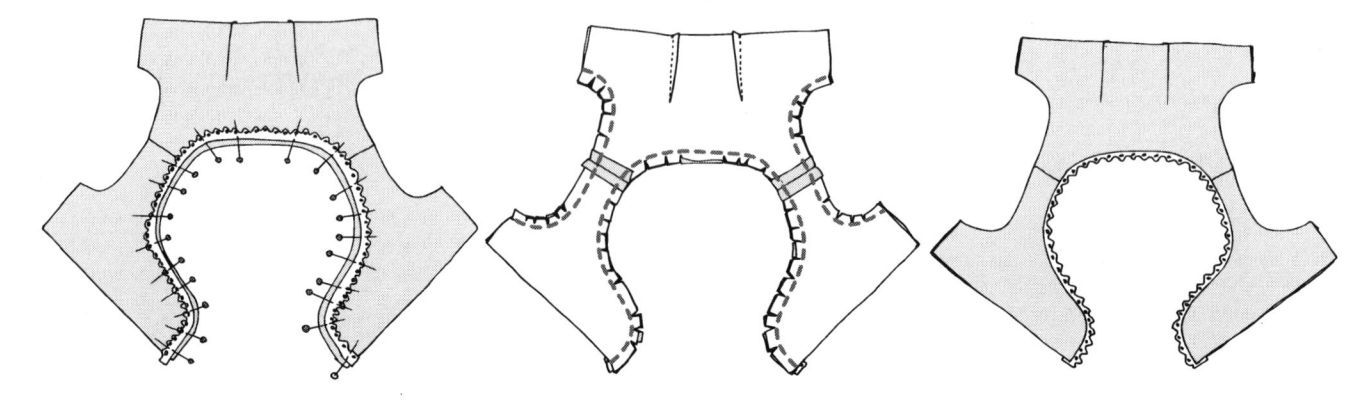

Page 124

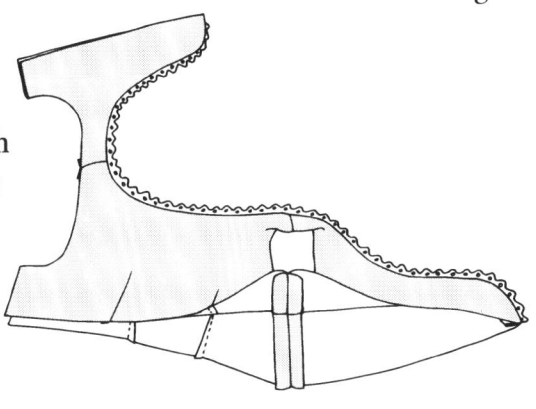

Step 21: With the right sides together, pin the sides of each bodice and bodice lining together as one seam. Stitch. Press the seam allowances open. Turn right side out and press.

Pinafore Skirting

Step 22: Finish the back and side seam allowances of the pinafore front and back skirting. Pin the pinafore skirt back and fronts right sides together, matching the notches. Stitch. Press the seam allowances open.

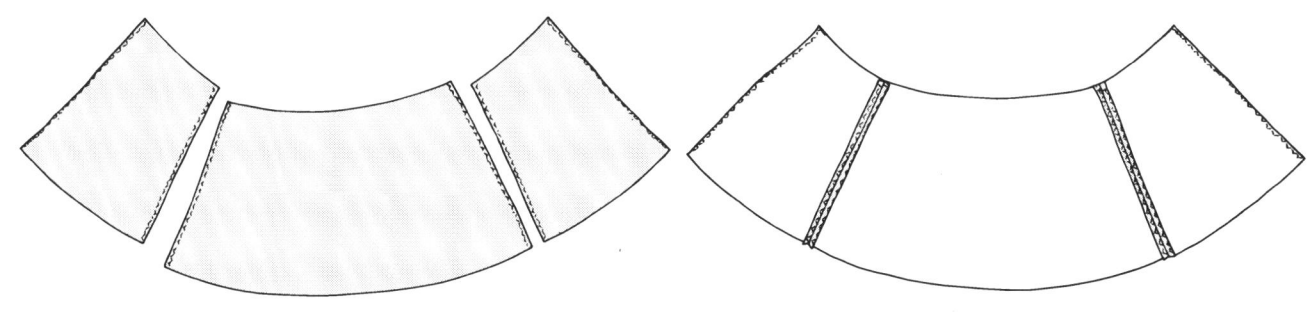

Step 23: With the right sides together, turn each back facing under at the bottom edge along the fold line. Pin in place. Stitch across the facing 1/2-inch (12 mm) from the bottom edge. Finish the bottom edge of the skirting. Turn the facing right side out, squaring the corners with a blunt needle. Press a 1/2- inch (12 mm) hem under along the bottom edge of the skirting and pin in place. Stitch the hem by machine or by hand.

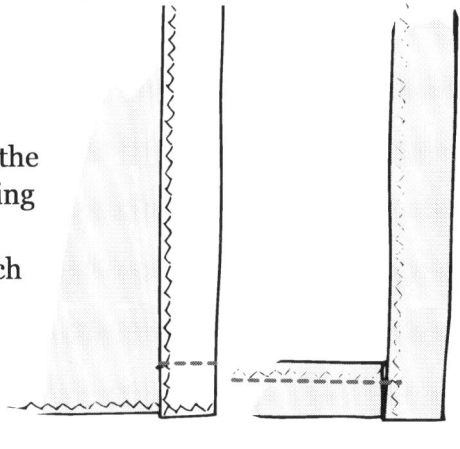

Step 24: Sew two rows of gathering stitches along the top edge of the skirting where indicated on the pattern.

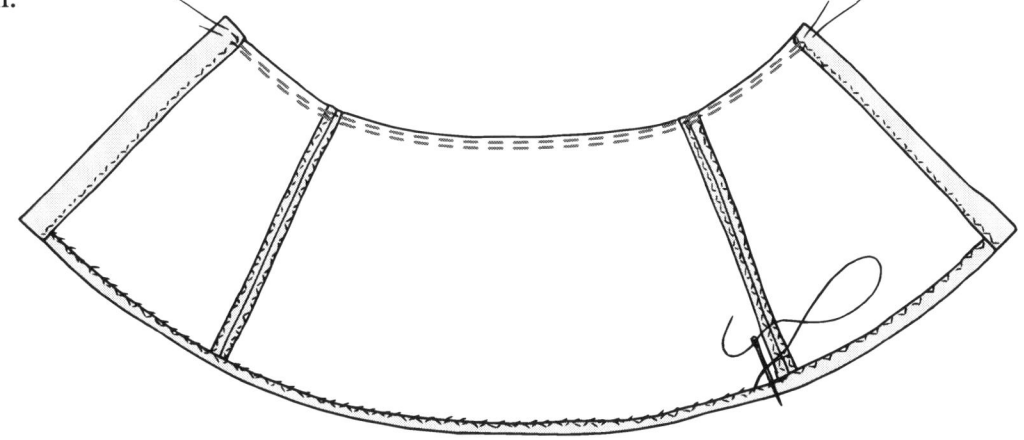

Step 25: With the right sides together, pin the pinafore skirting to the pinafore bodice between the front dots and matching the center back notches. Draw up the gathering stitches and arrange the gathers evenly along the bodice. Stitch, being careful not to catch the bodice lining in the seam. Press the seam allowance toward the bodice, being careful not to crush the gathers.

Step 26: Turn the bodice wrong side out along the front flaps. With the wrong sides together, pin the bodice lining to the bodice along the bottom edge of each front flap just past the front edges of the skirting. Stitch. Clip the corners and turn right side out, squaring the corners with a blunt needle. Press, following the seam lines. Turn the bottom edge of the lining under along the seam allowance and pin along the waistline seam. Hand stitch to secure.

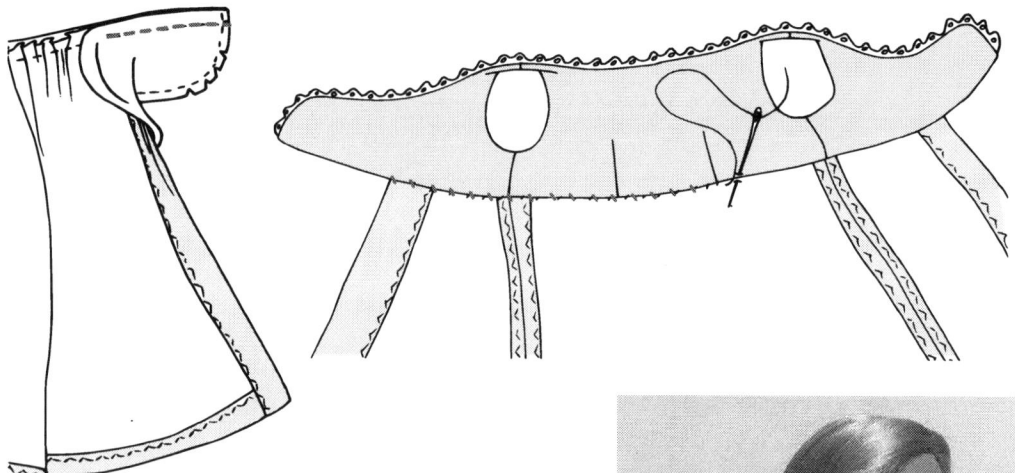

Finishing the Pinafore

Step 27: Attach decorative buttons where indicated on the pattern on the proper right flap. Attach snaps between the flaps directly under the buttons.

Fichu

Step 28: Pin the fichu pieces right sides together. Stitch, leaving the space between the dots on the inside curve open. Clip the corners and curves. Trim the seam allowance to 1/8-inch (3 mm).

Step 29: Turn the fichu right side out, squaring the corners and rounding the curves with a blunt needle. Press, following the seamlines. Turn the seam allowances of the opening inside and whipstitch it closed.

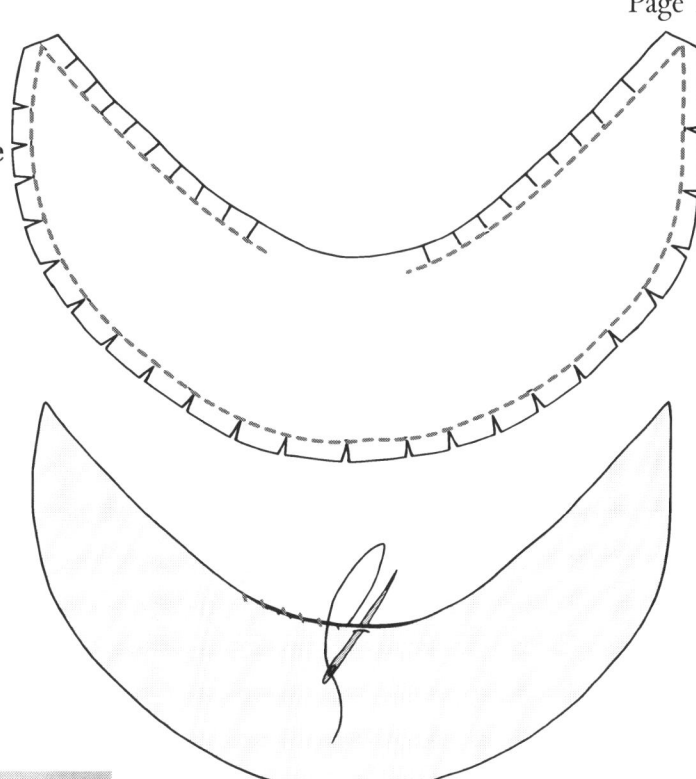

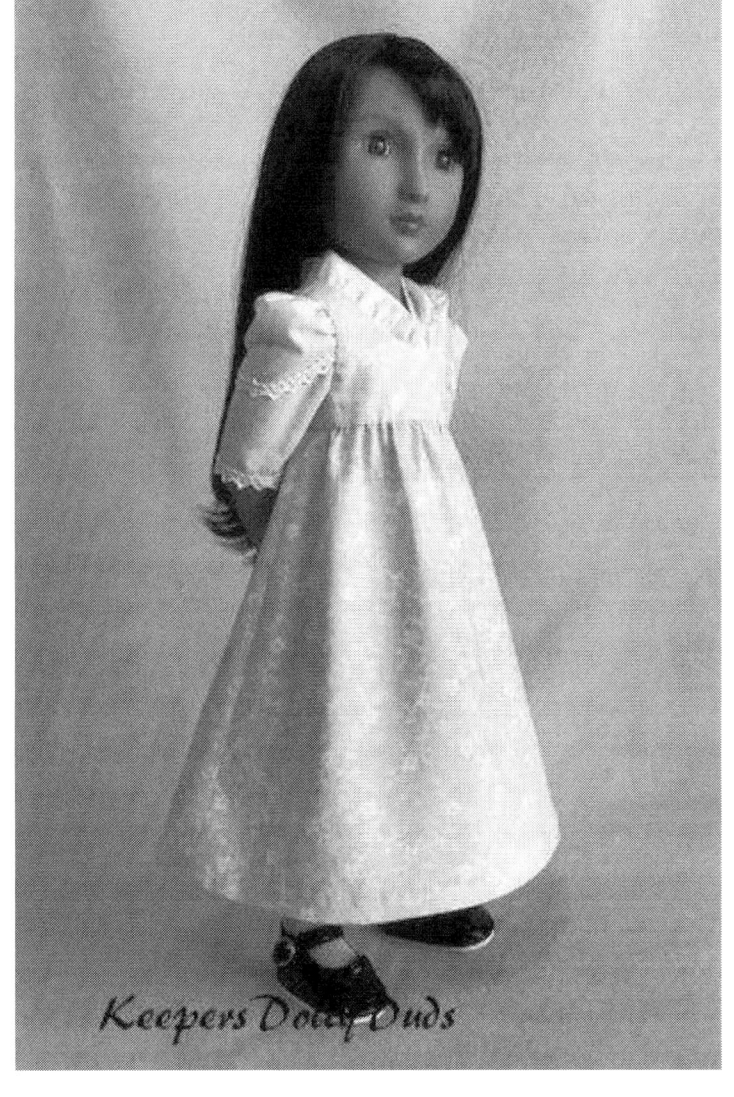

Regency Pinafore Dress and Fichu
Pattern Pieces

Cutting Layout for 45-inch (1.14 m) wide Fabric
11 Pieces

- 79 ~ Regency Dress Bodice Front
- 80 ~ Regency Dress Bodice Back
- 81 ~ Regency Neck Ruffle
- 82 ~ Regency Dress Sleeve
- 83 ~ Regency Dress Front Skirting
- 84 ~ Regency Dress Back Skirting
- 85 ~ Regency Pinafore Bodice Front
- 86 ~ Regency Pinafore Bodice Back
- 87 ~ Regency Pinafore Front Skirting
- 88 ~ Regency Pinafore Back Skirting
- 89 ~ Regency Fichu

Regency Dress
Use pieces: 79, 80, 83, and 84

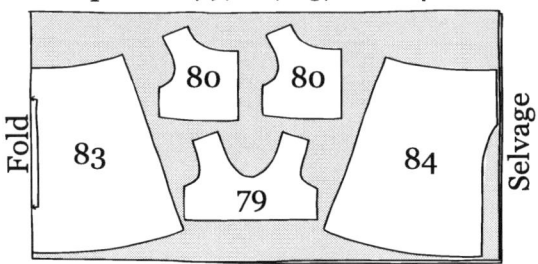

Regency Fichu
Use piece: 89

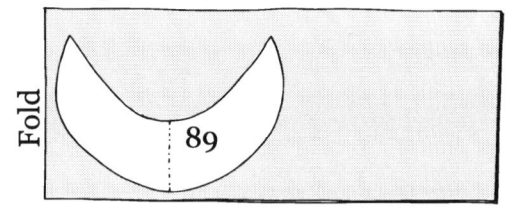

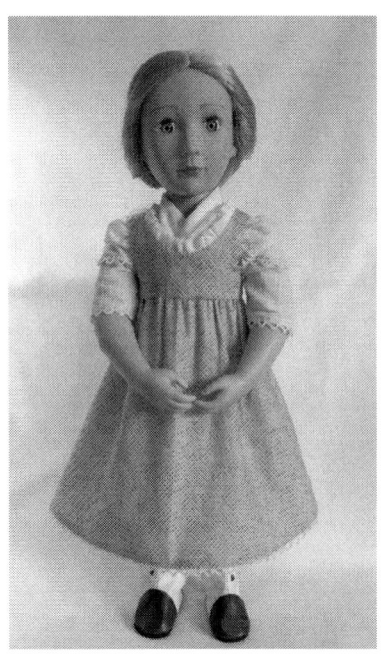

Regency Dress Contrast
Use pieces: 81 and 82

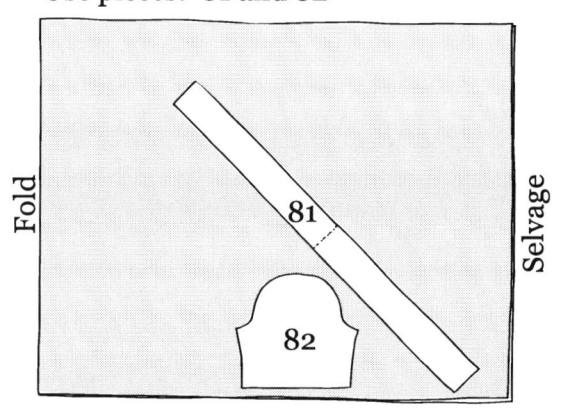

Regency Pinafore
Use pieces: 85, 86, 87, and 88

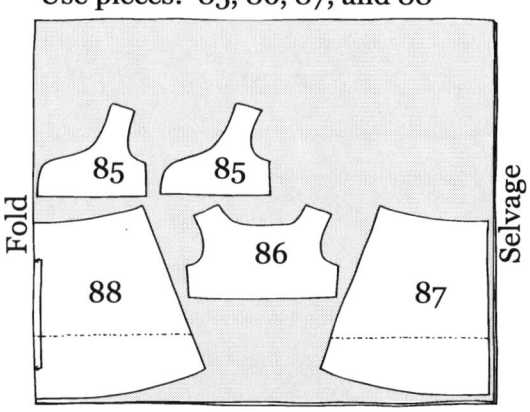

Regency Dress and Fichu

Page 129

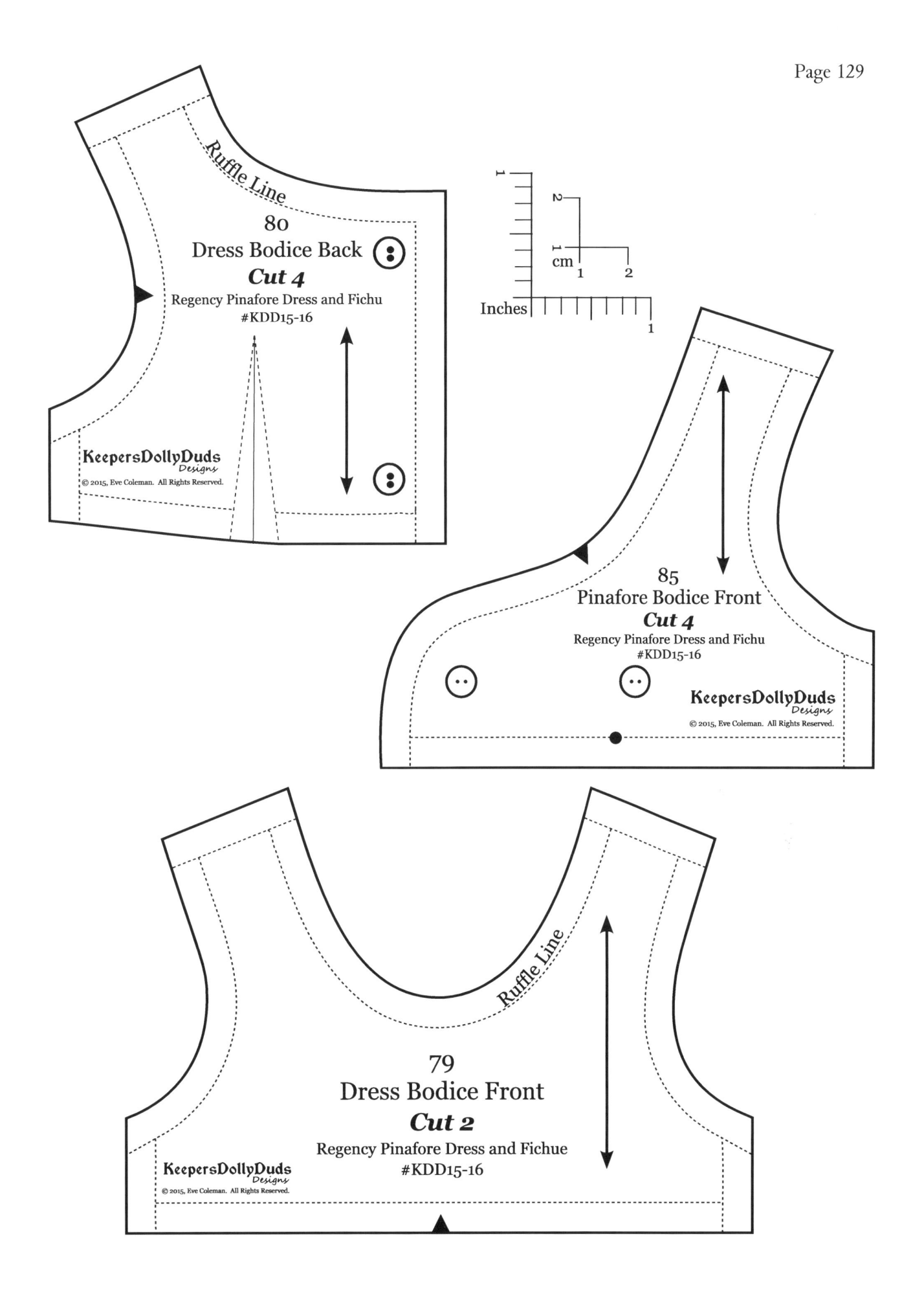

80
Dress Bodice Back
Cut 4
Regency Pinafore Dress and Fichu
#KDD15-16

Ruffle Line

85
Pinafore Bodice Front
Cut 4
Regency Pinafore Dress and Fichu
#KDD15-16

79
Dress Bodice Front
Cut 2
Regency Pinafore Dress and Fichue
#KDD15-16

Ruffle Line

KeepersDollyDuds Designs
© 2015, Eve Coleman. All Rights Reserved.

Page 131

Gather

Fold Line

84
Dress Back Skirting
Cut 2
Regency Pinafore Dress and Fichu
#KDD15-16

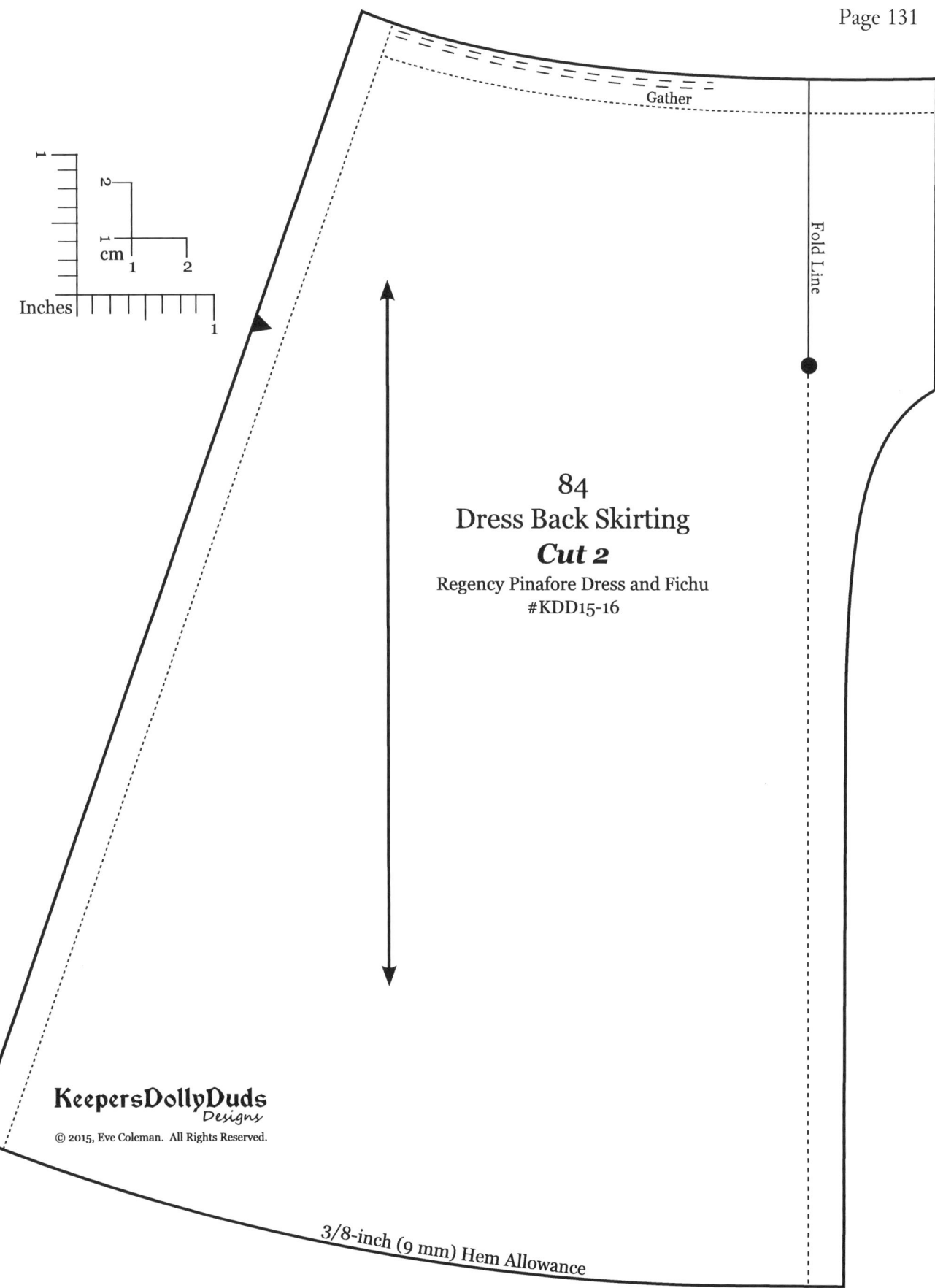

KeepersDollyDuds Designs
© 2015, Eve Coleman. All Rights Reserved.

3/8-inch (9 mm) Hem Allowance

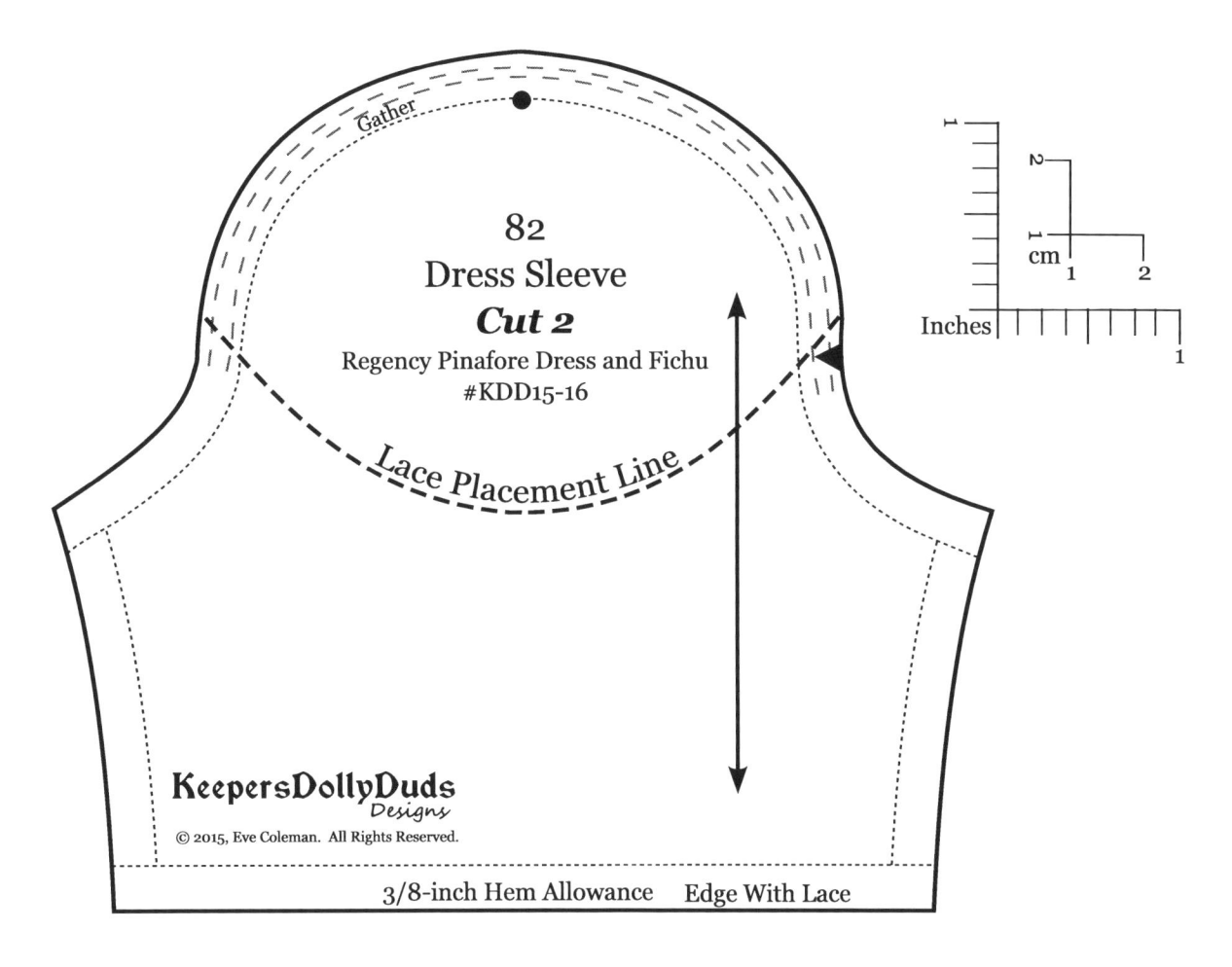

Page 133

**82
Dress Sleeve
Cut 2
Regency Pinafore Dress and Fichu
#KDD15-16**

Gather

Lace Placement Line

3/8-inch Hem Allowance   Edge With Lace

KeepersDollyDuds Designs
© 2015, Eve Coleman. All Rights Reserved.

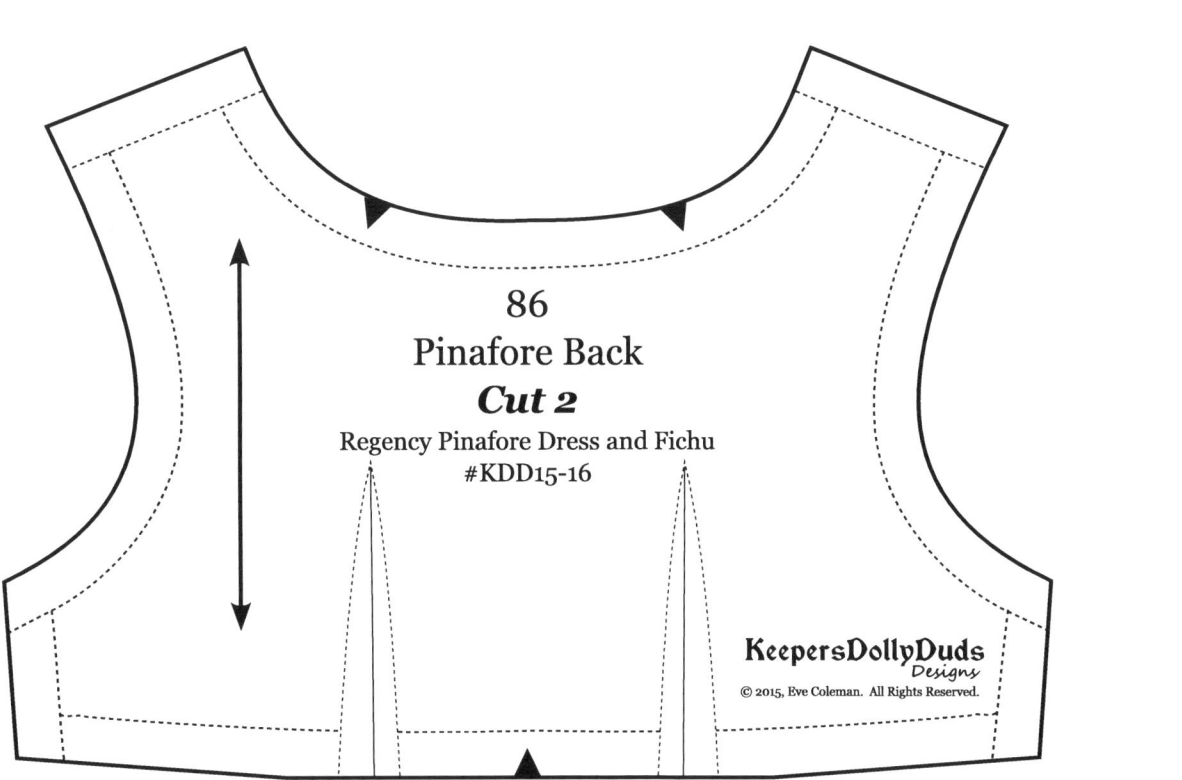

**86
Pinafore Back
Cut 2
Regency Pinafore Dress and Fichu
#KDD15-16**

KeepersDollyDuds Designs
© 2015, Eve Coleman. All Rights Reserved.

Page 135

Center Front — Gather

83
Dress Front Skirting
Cut 1 on Fold
Regency Pinafore Dress and Fichu
#KDD15-16

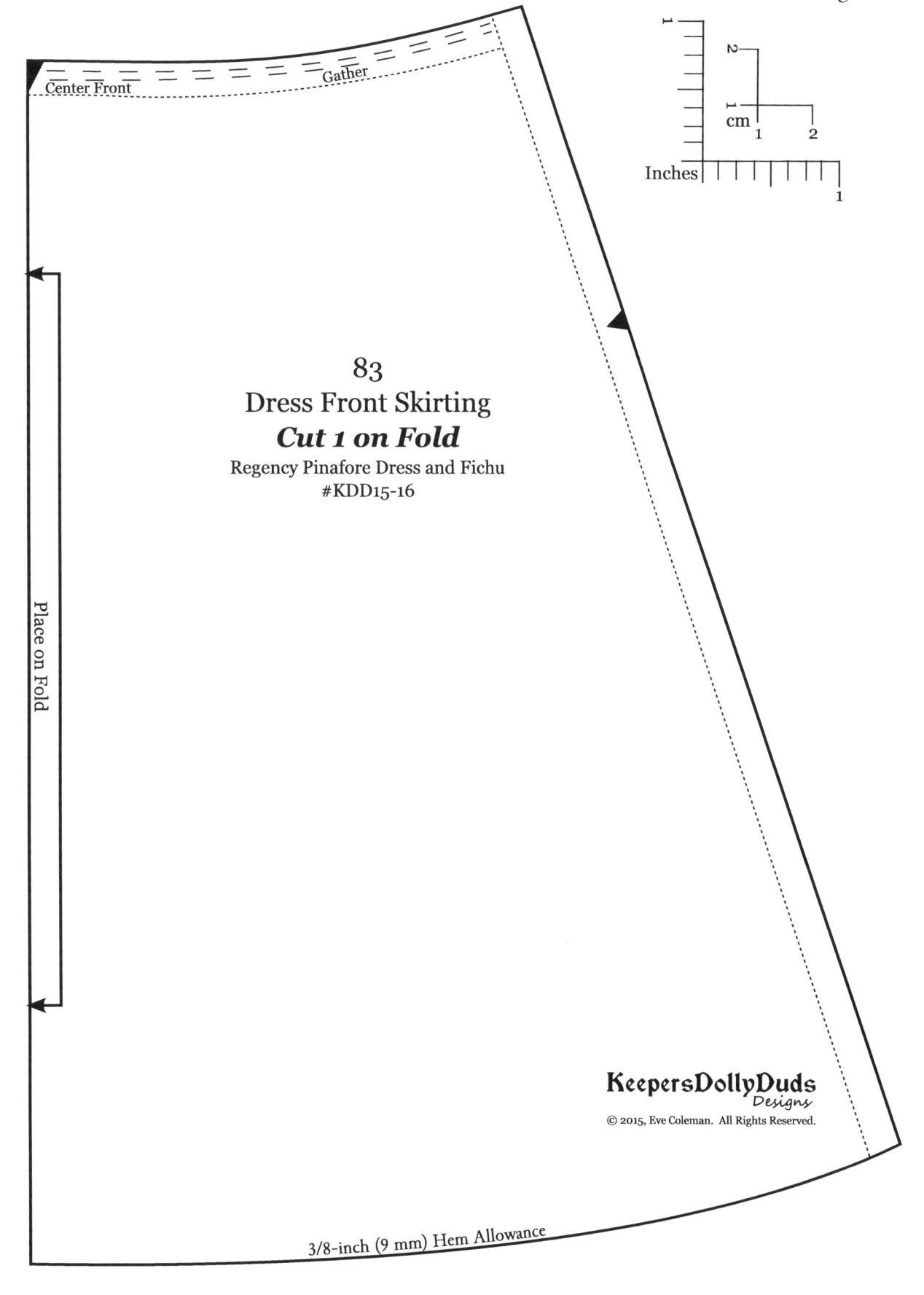

Place on Fold

KeepersDollyDuds Designs
© 2015, Eve Coleman. All Rights Reserved.

3/8-inch (9 mm) Hem Allowance

81 **Dress Neck Ruffle** (Section 1 of 2) *Cut 1* Regency Pinafore Dress and Fichu #KDD15-16

Fold Line

KeepersDollyDuds *Designs*
© 2015, Eve Coleman. All Rights Reserved.

Attach Section 2 Here

Attach Section 1 Here

81 **Dress Neck Ruffle** (Section 2 of 2) Regency Pinafore Dress and Fichu #KDD15-16

Fold Line

For Rotary Cutters
Total length = 16-1/2 in.
Width = 1-3/8 in.

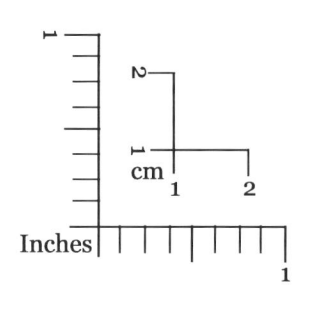

Page 137

87
Pinafore Front Skirting
Cut 2
Regency Pinafore Dress and Fichu
#KDD15-16

Fold Line

Facing

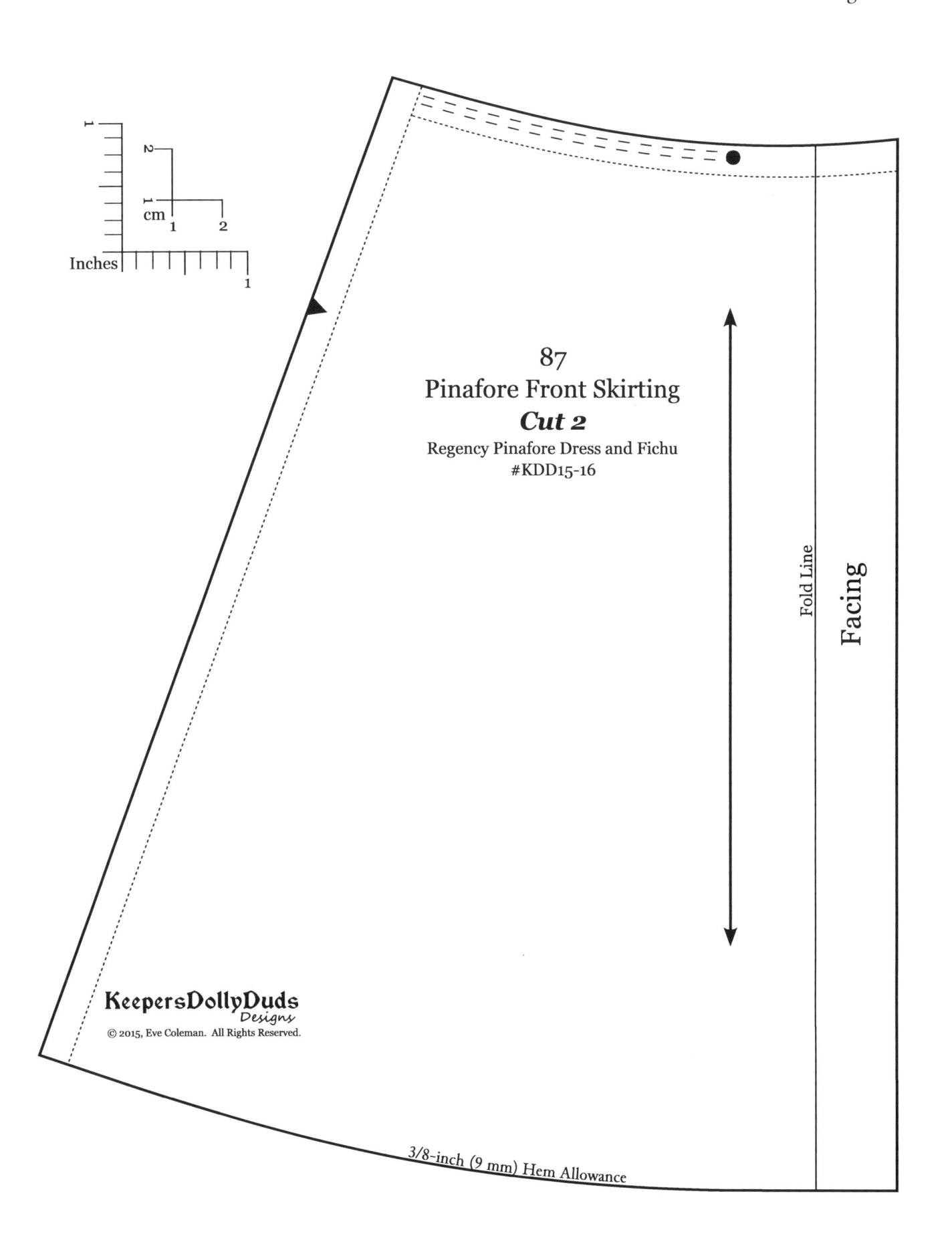

KeepersDollyDuds Designs
© 2015, Eve Coleman. All Rights Reserved.

3/8-inch (9 mm) Hem Allowance

Page 141

Center Back

Gather

88
Pinafore Back Skirting
Cut 1 on Fold
Regency Pinafore Dress and Fichu
#KDD15-16

Place on Fold

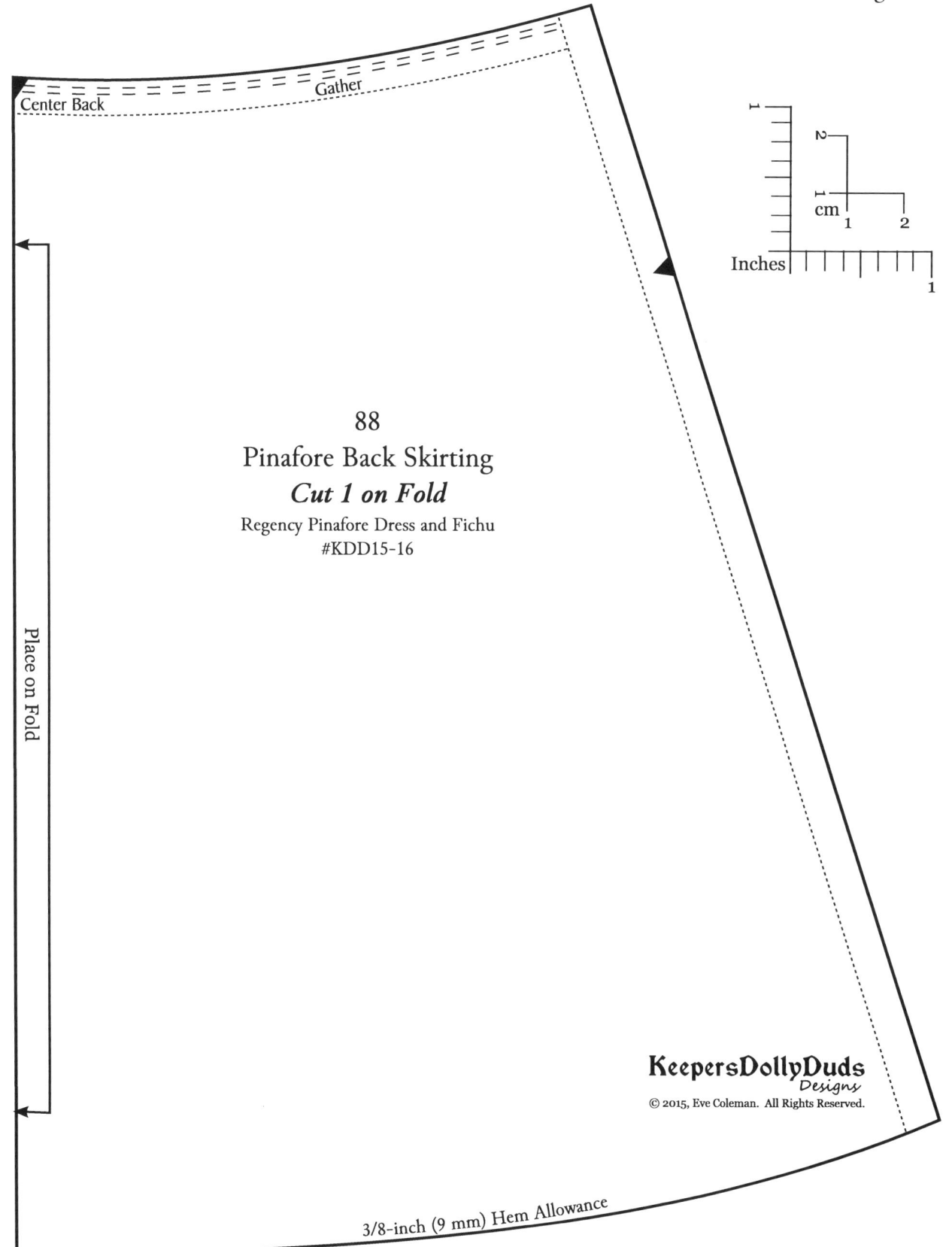

KeepersDollyDuds
Designs
© 2015, Eve Coleman. All Rights Reserved.

3/8-inch (9 mm) Hem Allowance

Page 143

KeepersDollyDuds
Designs
© 2015, Eve Coleman. All Rights Reserved.

89
Fichu
Cut 2
Regency Pinafore Dress and Fichu
#KDD15-16

Leave Open to Turn

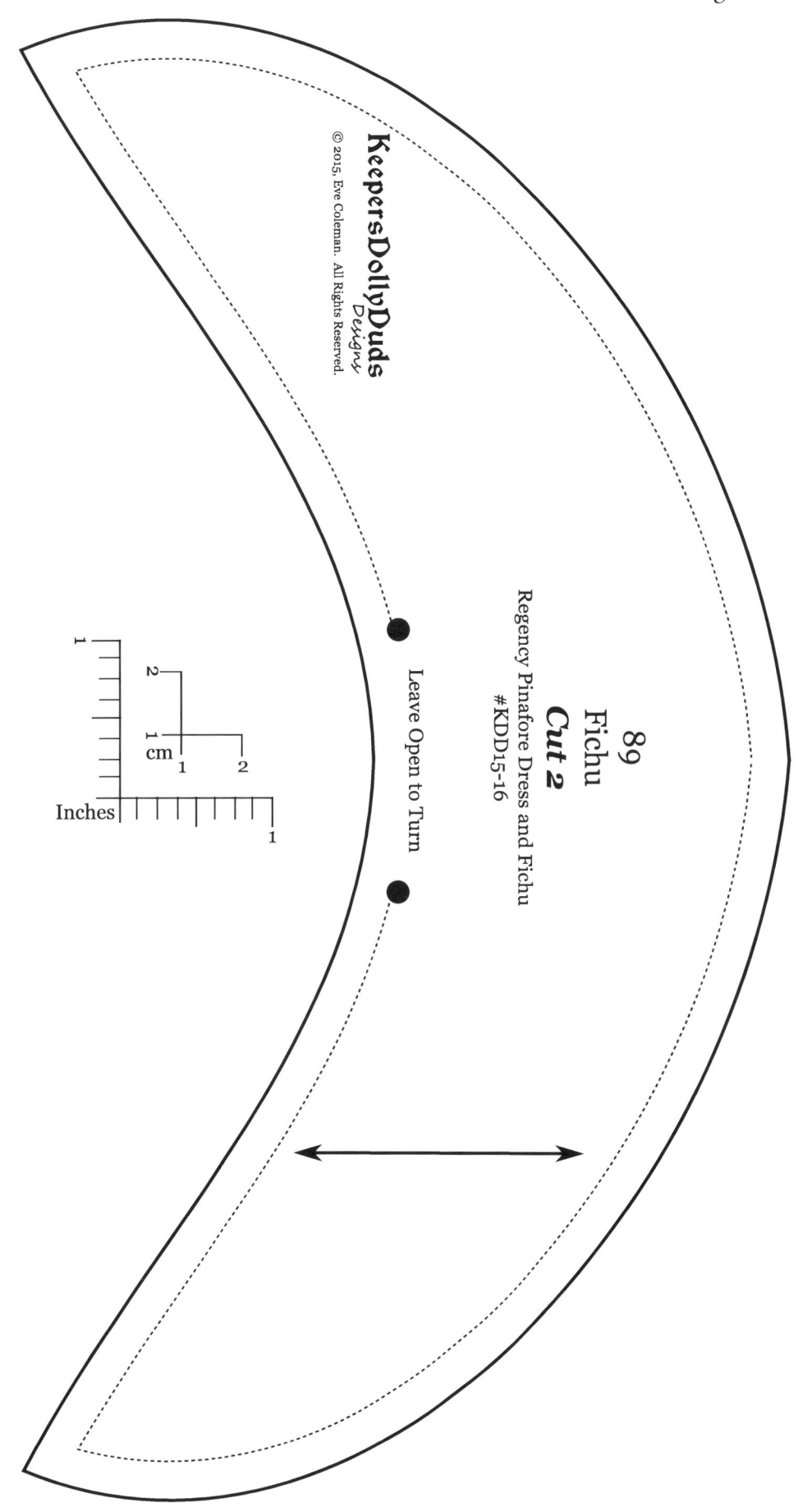

Page 145

Double Cape and Bonnet

Materials List
#KDD-17-16

Suggested Fabrics: **Cape and Bonnet** in wool, wool blend, linen, velvet, velveteen, or any medium weight woven fabric. Not Suitable for knits. **Lining** in polyester, satin, cotton, or homespun lining fabrics.

Fabric Yardage:
Cape and Bonnet ~ 1 yard (1 m) of fabric
Cape, Collar, and Overcape ~ 3/4 yard (0.75 m) of lining
Bonnet Lining, Ties, and Bias Trim ~ 1/2 yard (0.5 m) of contrasting fabric
Interfacing ~ 1/4 yard (0.25 m)

Notions:
___thread
___one hook and eye
___three 3/8-inch (9 mm) buttons

Page 146

Cape

Step 1: With the right sides together, pin the shoulder darts on the cape and cape lining. Stitch. Press the seam allowances open

Step 2: Stay-stitch around the neckline just insided the seam allowance. Finish the bottom edge of the cape and cape lining. Turn under a 3/8-inch (9 mm) hem on the ***lining only.*** Press flat and pin in place. Stitch by hand or machine.

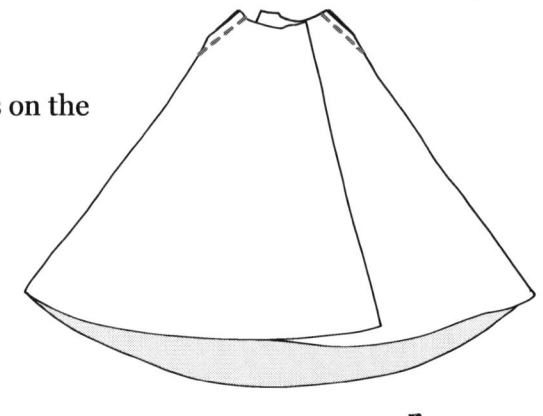

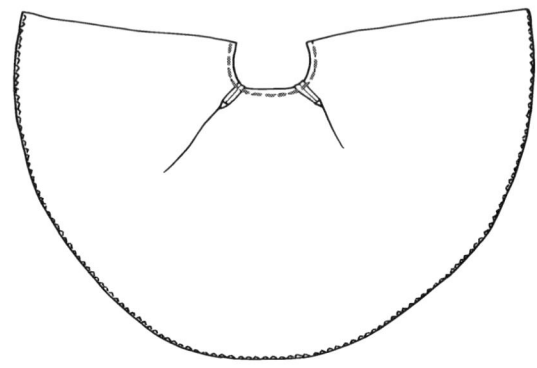

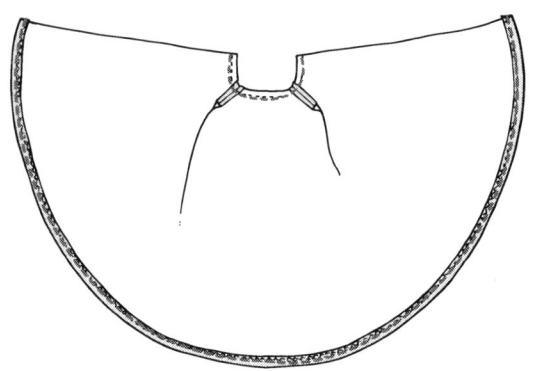

Finish the bottom edge of the lining ONLY at this time.

Collar

Step 3: With the wrong sides together, fold bias strips in half lengthwise. Press flat. Pin the raw edge of a 19-inch (48 cm) length of bias strip along the outside edge on the right side of one of the collar pieces. Baste in place to secure. Lace can be used instead of bias strips.

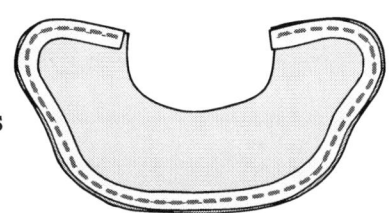

Step 4: With the right sides together, pin the two collar pieces along the outside edges. Stitch. Notch the curves and turn right side out. Press, following the seamline.

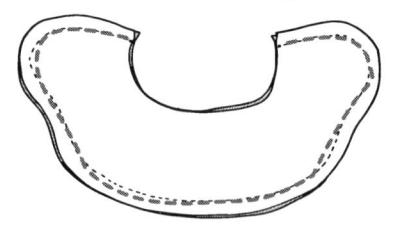

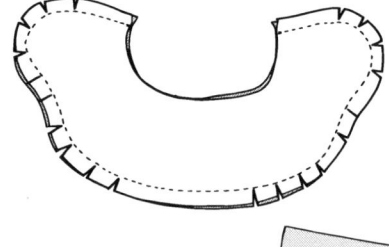

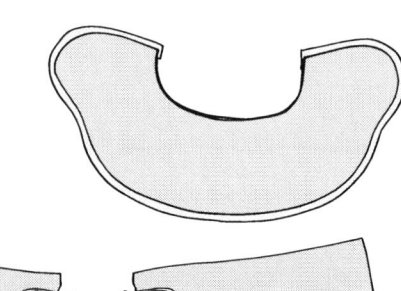

Step 5: Pin the collar to the neckline of the cape matching the dots in the front and the notches in the back.

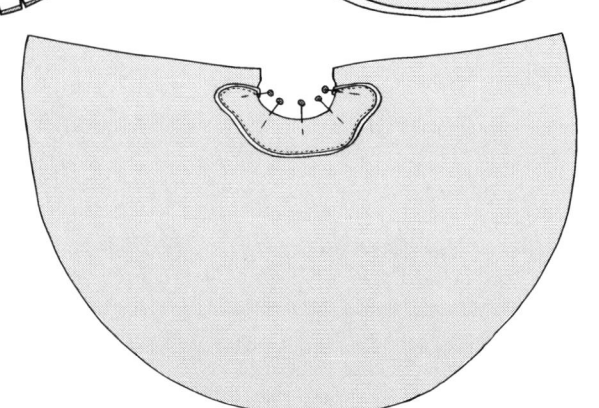

Cape Lining

Step 6: With the right sides together, pin the cape and lining together along the front edges. Stitch. Finish the seam allowances and press toward the lining.

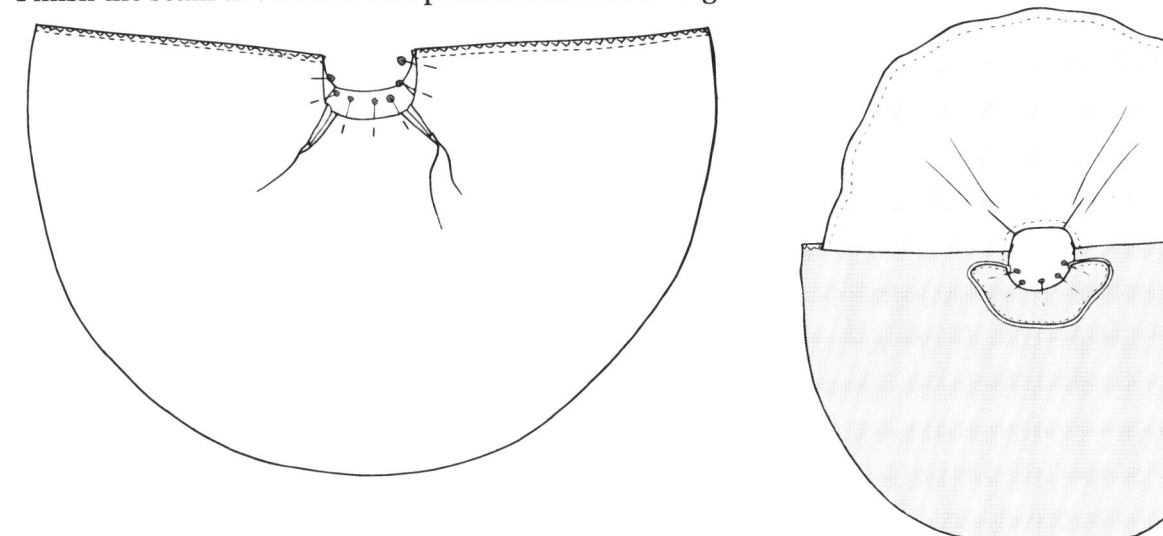

Step 7: Fold the front edges of the cape along the fold lines to create a facing. Matching the shoulder seams, pin the lining in place over the collar. Stitch and clip the inside curve of the collar. Stitch the facing down 3/8-inch (1/2 cm) from the bottom edge.

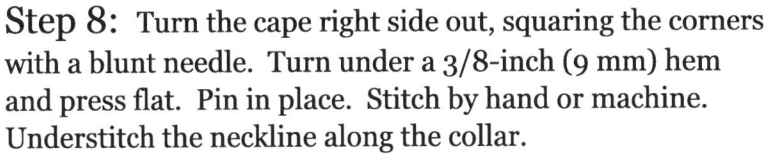

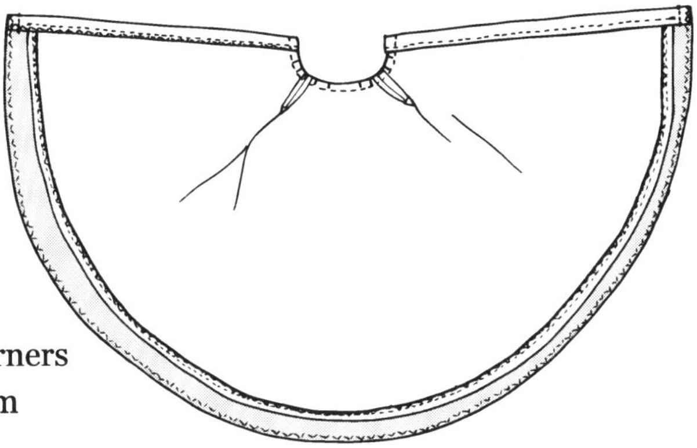

Step 8: Turn the cape right side out, squaring the corners with a blunt needle. Turn under a 3/8-inch (9 mm) hem and press flat. Pin in place. Stitch by hand or machine. Understitch the neckline along the collar.

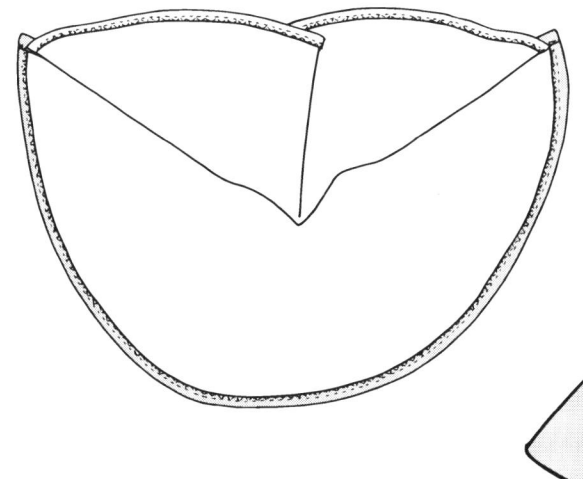

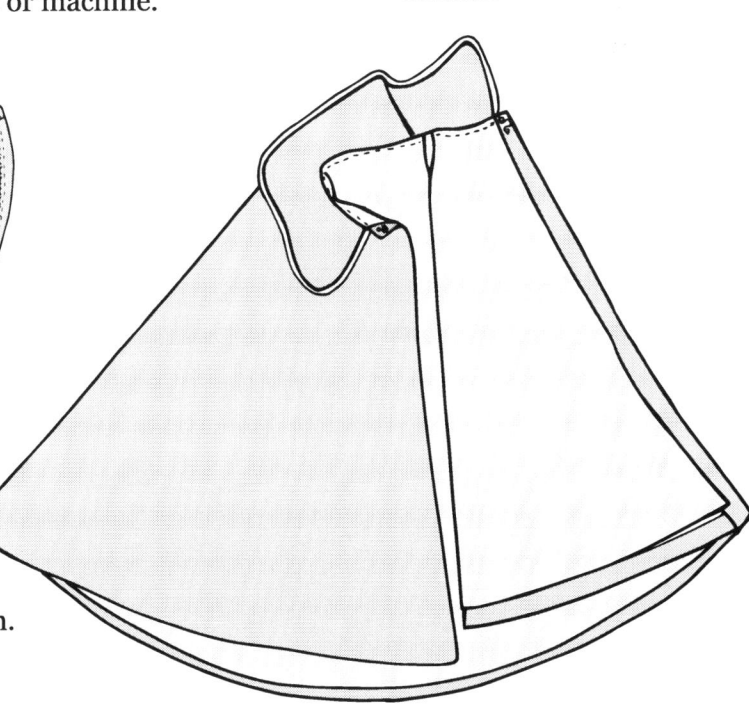

Step 9: Apply a hook and eye closure at the neckline where indicated on the pattern.

Page 148

Overcape

Step 10: Use a 29-inch (74 cm) long bias strip, joining two shorter pieces if necessary. Pin the raw edges of the bias strip along the outside edge on the right side of the overcape piece. Baste in place to secure. Lace can be used instead of bias strips.

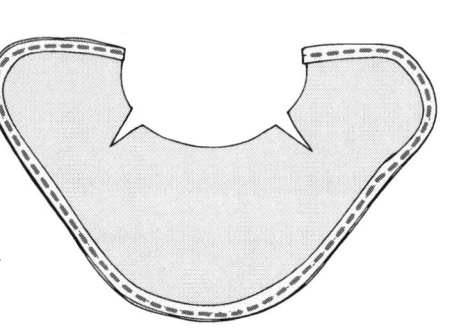

Step 11: With the right sides together, pin the shoulder darts on the overcape and overcape lining. Stitch. With the right sides together, pin the overcape and overcape lining pieces along the outside and neckline edges. Stitch, leaving the space between the dots at the neckline open for turning. Grade the seam allowances, notch the curves, clip the inside curves, and turn right side out. Press along the seamline. Whipstitch the neckline opening closed.

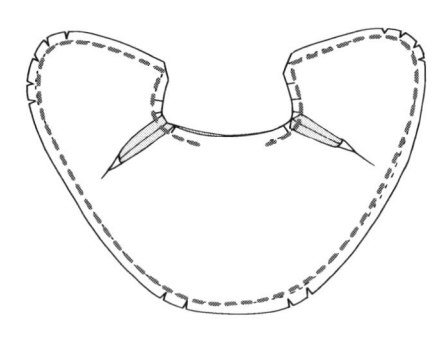

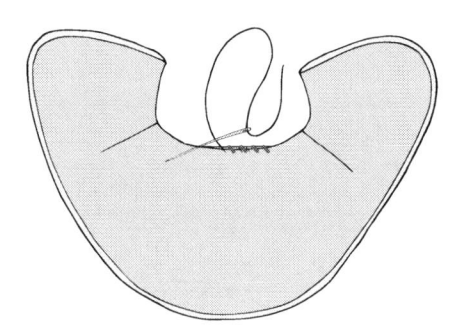

Step 12: Sew a button to the outside neckline on the proper left side where indicated on the pattern. Make a button loop on the inside of the neckline on the proper right side where indicated on the pattern, following the instructions below.

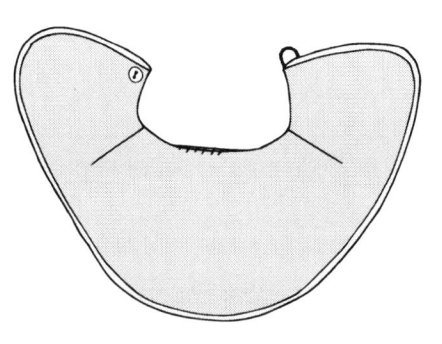

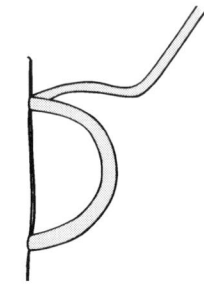

To make the button loop, use a single strand of button thread to make a loop that loosely fits the diameter of the button. Tack the loop in place at each end to secure. Do not cut the thread.

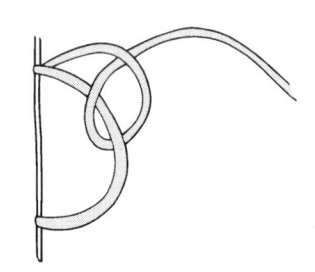

Starting at the end that the thread is attached, make a blanket stitch on the thread loop. Tighten the stitch snugly around the loop.

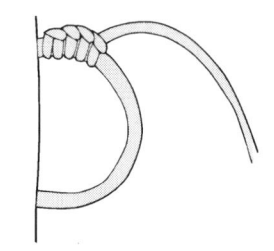

Continue adding stitches until the loop is completely covered.

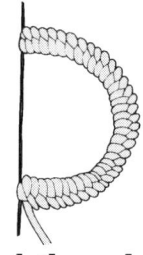

Tack the end of the thread at the end of the loop and draw it through the fabric to hide. Trim off the extra thread.

Bonnet

Step 13: Apply fusible interfacing to the wrong side of the bonnet brim, bonnet, and bonnet crown, following the manufacturer's instructions.

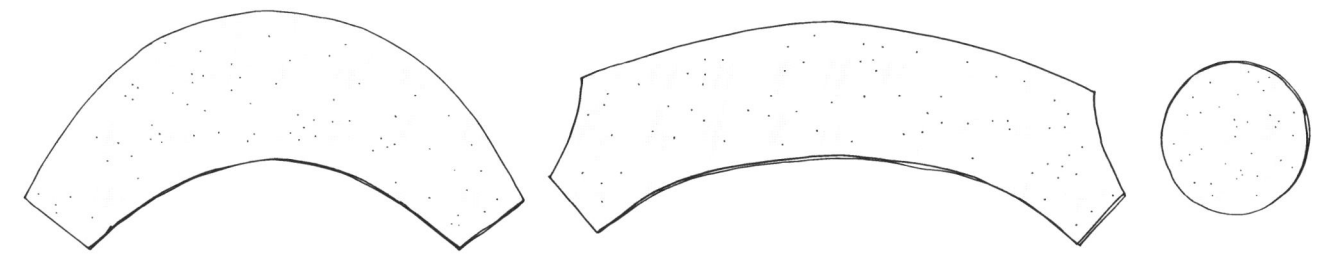

Step 14: With the right sides together and matching the notches, pin the back sides of the bonnet. Stitch. Press the seam allowances open. Stay-stitch the back edge of the bonnet and clip the the seam allowance up to the stay-stitching. Repeat with the lining.

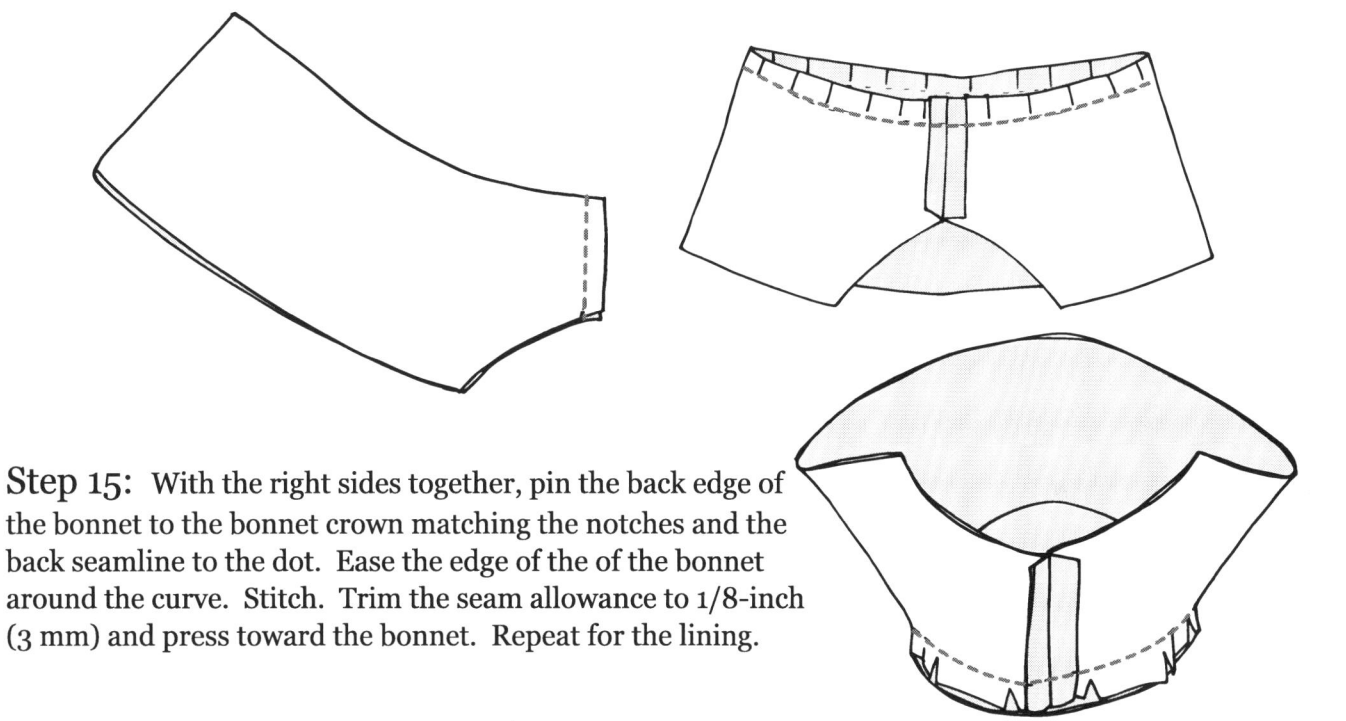

Step 15: With the right sides together, pin the back edge of the bonnet to the bonnet crown matching the notches and the back seamline to the dot. Ease the edge of the of the bonnet around the curve. Stitch. Trim the seam allowance to 1/8-inch (3 mm) and press toward the bonnet. Repeat for the lining.

Step 16: Pin the lower back edges of the bonnet and bonnet lining right sides together. Stitch. Clip curve and turn right side out. Pin the front edges of the bonnet together to secure. Topstitch the lower back edge.

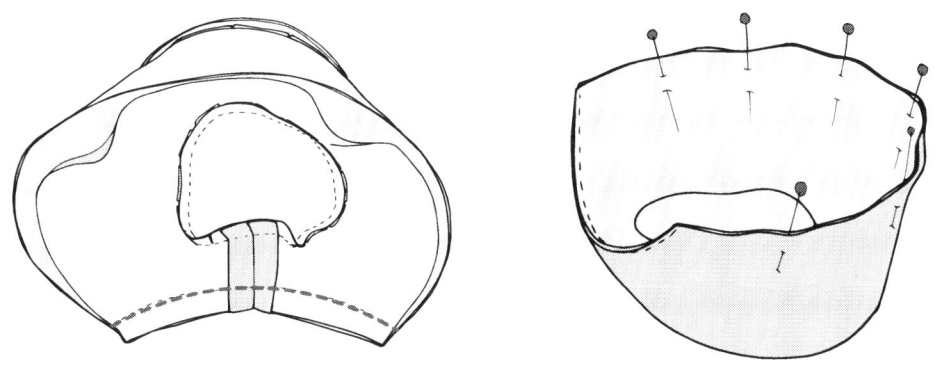

Step 17: Fold each bonnet tie right sides together along the fold line and pin along the length of the tie, leaving the flat end open. Stitch. Notch the corners and clip the curves. Trim the seam allowances to 1/8-inch (3 mm) and turn right side out. Square the corners with a blunt needle. Press following the seamlines.

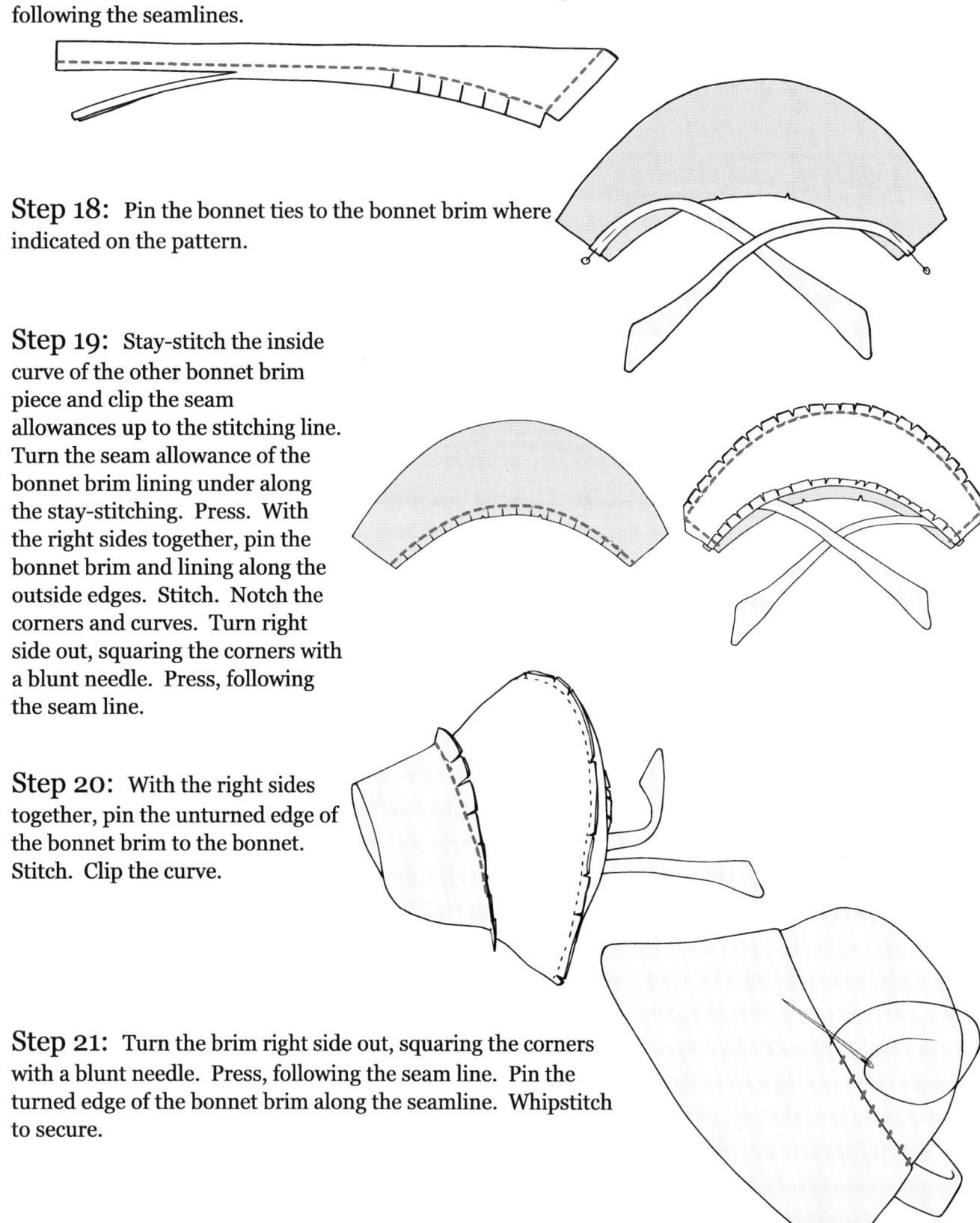

Step 18: Pin the bonnet ties to the bonnet brim where indicated on the pattern.

Step 19: Stay-stitch the inside curve of the other bonnet brim piece and clip the seam allowances up to the stitching line. Turn the seam allowance of the bonnet brim lining under along the stay-stitching. Press. With the right sides together, pin the bonnet brim and lining along the outside edges. Stitch. Notch the corners and curves. Turn right side out, squaring the corners with a blunt needle. Press, following the seam line.

Step 20: With the right sides together, pin the unturned edge of the bonnet brim to the bonnet. Stitch. Clip the curve.

Step 21: Turn the brim right side out, squaring the corners with a blunt needle. Press, following the seam line. Pin the turned edge of the bonnet brim along the seamline. Whipstitch to secure.

Page 151

Step 22: Pin the two bonnet band pieces right sides together. Stitch, leaving the space between the dots open for turning. Grade the seam allowances, notch the corners, and turn right side out. Press along the seamline. Whipstitch the opening closed.

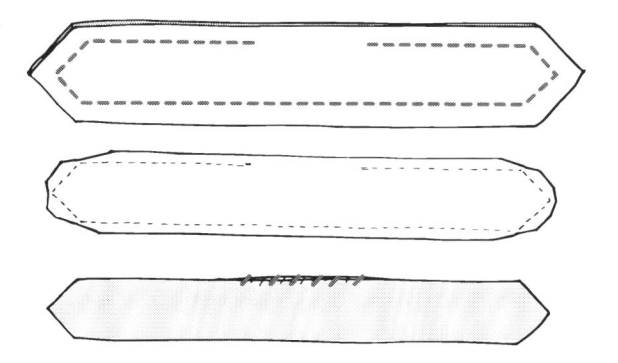

Step 18: Pin the bonnet band to the bonnet where indicated on the pattern. Secure at each end with a decorative button.

Page 152

Double Cape & Bonnet
Pattern Pieces

Cutting Layout for 45-inch (1.14 m) wide Fabric
8 Pieces

90 ~ Cape
91 ~ Collar
92 ~ Overcape
93 ~ Bonnet
94 ~ Bonnet Crown
95 ~ Bonnet Brim
96 ~ Bonnet Tie
97 ~ Bonnet Band

Cape and Bonnet
Use pieces: 90, 91, 92, 93, 94, and 95

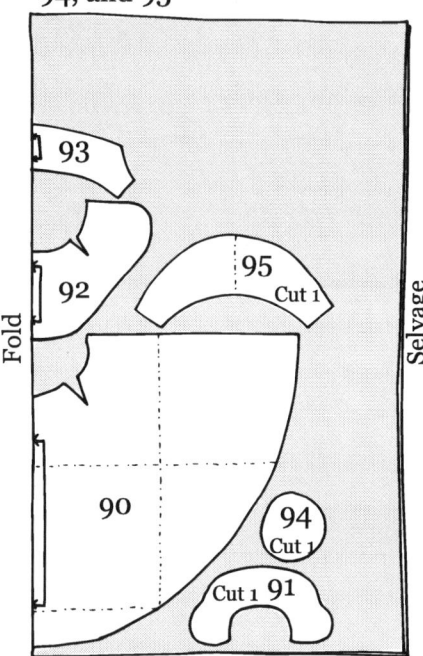

Cape Lining
Use pieces: 90, 91, and 92

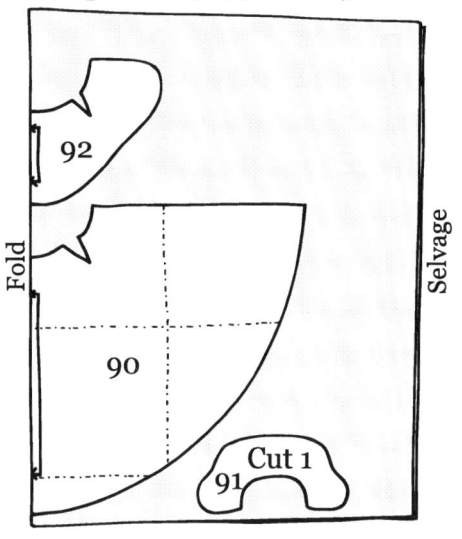

Cape & Bonnet Contrast Fabric
Use pieces: 93, 94, 95, 96, and 97

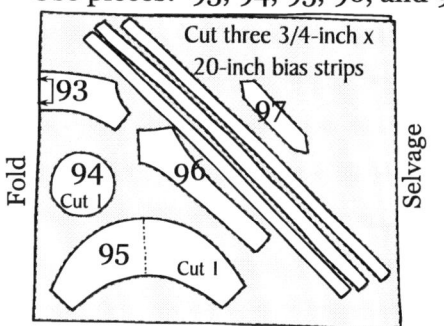

Cut three 3/4-inch x 20-inch bias strips

Interfacing
Use pieces: 93, 94, and 95

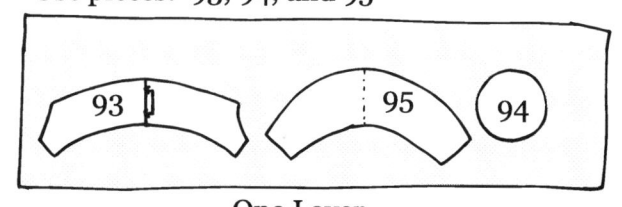

One Layer

Page 153

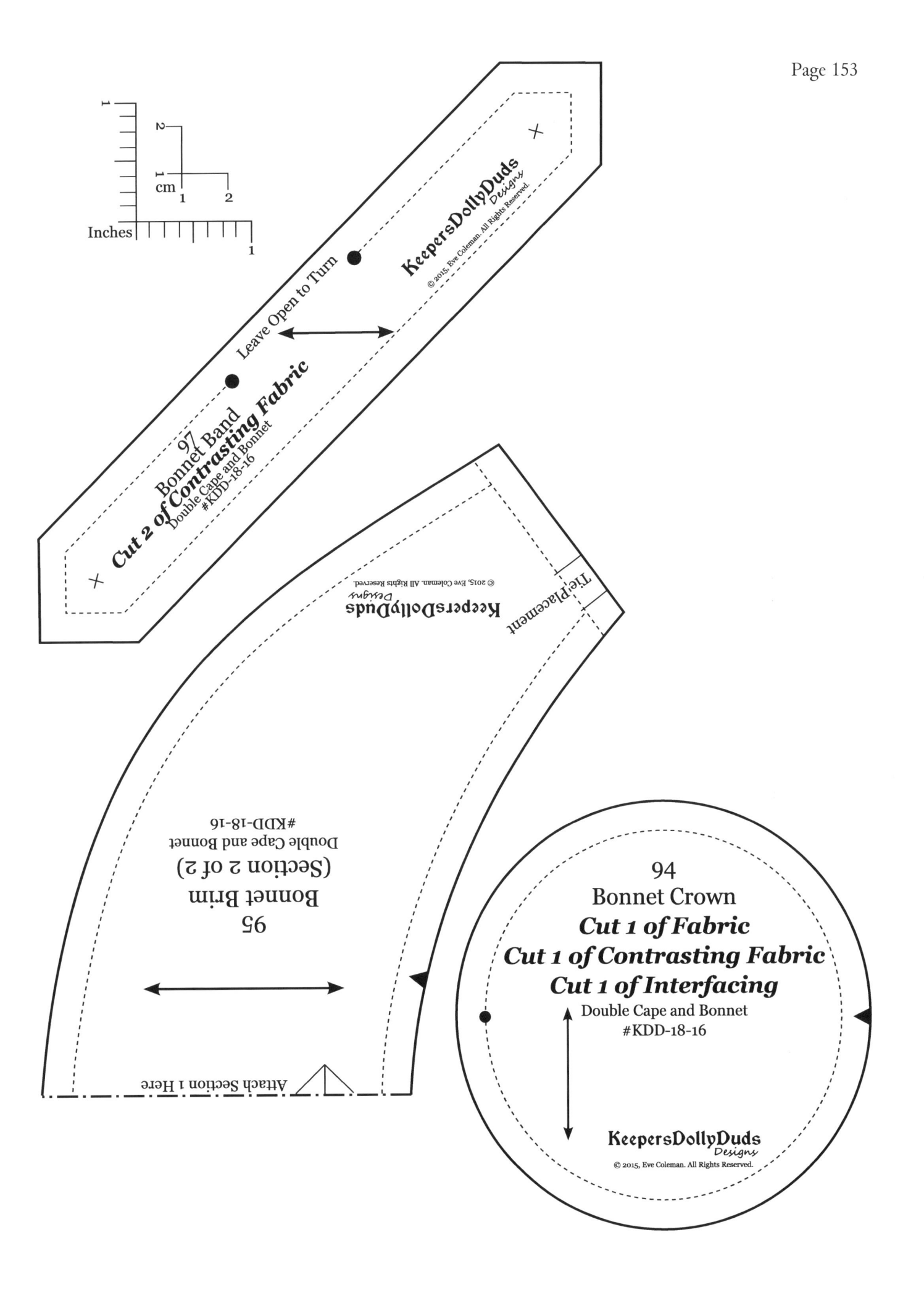

97
Bonnet Band
Cut 2 of Contrasting Fabric
Double Cape and Bonnet
#KDD-18-16

Leave Open to Turn

95
Bonnet Brim
(Section 2 of 2)
Double Cape and Bonnet
#KDD-18-16

Attach Section 1 Here

94
Bonnet Crown
Cut 1 of Fabric
Cut 1 of Contrasting Fabric
Cut 1 of Interfacing
Double Cape and Bonnet
#KDD-18-16

Tie Placement

KeepersDollyDuds Designs
© 2015, Eve Coleman. All Rights Reserved.

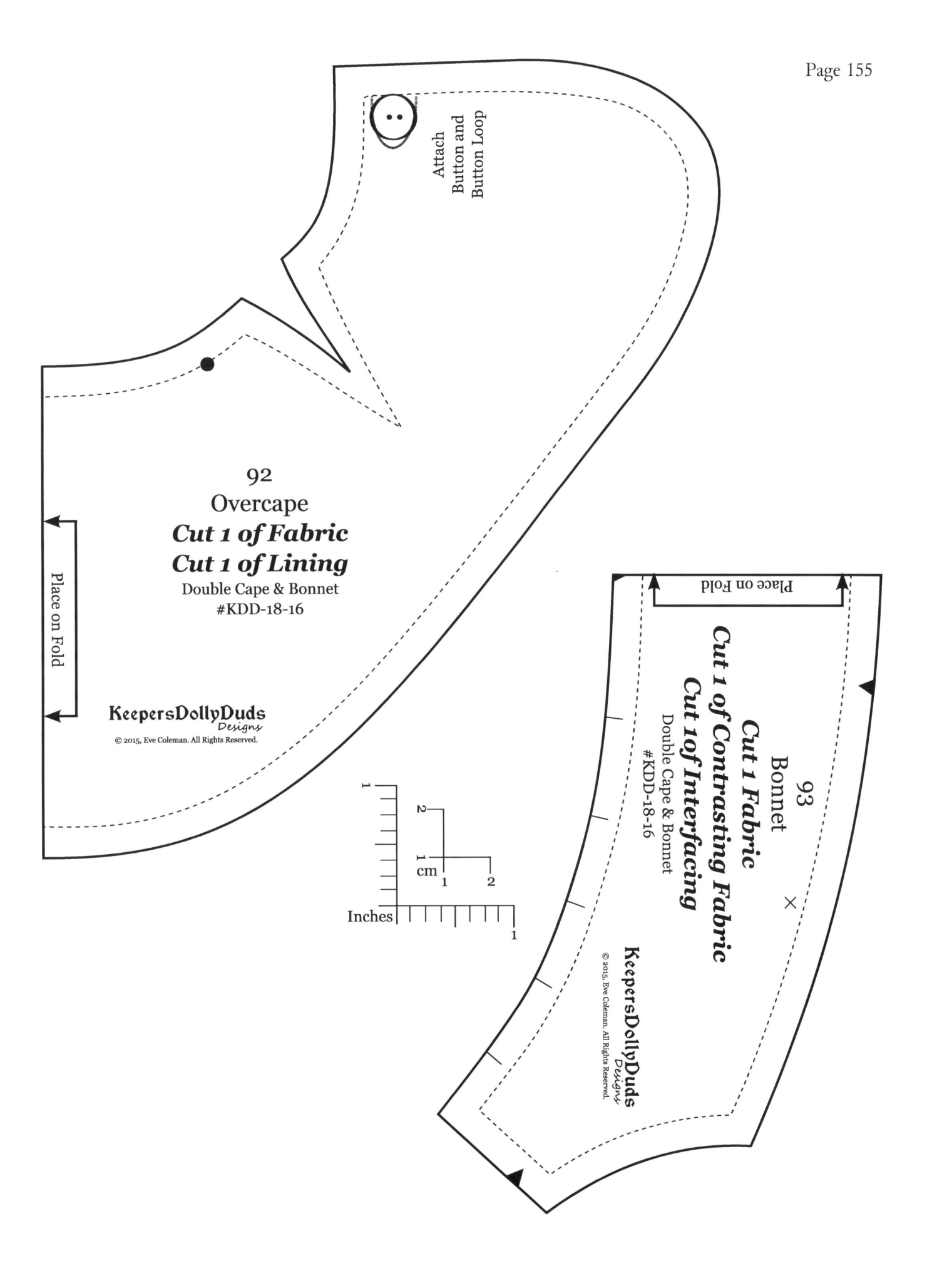

92
Overcape
Cut 1 of Fabric
Cut 1 of Lining
Double Cape & Bonnet
#KDD-18-16

KeepersDollyDuds Designs
© 2015, Eve Coleman. All Rights Reserved.

Place on Fold

Attach Button and Button Loop

93
Bonnet
Cut 1 Fabric
Cut 1 of Contrasting Fabric
Cut 1 of Interfacing
Double Cape & Bonnet
#KDD-18-16

Place on Fold

KeepersDollyDuds Designs
© 2015, Eve Coleman. All Rights Reserved.

Page 155

Place on Fold

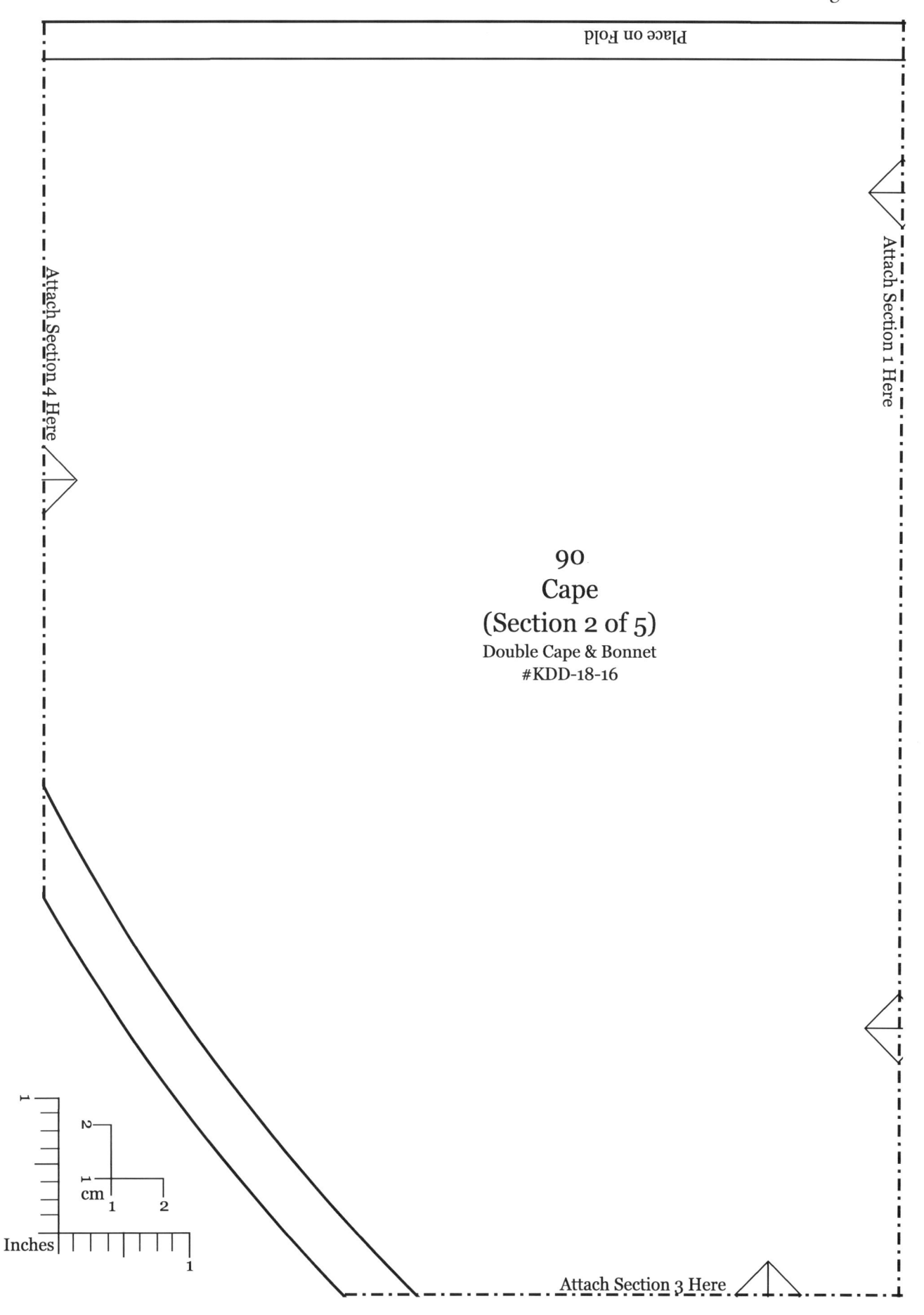

Attach Section 1 Here

Attach Section 4 Here

90
Cape
(Section 2 of 5)
Double Cape & Bonnet
#KDD-18-16

Attach Section 3 Here

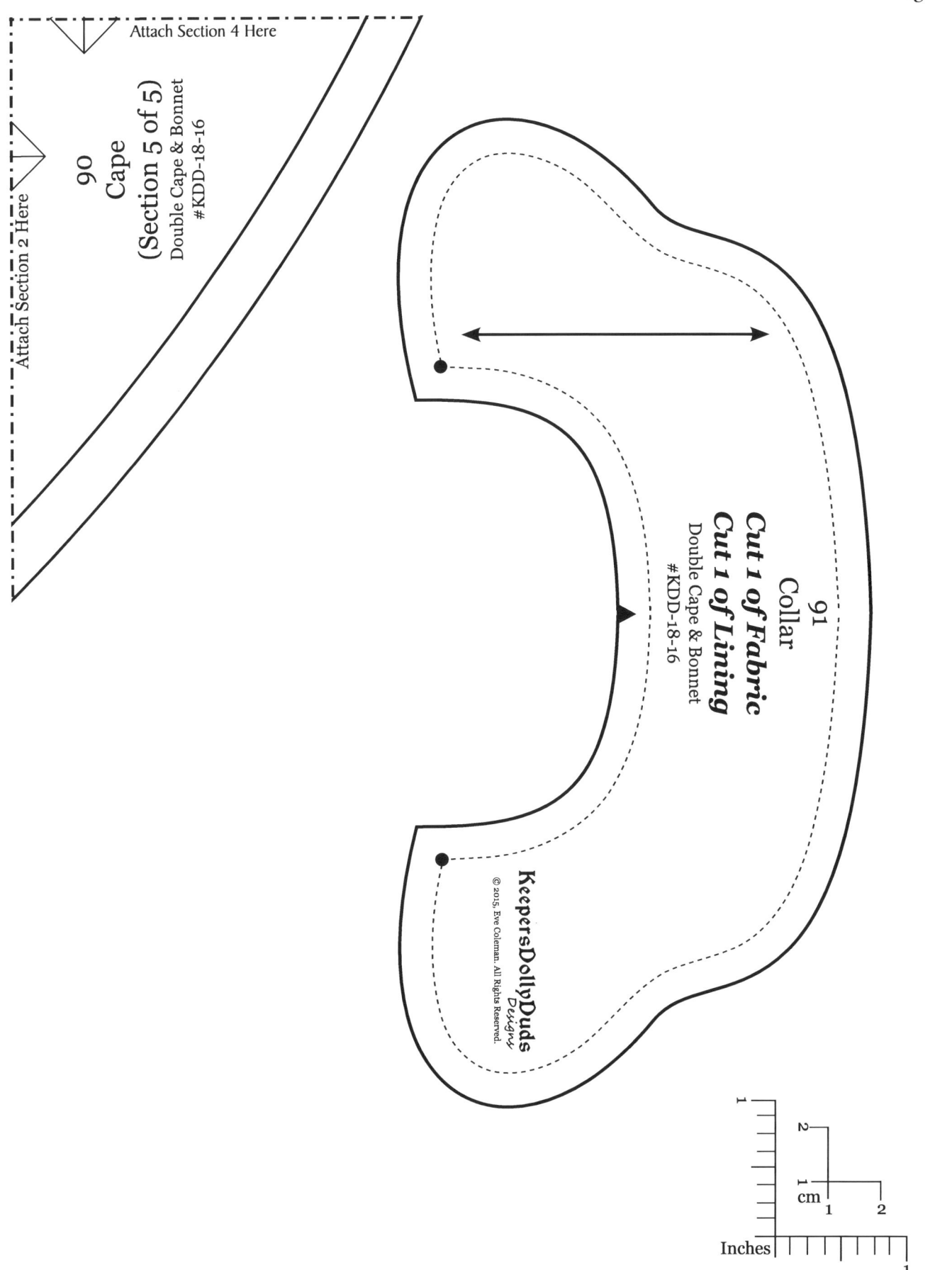

90
Cape
(Section 5 of 5)
Double Cape & Bonnet
#KDD-18-16

Attach Section 4 Here
Attach Section 2 Here

91
Collar
Cut 1 of Fabric
Cut 1 of Lining
Double Cape & Bonnet
#KDD-18-16

KeepersDollyDuds Designs
© 2015, Eve Coleman. All Rights Reserved.

Page 159

Page 161

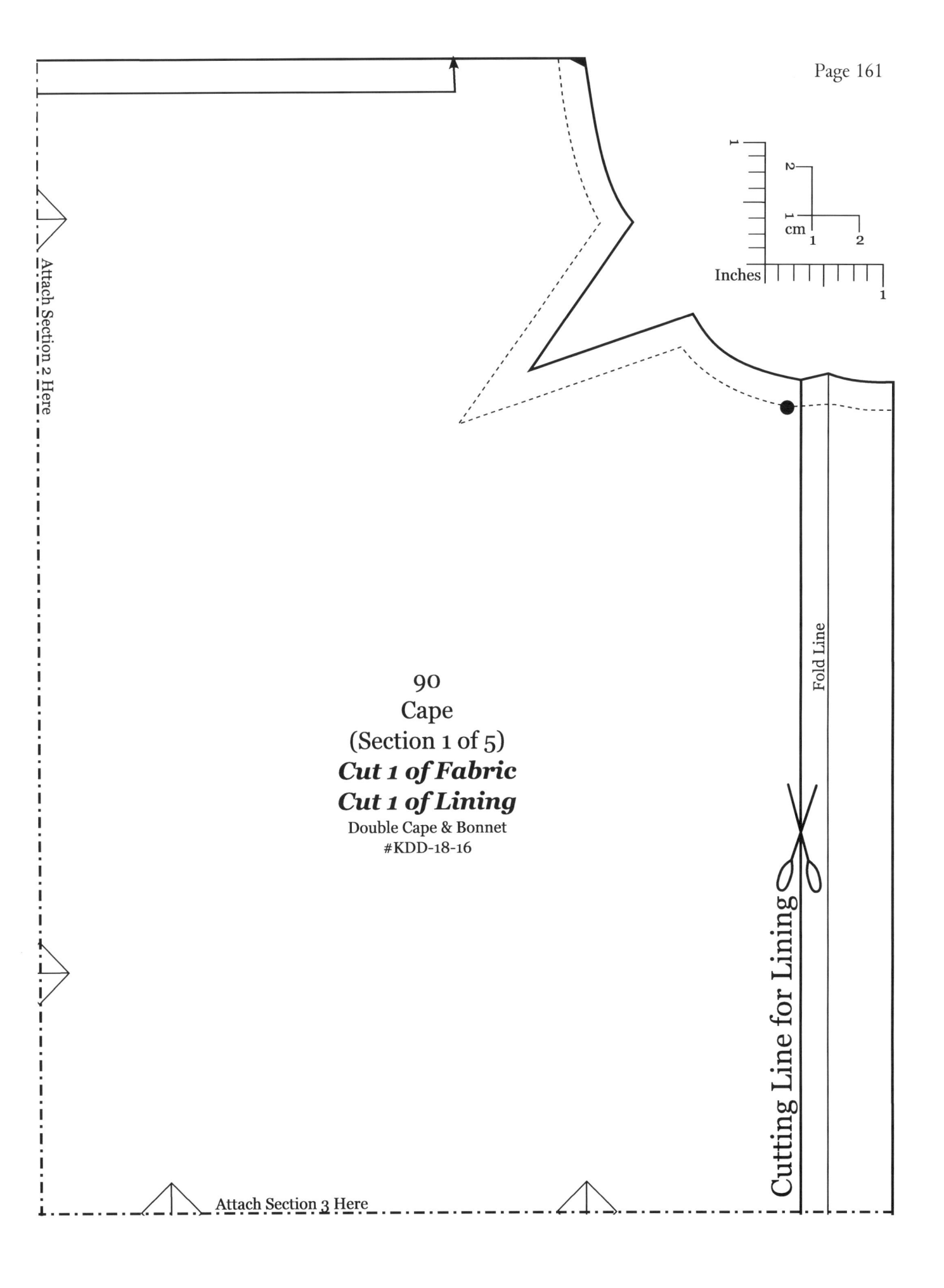

Attach Section 2 Here

90
Cape
(Section 1 of 5)
Cut 1 of Fabric
Cut 1 of Lining
Double Cape & Bonnet
#KDD-18-16

Fold Line

Cutting Line for Lining

Attach Section 3 Here

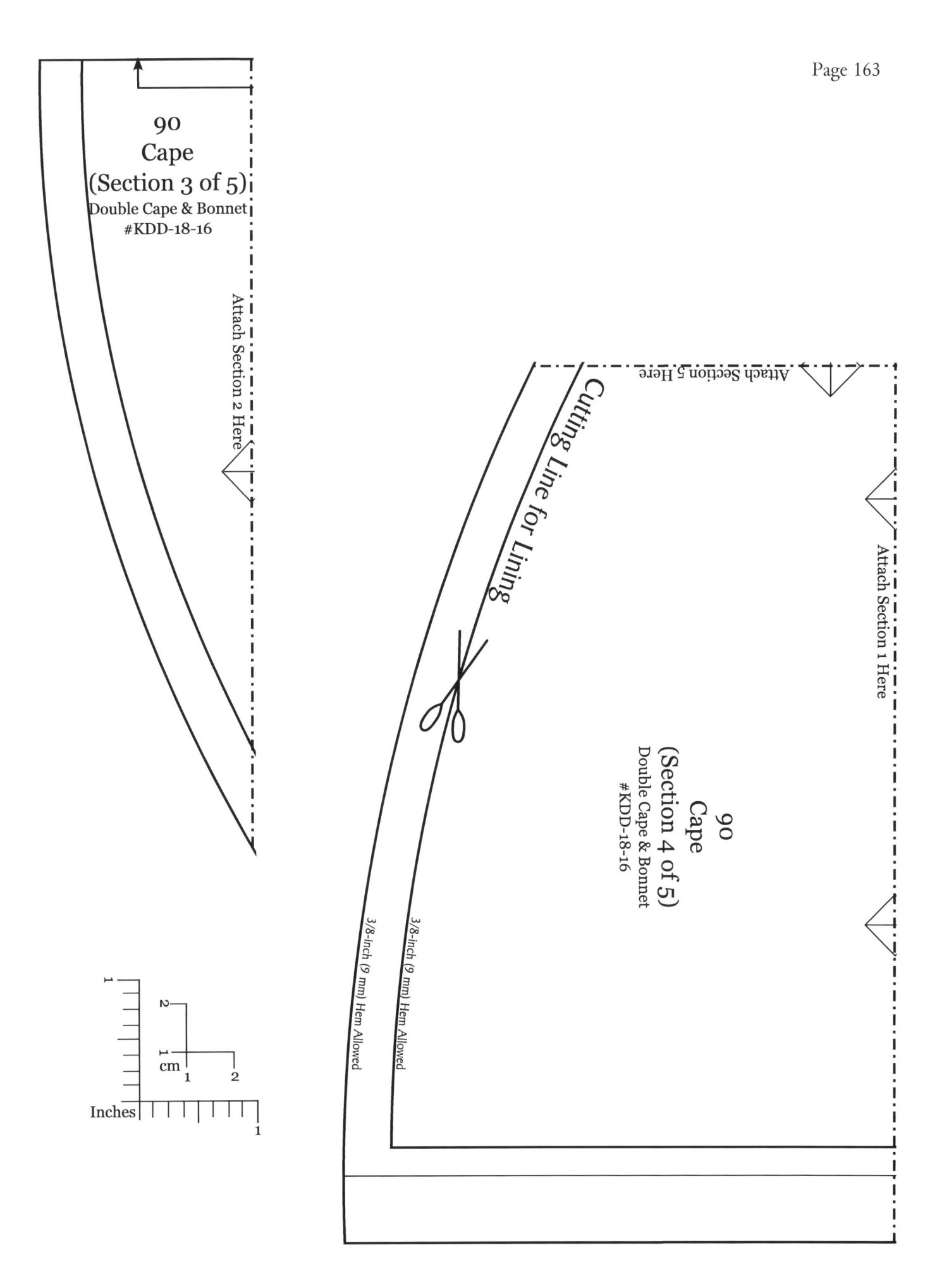

90
Cape
(Section 3 of 5)
Double Cape & Bonnet
#KDD-18-16

Attach Section 2 Here

90
Cape
(Section 4 of 5)
Double Cape & Bonnet
#KDD-18-16

Attach Section 5 Here

Attach Section 1 Here

Cutting Line for Lining

3/8-inch (9 mm) Hem Allowed

3/8-inch (9 mm) Hem Allowed

Page 165

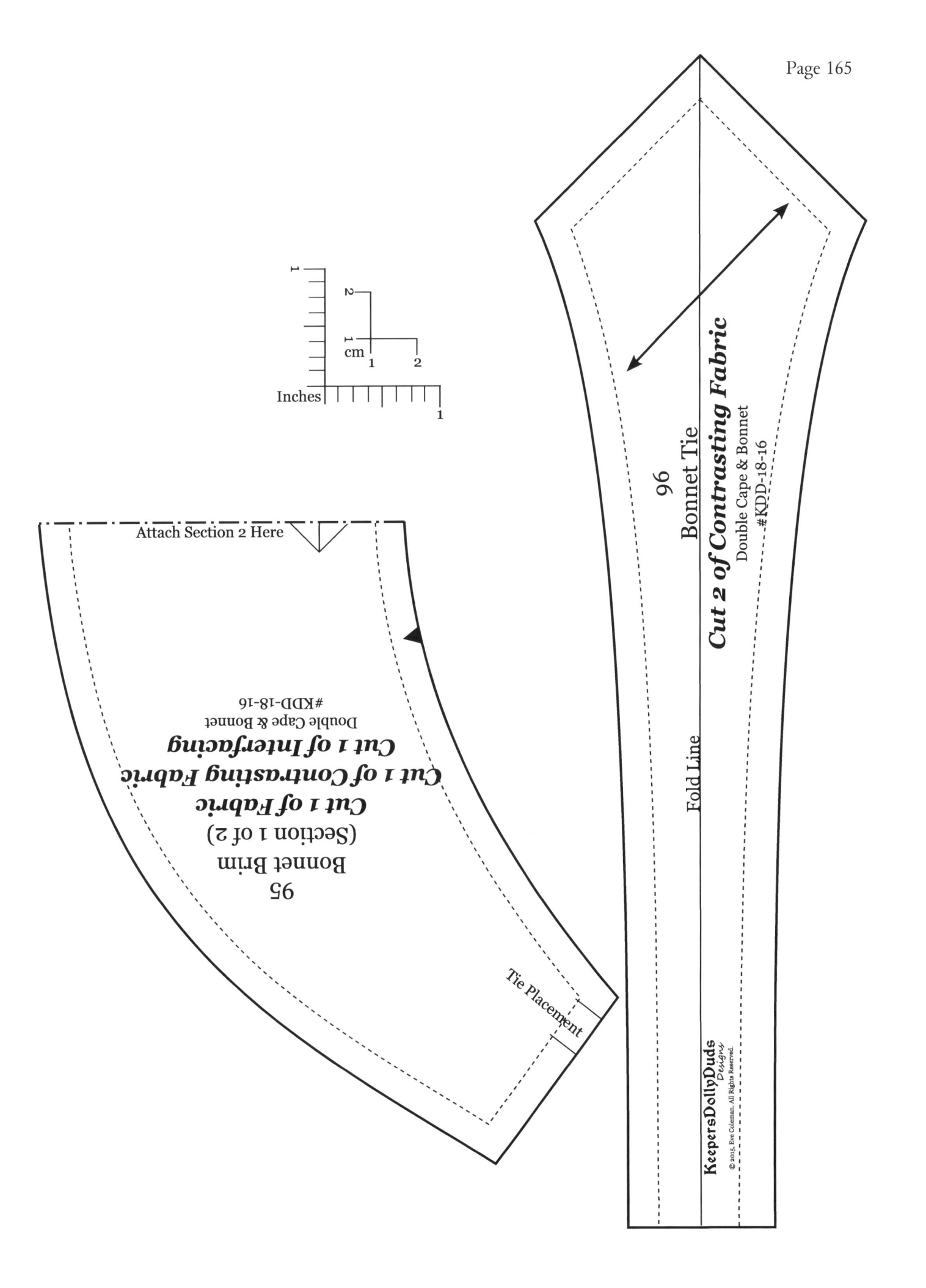

Bonnet Tie

Cut 2 of Contrasting Fabric

Double Cape & Bonnet
#KDD-18-16

96

Fold Line

Bonnet Brim
(Section 1 of 2)
Cut 1 of Fabric
Cut 1 of Contrasting Fabric
Cut 1 of Interfacing

Double Cape & Bonnet
#KDD-18-16

95

Attach Section 2 Here

Tie Placement

KeepersDollyDuds Designs
© 2015, Eve Coleman. All Rights Reserved.

Glossary

A

Armscye ~ The armhole or the opening in a bodice to which the sleeve is sewn.

B

Backstitch ~ A variation of the running stitch that doubles back on each stitch. It is is the most common hand stitch used as it makes a strong seam.

Back Tack ~ To stitch backwards a few stitches to anchor a seam

Baste ~ Temporary stitches made with a running stitch or a long machine stitch used to hold fabric in place before the final stitching.

Bias ~ Bias refers to any line diagonal to the horizontal and vertical grains of the fabric. Woven fabric stretches along the bias. The true bias, 45 degrees to the selvage, allows for the most stretch.

Bodice ~ The part of a garment which runs from the shoulders to the waist.

Button ~ A small disk or knob used as a fastening when passed through a buttonhole or loop.

Buttonhole ~ Holes in fabric that are finished with stitching or fabric which allow buttons to pass through and secure one piece of the fabric to another.

C

Clip ~ To cut small slashes inside the seam allowance of an inside curve to help rounded edges turn and lie neatly.

Cuff ~ A fold or band that trims or finishes the bottom of a sleeve.

Cutting Line ~ On a pattern, the outermost line that is to be cut.

D

Dart ~ A tuck of fabric that tapers into a point. Used to take in ease and give shape to a garment.

Double-fold Hem ~ A hem that is folded once for the hem allowance and a second time to enclose the raw edge.

E

Ease ~ The method of fitting a length of fabric into a slightly smaller space without resulting in gathers or puckers. Also, extra room added to a garment beyond the measurements to make the garment less restricting.

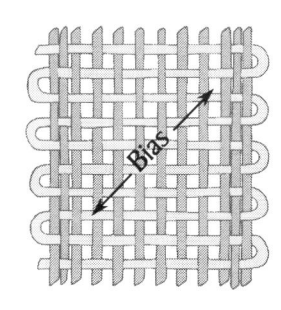

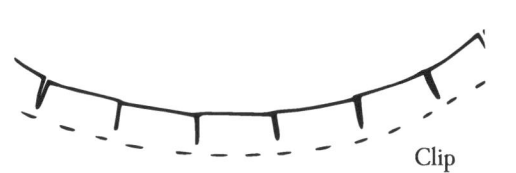

Easing Stitches ~ Parallel rows of running stitches sewn along the edge of the fabric to be eased. The stitching threads are drawn so that the fabric forms curves slightly along the threads.

F

Facing ~ A section of fabric, used to finish fabric edges and provide extra stability.

Finger Press ~A method of temporarily pressing a seam or creasing fabric using your fingertips.

Finished Seam Allowance ~ A seam allowance where the cut edge has been bound, most commonly done with a zig-zag stitch on a sewing machine or a serger.

Fold Line ~A line along which fabric is or is to be folded.

G

Gathering Stitches ~ Parallel rows of running stitches sewn along the edge of the fabric to be gathered. To create gathers, the stitching threads are drawn so that the fabric forms small folds along the threads.

Grainline ~This refers to the position of the horizontal and vertical threads in a woven piece of fabric. It also refers to the long arrow symbol on a pattern piece that corresponds with the vertical threads on a woven fabric.

H

Hem ~ A garment finishing method, where the edge of a piece of cloth is folded under and sewn to prevent the fabric from unraveling.

Hook and Loop Tape ~ A fastening tape consisting of a strip of nylon with a surface of minute hooks that fasten to a corresponding strip with a surface of uncut pile.

I

Interfacing ~ A secondary woven or non-woven fabric that is fused or sewn onto a primary fabric to add stability, body, reinforcement, or shape.

N

Narrow Hem ~A hem made with a 1/2-inch to 1/4-inch hem allowance that is folded in half twice to form a 1/4-inch to 1/8-inch wide hem. It can be finished with either topstitching or whipstitching.

Neckline ~ The edge of a garment at or below the neck.

Notch ~V shaped clips cut inside the seam allowance of an outside curve that help rounded edges turn out and lie neatly; also refers to pattern markings shaped like diamonds or triangles that are printed on the cutting line of a pattern to indicate where seams should meet.

P

Pattern ~ A template for the pieces of a garment that includes markings for specific details and construction guides.

Placket ~ Overlapping layers of fabric along a garment opening that supports or hides buttons and buttonholes or other closures.

Pocket ~ a bag or envelope like receptacle that is fastened to or inserted in a garment. Earlier in history, a pocket was a separate small pouch.

Proper Left ~ This refers to the wearer's left side.

Proper Right ~This refers to the wearer's right side.

R

Raw Edge ~ A cut edge of fabric that hasn't been finished.

Ribbon ~A long, narrow strip of trim, used for tying things together or for decoration.

Right Side of Fabric ~ This is the side of the fabric with the printed pattern or design. On unprinted or untextured fabrics, both sides may be the same, so the right side is determined by which side will be the visible. In pattern instructions, the right side is shaded in illustrations.

Rolled Hem ~ A hem made with a 1/4-inch hem allowance that is rolled under with the forefinger and thumb to form a 1/8-inch wide hem and finished with a simple blind stitch as the hem is rolled.

Ruffle ~ A strip of fabric, lace, or ribbon pleated or gathered on one edge and applied to a garment or other textile as a form of trimming.

Running Stitch ~ Also known as the straight stitch, the running stitch is the basic hand-sewing stitch on which all other stitches are based. The stitch is worked by passing the needle in and out of the fabric.

Running Stitch

S

Seam ~A line of stitching that holds two or more pieces of fabric together.

Selvage ~This is the tightly woven factory edge of fabric that runs parallel along each side of the lengthwise grain.

Skirt ~ A part of a garment that fastens around the waist and hangs down around the legs.

Snap ~ A two piece fastener that is engaged by pressing its two halves together.

Stay-Stitch ~ A straight stitch sewn through one layer of fabric that is most often used around a curve to reinforce a seam line and to prevent distortion.

T

Tack ~ To sew a few stitches in one spot, by hand or by machine, to secure one item to another.

Topstitch ~ A straight stitch along fabric edges or seam lines that helps to secure and strengthen an area; It can also be made with a decorative stitch to accentuate seams and style lines

W

Waistband ~ A band of fabric that encircles the waist of a garment.

Whipstitch ~ A sewing stitch that passes over an edge of cloth to join, finish, or gather.

Whipstitch

Wrong Side of Fabric ~ This is the side of the fabric that is unprinted or without intentional design. On unprinted or untextured fabrics, both sides may be the same so the wrong side is determined by which side will be the unseen. In pattern instructions, the wrong side is unshaded in illustrations.

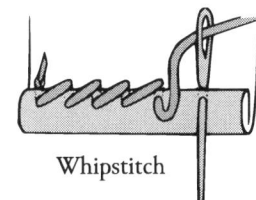

Printed in Great Britain
by Amazon